Russian
phrase book

Berlitz Publishing / Apa Publications GmbH & Co.
Verlag KG, Singapore Branch, Singapore

NO part of this book may be reproduced, stored in a retrieval system or transmitted in any form or means electronic, mechanical, photocopying, recording or otherwise, without prior written permission from Apa Publications.

Contacting the Editors
Every effort has been made to provide accurate information in this publication, but changes are inevitable. The publisher cannot be responsible for any resulting loss, inconvenience or injury. We would appreciate it if readers would call our attention to any errors or outdated information by contacting Berlitz Publishing, 95 Progress Street, Union, NJ 07083, USA. Fax: 1-908-206-1103
email: comments@berlitzbooks.com

Satisfaction guaranteed—If you are dissatisfied with this product for any reason, send the complete package, your dated sale receipt showing price and store name, and a brief note describing your dissatisfaction to: Berlitz Publishing, Langenscheidt Publishing Group, Dept. L, 46-35 54th Rd., Maspeth, NY 11378. You'll receive a full refund.

All Rights Reserved
© 2003 Berlitz Publishing/APA Publications GmbH & Co. Verlag KG, Singapore Branch, Singapore

Trademark Reg. U.S. Patent Office and other countries. Marca Registrada. Used under license from Berlitz Investment Corporation

Layout: Media Marketing, Inc.
Cover photo: ©Imageshop.com

Printed in Singapore

Contents

Pronunciation

This section is designed to make you familiar with the sounds of Russian using our simplified phonetic transcription. You'll find the pronunciation of the Cyrillic (Russian) letters and sounds explained below, together with their "imitated" equivalents. To use this system, found throughout the phrase book, simply read the pronunciation as if it were English, noting any special rules below.

The Russian language

Russian is a language with a long history. Like most other European languages it has its origin in Sanskrit and is part of the Indo-European group. The Cyrillic alphabet is named after St. Cyril, the apostle of the Slavs, who devised it for the translation of the Bible and the liturgy in the ninth century.

Russian is a phonetic language, and its pronunciation is much more systematic than that of English. It conforms fairly closely to consistent rules so that pronunciation problems, like the different pronunciations of the English "ough," as in "ought," "though," "cough," and "bough," do not occur. But the rules are complicated. The following information gives details about some of the more significant rules of pronunciation.

Pronunciation of Russian consonants

The pronunciation of Russian consonants can be either "hard" or "soft." Consonants are "soft" when followed by the vowels я, е, и, ё, ю, and the "soft sign," ь. When a letter is soft it is generally followed by a "y" before the vowel in our phonetic transcription. This "y" is pronounced like the "y" in "yet."

The letter ъ, known as the "hard sign," is rarely used in modern Russian. However, when it is used it always precedes a vowel and is also pronounced like the "y" in "yet." It also indicates that the preceding consonant is pronounced "hard."

As in English, certain consonants are termed "voiced" because their pronunciation is accompanied by a resonance of the voice. In Russian these "voiced" consonants are б, в, г, д, ж, and з (**b, v, g, d, zh**, and **z**, respectively). Each of them has an "unvoiced" equivalent, that is a consonant which is pronounced in exactly the same way, but without any resonance, almost as though whispered. These are п, ф, к, т, ш, and с (**p, f, k, t, sh**, and **s**, respectively).

This change from "voiced" to "unvoiced" consonant occurs at the end of a word, e.g., the word for "bread" – хлеб – is pronounced **khlyep**, and when immediately followed by an "unvoiced" consonant. Hence the preposition for "in/to" – в – is pronounced **f** when it precedes п, ф, к, т, ш, с, х, ц, ч, and щ, (**p**, **f**, **k**, **t**, **sh**, **s**, **kh**, **ts**, **ch**, and **shch**, respectively). For example, "in the park" – в парке – is pronounced **f parkye**.

Conversely, "unvoiced" consonants become "voiced" when they occur before another "voiced" consonant, except before в. Thus the verb for "to do" – сделать – is pronounced **zdyelat'**, but свидание is pronounced **sveedaneeya**.

Consonants

Letter	Approximate pronunciation	Symbol	Example	Pron.
б	like *b* in *b*it	b	был	*bill*
в	like *v* in *v*ine	v	ваш	*vash*
г	like *g* in *g*o	g	город	*gorat*
д	like *d* in *d*o	d	да	*da*
ж	like *s* in plea*s*ure	zh	жаркий	*zharkeey*
з	like *z* in *z*oo	z	завтра	*zaftra*
к	like *k* in *k*itten	k	карта	*karta*
л	like *l* in *l*ily	l	лампа	*lampa*
м	like *m* in *m*y	m	масло	*masla*
н	like *n* in *n*ot	n	нет	*nyet*
п	like *p* in *p*ot	p	парк	*park*
р	trilled (like a Scottish *r*)	r	русский	*rooskeey*
с	like *s* in *s*ee	s	слово	*slova*
т	like *t* in *t*ip	t	там	*tam*
ф	like *f* in *f*ace	f	ферма	*fyerma*
х	like *ch* in Scottish lo*ch*	kh	хлеб	*khlyep*
ц	like *ts* in si*ts*	ts	цена	*tseena*
ч	like *ch* in *ch*ip	.chy	час	*chyas*
ш	like *sh* in *sh*ut	sh	ваша	*vasha*
щ	like *sh* followed by *ch,* as in fre*sh ch*eese	shch	щи	*shchee*

Vowels

Vowels can be "stressed" and "unstressed". The vowels o, e, a, and я change their pronunciation when they are unstressed. This is reflected in the phonetic transcription.

Letter	Approximate pronunciation	Symbol	Example	Pron.
а	between *a* in c*a*t and *u* in c*u*t	*a*	как	*kak*
е	like *ye* in *ye*t	*ye*	где	*gdye*
ё	like *yo* in *yo*nder	*yo*	мёд	*myot*
и	like *ee* in s*ee*	*ee*	синий	*seenyeey*
й*	like *y* in bo*y*	*y*	бой	*boy*
о**	like *o* in h*o*t	*o*	стол	*stol*
у	like *oo* in b*oo*t	*oo*	улица	*ooleetsa*
ы	like *i* in *i*ll	*i*	вы	*vi*
э	like *e* in m*e*t	*e*	эта	*eta*
ю	like *you* in *you*th	*yoo*	юг	*yook*
я	like *ya* in *ya*rd	*ya*	мясо	*myasa*

* й is a semi-vowel and occurs with other full vowels. It is mainly used to form diphthongs.

** When o is unstressed it is pronounced like the Russian a.

Diphthongs

Letter	Approximate pronunciation	Symbol	Example	Pron.
ай	like *y* in m*y*	*ay*	май	*may*
яй	like *y* in m*y*, preceded by *y* in *y*es	*yay*	негодяй	*neegadyay*
ой	like *oy* in b*oy*	*oy*	вой	*voy*
ей	like *ey* in ob*ey*, preceded by *y* in *y*es	*yey*	соловей	*salavyey*
ий	like *ee* in s*ee*, followed by *y* in *y*es	*eey*	ранний	*ranneey*
ый	like *i* in *i*ll, followed by *y* in *y*es	*iy*	красивый	*kraseeviy*
уй	like *oo* in g*oo*d, followed by *y* in *y*es	*ooy*	дуй	*dooy*
юй	as уй above, preceded by *y* in *y*es	*yooy*	плюй	*plyooy*

Stress

Stress in Russian is irregular and must simply be learned. If a vowel or diphthong is not stressed, it often changes its pronunciation. However, for the purposes of the phrase book, the stress has been marked, the stressed syllable being underlined, and any pronunciation changes are reflected in the phonetic transcription.

The Russian alphabet

А	а	*a*	Р	р	*er*
Б	б	*be*	С	с	*es*
В	в	*ve*	Т	т	*te*
Г	г	*ge*	У	у	*oo*
Д	д	*de*	Ф	ф	*ef*
Е	е	*ye*	Х	х	*kha*
Ё	ё	*yo*	Ц	ц	*tse*
Ж	ж	*zhe*	Ч	ч	*chya*
З	з	*ze*	Ш	ш	*sha*
И	и	*ee*	Щ	щ	*shchya*
Й	й	*ee kratkaye*	Ъ	ъ	*tvyordiy znak*
К	к	*ka*	Ы	ы	*i*
Л	л	*el'*	Ь	ь	*myakhkeey znak*
М	м	*em*	Э	э	*ee abarotnaye*
Н	н	*en*	Ю	ю	*yoo*
О	о	*o*	Я	я	*ya*
П	п	*pe*			

Basic Expressions

ESSENTIAL

Yes./No	Да./Нет. *da/nyet*
Okay.	Хорошо/О кей. *kharasho/o ke*
Please.	Пожалуйста. *pazhalsta*
Thank you (very much).	Спасибо (большое). *spaseeba (bal'shoye)*

Greetings/Apologies
Приветствия и извинения

Hello./Hi!	Здравствуй(те)!/Привет! *zdrastvooy(tye)/preevyet*
Good morning.	Доброе утро. *dobraye ootra*
Good afternoon/evening.	Добрый день/вечер. *dobriy dyen'/vyechyeer*
Good night.	Спокойной ночи. *spakoyniy nochyee*
Good-bye.	До свидания. *da sveedaneeya*
Excuse me. (getting attention)	Извините./Простите. *eezveeneetye/ prasteetye*
Excuse me. (May I get past?)	Разрешите. (Разрешите пройти). *razreeshityе (razreeshityе praytee)*
Excuse me!/Sorry!	Извините!/Простите! *eezveeneetye/prasteetye*
Don't mention it.	Не за что. *nye za shta*
Never mind.	Ничего. *neechyeevo*

Communication difficulties
Трудности при разговоре

Do you speak English? — Вы говорите по-английски?
vi gava<u>ree</u>tye pa-an<u>glee</u>yskee

Does anyone here speak English? — Здесь кто-нибудь говорит по-английски?
zdyes' <u>kto</u>neebood' gava<u>ree</u>t pa-an<u>glee</u>yskee

I don't speak (much) Russian. — Я плохо говорю по-русски.
ya <u>plo</u>kha gava<u>ryoo</u> pa-<u>roo</u>skee

Could you speak more slowly? — Говорите медленнее, пожалуйста.
gava<u>ree</u>tye <u>mye</u>dleennee pa<u>zhal</u>sta

Could you repeat that? — Повторите, пожалуйста.
paf<u>tar</u>eetye pa<u>zhal</u>sta

Excuse me? [Pardon?] — Извините. *eezvee<u>nee</u>tye*

What was that? — Что такое? *shto ta<u>ko</u>ye*

Could you spell it? — Назовите по буквам, пожалуйста.
naza<u>vee</u>tye pa <u>book</u>vam pa<u>zhal</u>sta

Please write it down. — Напишите, пожалуйста.
napee<u>shi</u>tye pa<u>zhal</u>sta

Can you translate this for me? — Переведите мне это, пожалуйста.
peereevee<u>dee</u>tye mnye <u>e</u>ta pa<u>zhal</u>sta

What does this/that mean? — Что это/то значит?
shto <u>e</u>ta/to <u>zna</u>chyeet

Please point to the phrase in the book. — Пожалуйста, покажите эту фразу в книге.
pa<u>zhal</u>sta paka<u>zhi</u>tye <u>e</u>too <u>fra</u>zoo f <u>knee</u>gye

I understand. — Я понимаю.
ya panee<u>ma</u>yoo

I don't understand. — Я не понимаю.
ya nee panee<u>ma</u>yoo

Do you understand? — Вы понимаете?
vi panee<u>ma</u>yetye

– sto <u>treet</u>sat' pyat' roob<u>lyey</u>.
– ya nee panee<u>ma</u>yoo.
– sto <u>treet</u>sat' pyat' roob<u>lyey</u>.
– napee<u>shee</u>tyee pa<u>zhal</u>sta. ... aa, "135 rubles"!
vot pa<u>zhal</u>sta.

Questions Вопросы

You can form a simple question in Russian by repeating the same words of the positive statement, without altering the word order, but adding interrogatory intonation (letting the voice rise at the end of the sentence).

Здесь есть факс.
zdyes' yest' faks

There is a fax machine here.

Здесь есть факс?
zdyes' yest' faks

Is there a fax machine here?

Where? Где?/Куда?*

Where is it?	Где это? gdye eta
Where are you going?	Куда Вы идёте? kooda vi eedyotye
across the road	через дорогу chyeereez darogoo
around the town	по городу pa goradoo
at the meeting place [point]	в месте встречи v myestee fstryechyee
far from here	далеко от сюда daleeko atsyooda
from the U.S.	из Америки eez amyereekee
here (to here)	здесь (сюда) zdyes' (syooda)
in Russia	в России v raseeyee
in the car	в машине v mashinye
inside	внутри (position)/внутрь (motion) vnootree/vnootr'
near the bank	около банка okala banka
next to the post office	рядом с почтой ryadam s pochtay
opposite the market	напротив рынка naproteef rinka
on the left/right	направо/налево naprava/nalyeva
on the sidewalk [pavement]	на тротуаре na tratooarye
outside the café	около кафе okala kafe
there (to there)	там (туда) tam (tooda)
to the hotel	в гостиницу/отель v gasteeneetsoo/atyel
up to the traffic lights	до светофора da sveetafora

* Где is used to ask a question about where something is positioned; куда is used to ask a question about where something/someone is going.

When?   Когда?/Во сколько?

When does the museum open?	Когда открыт музей? *kagda atkrit moozyay*
When does the train arrive?	Во сколько приходит поезд? *va skol'ka* *preekhodeet poeest*
10 minutes ago	10 минут назад *dyeseet' meenoot nazat*
after lunch	после обеда *poslee abyeda*
always	всегда *fseegda*
around midnight	около полуночи *okala paloonachyee*
at 7 o'clock	в 7 часов *f syem' chyasof*
before Friday	до пятницы *da pyatneetsi*
by tomorrow	к завтрашнему дню *k zaftreeshneemoo dnyoo*
every week	каждую неделю *kazhdooyoo needyelyoo*
for 2 hours	2 часа *dva chyasa*
from 9 a.m. to 6 p.m.	с 9(и) утра до 6(и) вечера *z deeveetee ootra da sheestee vyechyeera*
in 20 minutes	через 20 минут *chyeereez dvatsat' meenoot*
never	никогда *neekagda*
not yet	нет ещё *nyet eeshchyo*
now	сейчас/теперь *seechyas/teepyer'*
often	часто *chyasta*
on March 8	8(ого) марта *vas'mova marta*
on weekdays	в будние (дни) *v boodneeye (dnee)*
sometimes	иногда *eenagda*
soon	скоро *skora*
then	затем/потом *zatyem/patom*
within 2 days	за 2 дня *za dva dnya*

What sort of …? Какой …?

I'd like something … — Я хотел(а)бы что-нибудь… *ya khatyel(a) bi shtoneebood'* …

It's … — Это … *eta* …

beautiful/ugly	красивый/некрасивый *kraseeviy/neekraseeviy*
better/worse	лучше/хуже *loochshe/khoozhe*
big/small	большой/маленький *bal'shoy/maleen'keey*
cheap/expensive	дешёвый/дорогой *deeshoviy/daragoy*
clean/dirty	чистый/грязный *chyeestiy/gryazniy*
dark/light	тёмный/светлый *tyomniy/svetliy*
delicious/revolting	вкусный/невкусный *fkoosniy/neefkoosniy*
early/late	ранний/поздний *ranneey/pozneey*
easy/difficult	лёгкий/трудный *lyokhkeey/troodniy*
empty/full	пустой/полный *poostoy/polniy*
good/bad	хороший/плохой *kharosheey/plakhoy*
heavy/light	тяжёлый/лёгкий *teezholiy/lyokhkeey*
hot/warm/cold	горячий/тёплый/холодный *garyachyeey/tyopliy/khalodniy*
narrow/wide	узкий/широкий *ooskeey/shirokeey*
next/last	следующий/последний *slyedooyooshchyeey/paslyedneey*
old/new	старый/новый *stariy/noviy*
open/shut	открытый/закрытый *atkritiy/zakritiy*
pleasant/nice/unpleasant	приятный/хороший/неприятный *preeyatniy/kharosheey/neepreeyatniy*
quick/slow	быстрый/медленный *bistriy/myedleenniy*
quiet/noisy	тихий/шумный *teekheey/shoomniy*
right/wrong	правильный/неправильный *praveel'niy/neepraveel'niy*
tall/short	высокий/низкий *visokeey/neezkeey*
thick/thin	толстый/тонкий *tolstiy/tonkeey*
vacant/occupied	свободный/занятый *svabodniy/zaneetiy*
young/old	молодой/старый *maladoy/stariy*

GRAMMAR

Russian nouns are either masculine, feminine, or neuter.
Unless they are indeclinable (these are mostly foreign "loan" words) they change their endings, and often their appearance, according to the case they are in, and according to whether they are singular or plural ➤ 169.

Masculine nouns:	usually end in a hard consonant, e.g., автобу<u>с</u>
Feminine nouns:	usually end in -a or -я, e.g., газет<u>а</u>, недел<u>я</u>
Neuter nouns:	usually end in -o or -e, e.g., мест<u>о</u>, здани<u>е</u>

How much/many? Сколько?

How much is that?	Сколько стоит? _skol'ka stoeet_
How many are there?	Сколько здесь? _skol'ka zdyes'_
1	один/одна _adeen/adna_
2	два/две _dva/dvye_
3/4/5	три/четыре/пять _tree/chyeet<u>ir</u>ee/pyat_
none	нисколько _neeskol'ka_
about 100 rubles [roubles]	около 100 рублей _okala sta roob<u>ley</u>ey_
a little	немного _neemnoga_
a lot of traffic	много машин _mnoga mashin_
enough	достаточно _dastatachna_
few/a few of them	несколько _nyeskal'ka_
many people	много людей _mnoga lyoodyey_
more than that	больше, чем _bol'she chyem_
less than that	меньше, чем _myen'she chyem_
much more	намного больше _namnoga bol'she_
nothing else	ничего больше _neechyeevo bol'she_
too much	слишком много _sleeshkam mnoga_

Why? Почему?

Why is that?	Почему это так? _pachyeemoo eta tak_
Why not?	Почему нет? _pachyeemoo nyet_
It's because of the weather.	Из-за погоды. _eez-za pagodi_
It's because I'm in a hurry.	Потому что я спешу. _patamooshto ya speeshoo_
I don't know why.	Я не знаю почему. _ya nee znayoo pachyeemoo_

Who?/Which? Кто?/Какой?

Who is it for?	Кому это? *kamoo eta*
(for) her/him	ей/ему *yey/eemoo*
(for) me	мне *mnye*
(for) you	Вам/тебе *vam/teebye*
(for) them	им *eem*
no one	никому *neekamoo*
Which one do you want?	Какой Вы хотите? *kakoy vi khateetye*
that one/this one	вон тот (та)/вот этот (эта) *von tot (ta)/vot etat (eta)*
one like that	такой как тот (та) *takoy kak tot (ta)*
not that one	не тот (та) *nye tot (ta)*
something	что-то *shtoto*
nothing	ничего *neecheevo*

Whose? Чей?

Whose is that?	Чьё это?* *chyo eta*
It's …	Это *eta*
mine (masculine/feminine)	мой/моя *moy/maya*
ours (masculine/feminine)	наш/наша *nash/nasha*
yours (masculine/feminine)	ваш/ваша *vash/vasha*
his/hers/theirs	его/её/их *eevo/eeyo/eekh*
It's … turn.‡	Это … очередь.‡ *eta … ochyeereed'*
my/our/your	моя/наша/ваша *maya/nasha/vasha*
his/her/their	его/её/их *eevo/eeyo/eekh*

* чей = *whose* (masculine singular), чья = *whose* (feminine singular),
чьё = *whose* (neuter singular)

‡ The word for "turn" – очередь – is feminine and takes the feminine form of the possessive adjective. The words for "his," "her," and "their" are indeclinable and are identical with the possessive pronouns "his," "hers," and "theirs."

GRAMMAR

As nouns in Russian decline according to gender, plurality, and case, so do pronouns. Personal pronouns can look very different from their base forms according to what "role" they play in the sentence. Possessive pronouns behave like adjectives, and vary according to the gender, plurality, and case of the noun they modify ➤ 169

How? Как?

How would you like to pay?	Как будете платить? *kak boodeetye plateet'*
by cash	наличными *naleechnimy*
by credit card	кредитной карточкой *kreedeetnoy kartachkoy*
How are you getting here?	Как Вы добираетесь сюда? *kak vi dabeeraeetyes' syooda*
by car/bus/train	машиной/автобусом/поездом *masheenay/aftoboosam/poeezdam*
on foot	пешком *peeshkom*
quickly	быстро *bistra*
slowly	медленно *myedleena*
too fast	слишком быстро *sleeshkam bistra*
totally	полностью *polnastyoo*
very	очень *ochyeen'*
with a friend	с другом *z droogam*
without a passport	без паспорта *byes pasparta*

Is it …?/Are there …? Есть

Is it free of charge?	Бесплатно? *Beesplatna*
It isn't ready.	Не готово. *nee gatova*
Is there a shower in the room?	В комнате есть душ? *f komnatye yest' doosh*
Is there a bus into town?	Есть автобус в город? *yest' aftoboos v gorad*
There it is/they are.	Вон там./Вон они. *von tam/vot anee*
There is a good restaurant near here.	Здесь рядом есть хороший ресторан. *zdyes' ryadam yest' kharosheey reestaran*
Here it is.	Вот, пожалуйста. *vot pazhalsta*
Here they are.	Вот они. *vot anee*

GRAMMAR

The verb *to be* is not used in the present tense. Therefore the words *am*, *is*, and *are* are omitted. However, the word есть is sometimes used to translate *is* and *are*. Besides meaning *no*, the word нет also means *there is not* and *there are not*.

Can/May? Можно?

Can I …?	Можно мне …? _mozhna mnye …_
Can we …?	Можно нам …? _mozhna nam …_
Can you show me …?	Покажите мне … _pakazheetye mnye …_
Can you tell me?	Скажите, пожалуйста. _skazhitye pazhalsta_
Can you help me?	Помогите мне. _pamageetye mnye_
May I help you?	Вам помочь? _vam pamoch'_
Can you direct me to …?	Покажите мне дорогу к … _pakazhitye mnye darogoo k …_
I can't.	Я не могу. _ya nee magoo_

What do you want? Что Вы хотите?

I'd like …	Я хотел(а) бы … _ya khatyel(a) bi …_
Could I have …?	Можно мне …? _mozhna mnye …_
We'd like …	Мы хотели бы … _mi khatyelee bi …_
Give me …	Дайте мне … _daytye mnye …_
I'm looking for …	Я ищу … _ya eeshchyoo …_
I need to …	Мне нужно … _tnye noozhna …_
go	пойти _paytee_
find	найти _naytee_
see	посмотреть _pasmatryet'_
speak to …	поговорить с … _pagavareet' s …_

– eezveenityee pazhalsta.
– da? vam pamoch'?
– mozhna mnye pagavareet'
s gaspadeenom Eevanovim.
– da kanyeshna.

18

Other useful words
Другие нужные слова

fortunately	к счастью	*k shchyastyoo*
hopefully (*lit.* I hope)	я надеюсь	*ya adyeyoos'*
of course	конечно	*kanyeshna*
perhaps	может быть	*mozhet' bit'*
unfortunately	к сожалению	*k sazhalyeneeyoo*
also/but	также/но	*tagzhe/no*
and/or	и/или	*ee/eelee*

Exclamations Восклицания

At last!	Наконец!	*nakanyets*
Go on.	Дальше.	*dal'she*
Nonsense!	Ерунда!	*eeroonda*
That's true!	Совершенно правильно!	*saveershenna praveel'na*
No way!	Вы шутите!	*vi shooteetye*
How are things?	Как дела?	*kag deela*
great/terrific	замечательный	*zamyechateel'niy*
very good	отлично	*atleechna*
fine	прекрасно	*preekrasna*
not bad	неплохо	*neeplokha*
okay	хорошо	*kharasho*
not good	не очень хорошо	*nee ocheen' kharasho*
fairly bad	довольно плохо	*davol'na plokha*
terrible	ужасно	*oozhasna*

GRAMMAR

Russian has no articles, i.e., no words for *a/an* or *the*. Thus *a telephone* or *the telephone* are simply conveyed as:

(a/the) telephone   телефон **teeleefon**

However, remember that this noun (masculine) will change according to number and case ➤ 169

Accommodations

Arrangements. You must make hotel reservations before leaving your own country. Russian visas are only issued after reservations have been confirmed. If at all possible, arrange to be met at the airport by a representative from your hotel. Travelers with Intourist will be met by a representative upon exiting customs. If no one is meeting you, try to use public transportation to get to your hotel. Avoid using a "taxi" offered by a taxi-tout. Many travelers have been robbed when using these "taxis," especially in Moscow after dark.

The travel bureau. Intourist no longer holds a monopoly on accommodations in Russia, and in major cities an increasing number of new or newly renovated hotels are now jointly run with Western companies. These first-class ventures offer a new, if pricey, degree of choice accommodation to the traveler. If you are on an Intourist package tour, you can state your preference of hotel, but the final arrangements rest with Intourist, which will let you know where you are staying upon arrival at the airport.

Arrival. Upon arrival at the hotel, check in at reception and hand over all your documents and vouchers. The desk clerk won't give you a key to your room but a hotel pass (пропуск **propoosk**) that gives your name, length of stay, and room number. You have to present this to the doorman every time you enter the hotel and hand it to the "floor manager" (дежурная **deezhoornaya**), who not only keeps the keys but an eye on the guests, too. These are mostly middle-aged women who will also make tea, call a taxi for you, and solve any other problem.

Intourist hotels. These hotels have service bureaus (бюро обслуживания **byooro apsloozheevanya**) manned by multilingual staff who provide information, arrange outings and excursions, make reservations, and give general assistance.

Other accommodation. Apart from big hotels, no other form of accommodation is available. However, foreigners are now allowed to stay in the home of a Russian friend or contact, but a letter of invitation must accompany your visa application.

Reservations Заказ

In advance Предварительно

Travelers with Intourist will be met by a representative upon
exiting customs.

Can you recommend a hotel in …?	Какой отель Вы рекомендуете в ...? *kakoy atyel' vi reekameendooeetye v …*
Is it near the center of town?	Это близко от центра города? *eta bleeska at tsentra gorada*
How much is it per night?	Сколько стоит номер в сутки? *skol'ka stoeet nomeer f sootkee*
Do you have a cheaper room?	Дешевле нет? *deeshevlye nyet*
Could you reserve me a room there, please?	Можно мне заказать номер? *mozhna mnye zakazat' nomeer*
How do I get there?	Как туда добраться? *kak tooda dabrat'sa*

At the hotel В гостинице

Do you have a room?	Есть свободные места? *yest' sfabodniye meesta*
I'm sorry, we're full.	Извините, мест нет. *eezveeneetye myest nyet*
Is there another hotel nearby?	Здесь рядом есть другая гостиница? *zdyes' ryadam yest' droogaya gasteeneetsa*
I'd like a single/double room.	Я хотел(а) бы одноместный/ двухместный номер. *ya khatyel(a) bi adnamyestniy/dvookhmyestniy nomeer*
Can I see the room, please?	Можно посмотреть комнату? *mozhna pasmatryet' komnatoo*
I'd like a room with …	Я хотел(а) бы номер с ... *ya khatyel (a) bi nomeer s …*
twin beds	двумя кроватями *dvoomya kravatyamee*
a double bed	двуспальной кроватью *dvoospal'ni kravatyoo*
a bath/shower	ванной/душем *vanni/dooshem*

– yest' sfabodniye meesta?
– *eezveeneetye myest nyet.*
– zdyes' ryadam yest' droogaya gasteeneetsa?
– *da yest'. paprobooyeetye v Ambasadorye chyeryez darogoo.*

Reception Приём

I have a reservation.	У меня заказ.
	Oo meenya zakas
My name is …	Моя фамилия …
	maya fameeleeya …
We've reserved a double and a single room.	Мы заказали двухместный и одноместный номер. *Mi zakazalee dvookhmyestniy ee adnamyestniy nomeer*
I've reserved a room for two nights.	Я заказал номер на двое суток.. *ya zakazal nomeer na dvoye sootok*
I confirmed my reservation by mail.	Я послал(а) подтверждение письмом. *ya paslal(a) pattveerzhdyeneeye pees'mom*
Could we have adjoining rooms?	Можно нам рядом номера? *Mozhna nam ryadam nomeera*

Amenities and facilities Удобства и комфорт

Is there (a/an) … in the room?	В номере есть …? *v nomeerye yest' …*
air conditioning	кондиционер *kandeetseeonyer*
TV/telephone	телевизор/телефон *teeleeveezar/teeleefon*
Does the hotel have a(n) …?	В гостинице есть …? *v gasteeneetse yest' …*
fax	факс *faks*
laundry service	прачечная *prachyeechnaya*
satellite TV	спутниковое телевидение *spootneekavaye tyelyeveedyeneeye*
sauna	сауна *saoona*
swimming pool	бассейн *bassyeyn*
Could you put … in the room?	Можно поставить … в комнату? *mozhna pastaveet' … f komnatoo*
an extra bed	ещё одну кровать *eeshcho adnoo kravat'*
a crib [a child's cot]	детскую кроватку *dyetskooyoo kravatkoo*
Do you have facilities for children/the disabled?	Здесь есть удобства для детей/инвалидов? *zdyes' yest' oodobstva dlya deetyey/eenvaleedaf*

How long …?   Как долго ...?

We'll be staying …	Мы пробудем … *mi praboodeem …*
overnight only	только одну ночь *tol'koo adnoo noch'*
a few days	несколько дней *nyeskal'ka dnyey*
a week (at least)	неделю (по крайней мере) *needyelyoo (pa kraynyee myerye)*
I'd like to stay an extra night.	Я хотел(а) бы остаться ещё на одну ночь. *ya khatyel(a) bi astat'sa eeshchyo na adnoo noch'*

– oo meenya zakas. maya fameeleeya nyooton.
– *zdrastvooytye gaspadeen nyooton.*
– mi praboodeem nyeskal'ka dneyey.
– *kharasho. pazhalsta raspisheetyes' zdyes'.*

May I see your passport, please?	Ваш паспорт, пожалуйста.
Please fill out this form/ sign here.	Заполните бланк/распишитесь здесь.
What is your car license number?	Какой номер Вашей машины?

комната только ... рублей	room only … rubles
завтрак входит в цену	breakfast included
ресторан к вашим услугам	meals available
фамилия/имя	last name/first name
адрес	home address
национальность/профессия	nationality/profession
дата/место рождения	date/place of birth
номер паспорта	passport number
номер машины	car license number
место/дата	place/date
подпись	signature

Price Цена

All accommodation must be paid for in advance. The price usually includes full board. When checking out you get a pass proving that you have paid your bill.

How much is it …?	Сколько стоит …? _skol'ka stoeet_ …
per night/week	в сутки/ в неделю f _soot_kee/v _need_yelyoo
for bed and breakfast	с завтраком z _zaf_trakam
excluding meals	без питания byes peet_aneeya_
for full board (American Plan [A.P.])	с полным питанием s _pol_neem peet_aneeyem_
for half board (Modified American Plan [M.A.P.])	с завтраком и ужином z _zaf_trakam ee _oo_zhinam
Does the price include …?	Цена включает…? _fkho_deet v _sto_eemast' …
breakfast	завтрак _zaf_trak
service	услуги oos_loo_gee
sales tax [VAT]	НДС en de es
Do I have to pay a deposit?	Нужно платить аванс? _noozh_na plat_eet'_ avans
Is there a discount for children?	Есть скидка для детей? yest' _skeet_ka dlya deet_yey_

Decision Выбор номера

May I see the room?	Можно мне посмотреть комнату? _mozh_na mnye pasmat_ryet'_ _kom_natoo
That's fine. I'll take it.	Хорошо. Подойдёт. khara_sho_ padayd_yot_
It's too …	Слишком … _sleesh_kam …
dark/small	темно/тесно teem_no_/_tyes_no
noisy	шумно _shoom_na
Do you have anything …?	Есть что-нибудь …? yest' _shto_neebood' …
bigger/cheaper	побольше/подешевле pa_bol'_she/padee_shev_lye
quieter/warmer	потише/потеплее pa_tee_she/pate_eplye_ye
No, I won't take it.	Нет, это не подойдёт. nyet _eta_ nee padayd_yot_

24

Problems Проблемы

The ... doesn't work.	... не работает. ... nee ra*botayet*
air conditioning	кондиционер *kandeetseeonyer*
fan	вентилятор *veenteelyatar*
heating	отопление *ataplyeneeye*
light	свет *svyet*
I can't turn the heat [heating] on/off.	Я не могу включить/выключить отопление. *ya nee magoo fklyoochyeet'/viklyoochyeet'*
There is no hot water/ toilet paper.	Нет горячей воды/туалетной бумаги. *nyet garyachyee vadi/tooal'etni boomagee*
The faucet [tap] is dripping.	Кран течёт. *kran teechyot*
The sink/toilet is blocked.	Раковина/туалет засорен(а). *rakaveena/tooalyet zasoreena*
The window/door is jammed.	Окно/дверь не закрывается. *akno/dvyer' nee zakrivaeetsa*
My room has not been made up.	Мой номер не убран. *moy nomeer nee oobran*
The ... is/are broken.	... сломан(а)/(ы). ... *sloman(a)/(i)*
blinds/shutters	жалюзи/ставни *zhalyoozee/stavni*
lamp	лампа *lampa*
lock	замок *zamok*
There are insects in our room.	У нас в комнате насекомые. *oo nas f komnatye naseekomiye*

Action Просьбы

Could you have that seen to?	Не могли бы Вы посмотреть? *nee maglee bi vi pasmatryet'*
I'd like to move to another room.	Я хотел(а) бы другую комнату. *ya khatyel(a) bi droogooyoo komnatoo*
I'd like to speak to the manager.	Я хотел(а) бы поговорить с директором. *ya khatyel(a) bi pagavareet' z deerektaram*

Requirements Общие требования

While 220 volts AC tends to be standard, you'll still find 110-120 volts AC in some places. Western plugs aren't the same as Russian ones, but large hotels often have sockets suited to Western plugs. However, suitable adapters are sometimes still hard to find in Russia, especially outside the big urban centers, so it is wise to take one with you.

About the hotel О гостинице

Where's the …?	Где ...? gdye …
bar	бар *bar*
bathroom	ванная *vanaya*
bathroom [toilet]	туалет *tooalyet*
dining room	ресторан *restaran*
elevator [lift]	лифт *leeft*
parking lot [car park]	автостоянка *aftastayanka*
shower room	душ *doosh*
swimming pool	бассейн *baseyn*
tour operator's bulletin board	доска объявлений *daska abyeevlyeneeye*
Does the hotel have a garage?	В отеле есть гараж? *v atyelye yest' garash*
Can I use this adapter here?	Здесь можно использовать этот адаптер? *zdyes' mozhna eespol'zavat etat adapteer*

ТОЛЬКО ДЛЯ БРИТВ	Razors [shavers] only.
ПОЖАРНЫЙ ВЫХОД	Emergency exit/ Fire exit
НЕ БЕСПОКОИТЬ	Do not disturb.
НАБЕРИТЕ ... В ГОРОД	Dial ... for an outside line.
НАБЕРИТЕ ... В БЮРО ОБСЛУЖИВАНИЯ	Dial ... for reception.
НЕ УНОСИТЕ ПОЛОТЕНЦА ИЗ НОМЕРА	Don't remove towels from room.

Personal needs Личные нужды

The key to room …, please.
Ключ от номера …, пожалуйста. *klyooch at <u>no</u>meera … pazha<u>l</u>sta*

I've lost my key.
Я потерял(а) ключ. *ya patee<u>ryal</u>(a) klyooch*

I've locked myself out of my room.
Я случайно захлопнул(а) дверь. *ya sloo<u>chya</u>yna za<u>khlop</u>nool(a) dvyer'*

Could you wake me at …?
Разбудите меня в … *razboo<u>dee</u>tye mee<u>nya</u> v …*

I'd like breakfast in my room.
Я хотел(а) бы завтрак в номер. *ya kha<u>tyel</u>(a) bi <u>zaf</u>trak v <u>no</u>meer*

Can I leave this in the safe?
Можно оставить это в сейфе? *<u>mozh</u>na a<u>sta</u>veet' eta v <u>syey</u>fye*

Could I have my things from the safe?
Можно взять вещи из сейфа? *<u>mozh</u>no vzyat' <u>vyesh</u>chyee eez <u>syey</u>fa*

Where can I find (a) …?
Где я могу найти …? *gdye ya ma<u>goo</u> <u>nay</u>tee …*

maid
горничную *<u>gor</u>neechnayoo*

our tour guide
экскурсовода *ekskoorsa<u>vo</u>da*

May I have (an) extra …?
Можно (ещё одно)…? *<u>mozh</u>na (ee<u>shchyo</u> ad<u>no</u>) …*

bath towel
большое полотенце *bal'<u>sho</u>ye pala<u>tyen</u>tse*

blanket
одеяло *adee<u>ya</u>la*

hanger
вешалку *<u>vee</u>shalkoo*

pillow
(ещё одну) подушку *(ee<u>shchyo</u> ad<u>noo</u>) pa<u>doosh</u>koo*

soap
мыло *<u>mi</u>la*

Is there any mail for me?
Есть почта для меня? *yest' <u>poch</u>ta dlya mee<u>nya</u>*

Are there any messages for me?
Мне что-нибудь передавали? *mnye <u>shto</u>neebood' peeree<u>da</u>valee*

Could you mail this for me, please?
Вы могли бы отправить вот это, пожалуйста? *vi ma<u>glee</u> bi at<u>pra</u>veet' vot <u>e</u>ta pa<u>zhal</u>sta*

BREAKFAST ➤ 43; CHANGING MONEY ➤ 138

Renting Съём квартиры/ дачи

We reserved an apartment/cottage …	Мы сняли квартиру/дачу … *mi snyalee kvarteeroo/dachyoo …*
in the name of …	на имя … *na eemya …*
Where do we pick up the keys?	Где взять ключи? *gdye vzyat' klyoochyee'*
Where is the…?	Где …? *gdye …*
electricity meter	счётчик *shchyotchyeek*
fuse box	распределительный щит *raspreedeeleeteel'niy shchyeet*
valve [stopcock]	запорный кран *zaporniy kran*
water heater	водонагреватель *vadanagreevateel'*
Are there any spare …?	Есть запасные ...? *yest' zapasniye …*
fuses	пробки *propkee*
gas bottles	газовые баллоны *gazaviye baloni*
sheets	простыни *prostinyee*
Which day does the maid come?	В какой день приходит уборщица? *f kakoy dyen' preekhodeet ooborshchyeetsa*
When do I put out the trash [rubbish]?	Когда выносить мусор? *kagda vinaseet' moosar*

Problems Проблемы

Where can I contact you?	Где я могу Вас найти? *gdye ya magoo vas naytee*
How does the stove [cooker]/ water heater work?	Как работает плита/водонагреватель? *kak rabotayet pleeta/vadanagreevateel'*
The … is/are dirty.	… грязно. *… gryazna*
The … has broken down.	… не работает. *… nee rabotayet*
We accidentally broke/lost …	Мы случайно сломали/потеряли … *mi sloochyayna slamalee/pateeryalee …*
That was already damaged when we arrived.	Это было уже сломано, когда мы приехали. *eta bila oozhe slomana kagda mi preeyekhalee*

28

HOUSEHOLD ARTICLES ➤ 148

Useful terms На даче

boiler	бойлер _boyleer_
crockery	посуда pa_soo_da
cutlery	прибор pre_ebor_
freezer	морозильная камера mara_zeel'_naya _kameera_
frying pan	сковорода skava_rada_
kettle	чайник _chyay_neek
lamp	лампа _lampa_
refrigerator	холодильник khala_deel'_neek
saucepan	кастрюля kast_ryoo_lya
stove [cooker]	плита _pleeta_
washing machine	стиральная машина stee_ral'_naya _mashina_

Rooms Комнаты

balcony	балкон bal_kon_
bathroom	ванная _vannaya_
bedroom	спальня _spal'_nya
dining room	столовая sta_lo_vaya
kitchen	кухня _kookh_nya
living room	гостиная gas_tee_naya
toilet	туалет tooa_lyet_

Youth hostel Общежитие

Sputnik, the Russian youth travel association, organizes group tours for students with accommodation in youth hostels (молодёжная турбаза **mala_dyozh_naya toor_ba_za**).

Do you have any places left for tonight?	Есть свободные места сегодня? yest' sva_bod_niye me_esta_ see_vodnya_
Do you rent [hire] out bedding?	Вы даёте напрокат постельное бельё? vi da_yotye_ napra_kat_ pas_tyel'_naye beel_yo_
What time are the doors locked?	Во сколько закрывается вход? va skol'ka zakri_vaeetsa fkhot
I have an International Student Card.	У меня студенческий билет. oo mee_nya_ stoo_dyen_chyeeskyee bee_lyet_

REQUIREMENTS ➤ 26; CAMPING ➤ 30

Camping Кемпинг

During the summer season – June to August and, in some areas, part of September – authorized campsites are operated near many cities. Campers may park a car and pitch a tent for a fixed rate that includes such amenities as showers and cooking facilities, plus a guided tour of nearby attractions. Arrangements must be made in advance through travel agents outside Russia. Note: Ask your travel agent to check on the security at your chosen campsite before you go.

Reservations Приезд

Is there a camp site near here?	Здесь есть кемпинг поблизости? *zdyes' yest' kyempeeng pableezastee*
Do you have space for a tent/trailer [caravan]?	Есть место для палатки/трейлера? *yest' myesta dlya palatkee/tryeyleera*
What is the charge …?	Сколько стоит ...? *skol'ka stoeet* …
per day/week	в день/в неделю *v dyen'/v needyelyoo*
for a tent/car	за палатку/машину *za palatkoo/mashinoo*
for a trailer [caravan]	за трейлер *za tryeyleer*

Facilities Удобства

Are there cooking facilities on site?	Здесь можно готовить? *zdyes' mozhna gatoveet'*
Are there any electrical outlets [power points]?	Здесь есть розетки? *zdyes' yest' razyetkee*
Where is/are the …?	Где ...? *gdye* …
drinking water	питьевая вода *peeteevaya vada*
trash cans [dustbins]	мусорные баки *moosarniye bakee*
laundry facilities	прачечная *prachyeechnaya*
showers	душ *doosh*
Where can I get some butane gas?	Где можно достать газовые баллоны? *gdye mozhna dastat' gazaviye baloni*

СТОЯНКА ТУРИСТОВ ЗАПРЕЩЕНА	no camping
ПИТЬЕВАЯ ВОДА	drinking water
РАЗЖИГАТЬ КОСТРЫ ЗАПРЕЩАЕТСЯ	no fires

Complaints Жалобы

It's too sunny here.
Здесь слишком на солнце.
zdyes sleeshkam na-sontse.

It's too shady/crowded here.
Здесь слишком в тени/
тесно. *zdyes sleeshkam f
tyenee/tyesno*

The ground's too hard/uneven.
Почва слишком твердая/неровная.
pochva sleeshkam tvyordaya/neerovnaya

Is there a more level spot?
Есть место поровнее?
yest' myesta paravnyeye

You can't camp here.
Здесь нельзя ставить палатки.
zdyes' neel'zya staveet' palatkoo

Camping equipment Снаряжение

butane gas	газовый баллон *gazaviy ballon*
campbed	раскладушка *raskladooshka*
charcoal	уголь *oogal'*
flashlight [torch]	фонарь *fanar'*
groundcloth [groundsheet]	полотнище *palotneeshchye*
guy rope	оттяжка *atyashka*
hammer	молоток *malatok*
kerosene [primus] stove	примус *preemoos*
knapsack	рюкзак *ryoogzak*
mallet	деревянный молоток *deereevyanniy malatok*
matches	спички *speechkee*
(air) mattress	(надувной) матрас *(nadoovnoy) matras*
paraffin	керосин *keeraseen*
sleeping bag	спальный мешок *spal'niy meeshok*
tent	палатка *palatka*
tent pegs	колышки *kolishkee*
tent pole	шест *shest*

Checking out Отъезд

When checking out, you'll get a pass proving that you have paid your bill.

What time do we have to check out by?	Во сколько надо освободить комнату? *va skol'ka nada asvabadeet' komnatoo*
Could we leave our baggage [luggage] here until ... p.m.?	Здесь можно оставить багаж до ...? *zdyes' mozhna astaveet' bagash da ...*
I'm leaving now.	Я уезжаю сейчас. *ya ooyeezhzhayoo seechyas*
Could you order me a taxi, please?	Вы могли бы заказать мне такси? *vi maglee bi zakazat' mnye taksee*
It's been a very enjoyable stay.	Мне (нам) очень понравилось здесь. *mnye (nam) ochyeen' panraveelas' zdyes'*

Paying Оплата

In Russia it is customary to tip taxi drivers and restaurant waiters. The size of the tip is optional but usually does not exceed 15%. Service is never included in any bill.

May I have my bill, please?	Можно счёт, пожалуйста? *mozhna shchyot pazhalsta*
How much is my telephone bill?	Сколько за телефон? *skol'ka za teeleefon*
I think there's a mistake in this bill.	Мне кажется, Вы ошиблись. *mnye kazhetsa vi ashiblees'*
I've made ... telephone calls.	Я звонил(а) ... раз(а). *ya zvaneel(a) ... raz(a)*
I've taken ... from the mini-bar.	Я брал(а) ... из мини-бара. *ya bral(a) ... eez meeneebara*
Can I have an itemized bill?	Можно счёт по пунктам? *mozhna shchyot pa poonktam*
Could I have a receipt, please?	Можно чек, пожалуйста? *mozhna chyek pazhalsta*

Eating Out

Restaurants Ресторан

Бар *bar*
Bar. These are usually found in hotels and only accept foreign currency.

Блинная *bleenaya*
Blini bar. Serves Блины (**bleeni**), Russian pancakes, with various toppings,
sweet and savory.

Буфет *boofyet*
Snack bar. These are found in hotels, theaters, at stations, etc., and are good
for light meals. You can buy food and drink and eat at one of the tables or
take your food away with you.

Закусочная *zakoosachnaya*
A kind of snack bar.

Кафе *kafye*
Café. Despite its name, a Russian "café" is the equivalent of a Western
restaurant. Many close by 9 p.m., 11 p.m. at the latest.

Кафе-кондитерская *kafye-kandeetyerskaya*
Also called simply Кондитерская; these cafés serve coffee and cakes.

Кафе-мороженое *kafye-marozhenaya*
Ice-cream parlor. These establishments serve ice cream, drinks, and
cocktails.

Кафетерий *kafeetyereey*
Cafeteria. Usually with no seats, serving small dishes, snacks, and salads.

Пельменная *peelmyenaya*
Small restaurants serving mainly пельмени (**peelmyenee**), a kind of meat dumpling.

Пивной бар *peevnoy bar*
Beer bar. Serves beer and appetizers, always crowded.

Пирожковая *peerashkovaya*
Snack bar. Sells only пирожки (**peerashkee**), savory pastries with various fillings (meat, cabbage, rice, jam, etc.).

Ресторан *reestaran*
Restaurant. In most cases it's a place where you go not just for a meal but for a whole evening's entertainment, with music and dancing. It is advisable to reserve a table in advance.

If you have a chance, don't restrict yourself to Russian food, but try restaurants where they serve Georgian, Armenian, Azerbaijani, or Uzbek specialities.

All restaurants close by midnight. Many close at 5 p.m. and re-open at 7 p.m.

Столовая *stalovaya*
Cafeteria or canteen (public establishment). Self-service, low prices, no alcohol.

Чайная *chaynaya*
Tearoom or small café.

Шашлычная *shashlichnaya*
An establishment serving шашлык (**shashlik**), pieces of lamb grilled on skewers, as well as other typical dishes from the Caucasus and Central Asia.

Meal times Часы работы

Breakfast (завтрак **zaftrak**): served from 7 a.m. to 10 a.m.

Lunch (обед **abyet**): served from about 11 a.m. to 4 p.m.

Dinner (ужин **oozhin**): served from about 6 p.m. to 10 or 10:30 p.m.
As restaurants close at 11 p.m. (midnight at the latest), Russians usually arrive early.

Russian cuisine Русская кухня

The country's geographical, climatic, and ethnic variety is reflected in a rich and varied cuisine. The Russians have a "sweet tooth" and are very fond of desserts and pastries, as well as their excellent ice cream.

Eating plays an important part in Russian social life, and it is while dining that you'll find Russians at their most hospitable. Don't forget to wish your table companions a hearty appetite – Приятного аппетита! (*preeyatnava apeeteeta*).

A table for…	Столик на … *stoleek na …*
1/2/3/4	одного/двоих/троих/четверых *adnavo/dvaeekh/traeekh/cheetveerikh*
Thank you.	Спасибо. *spaseeba*
The bill, please.	Пожалуйста, счёт. *pazhalsta shchyot*

Finding a place to eat
Где можно поесть?

Can you recommend a good restaurant?	Какой ресторан Вы рекомендуете? *kakoy reestaran vi reekameendooeetye*
Is there a(n) … near here?	Здесь есть … поблизости? *zdyes' yest' … pableezastee*
traditional local restaurant	национальный ресторан *natsianal'niy reestaran*
Chinese restaurant	китайский ресторан *keetayskeey reestaran*
fish restaurant	рыбный ресторан *ribniy reestaran*
Russian/Georgian restaurant	русский/грузинский ресторан *roosskeey/groozeenskeey reestaran*
Italian restaurant	итальянский ресторан *eetalyanskeey reestaran*
inexpensive restaurant	недорогой ресторан *needaragoy reestaran*
vegetarian restaurant	вегетарианский ресторан *veegeetaryanskiy reestaran*
Where can I find a(n) …?	Где находится …? *gdye nakhodeetsa …*
burger stand	кафе-гамбургер *kafe gamboorgeer*
café	кафе *kafe*
ice-cream parlor	кафе-мороженое *kafe marozheenaye*
pizzeria	пиццерия *peetseereeya*

Reserving a table Заказ столика

I'd like to reserve a table for two.	Я хотел(а) бы заказать столик на 2. *ya kha<u>tyel</u>(a) bi zaka<u>zat'</u> <u>sto</u>leek na dva<u>eekh</u>*
For this evening/tomorrow at …	на сегодня вечером/завтра на … *na see<u>vo</u>dnya <u>vye</u>cheeram/<u>zaf</u>tra na …*
We'll come at 8:00.	Мы будем в 8 часов. *mi <u>boo</u>dem v <u>vo</u>seem' chya<u>sof</u>*
A table for two, please.	Столик на двоих, пожалуйста. *<u>sto</u>leek na dva<u>eekh</u> pa<u>zhal</u>sta*
We have a reservation.	У нас заказ. *oo nas za<u>kas</u>*

Ваша фамилия?	What's the name, please?
Во сколько Вы будете?	What time will you be arriving?
Извините, мест нет.	I'm sorry. We're very busy/full up.
Столик освободится через … минут.	We'll have a free table in … minutes.
Вам придётся прийти через … минут.	You'll have to come back in … minutes.

Where to sit Где можно сесть?

Could we sit …?	Можно нам сесть …? *<u>mozh</u>na nam syest' …*
over there/outside	вон там/на улице *von tam/na <u>oo</u>leetse*
in a non-smoking area	где не курят *gdye nyee <u>koo</u>ryat*
by the window	у окна *oo ak<u>na</u>*
Smoking or non-smoking?	Курящий или некурящий? *koo<u>rya</u>shchyeey <u>ee</u>lee neekoo<u>rya</u>shchyeey*

– ya kha<u>tyel</u>(a) bi zaka<u>zat'</u> <u>sto</u>leek.
  –*na <u>skol</u>'ka chyela<u>vyek</u>?*
  – nas chyet<u>vee</u>ro.
  – *vo <u>skol</u>'ka vi <u>boo</u>deetye?*
– mi <u>boo</u>dyeem v <u>vo</u>seem chya<u>sof</u>.
  – *vasha fa<u>mee</u>leeya pa<u>zhal</u>sta?*
  – smeet.
  – *kha<u>ra</u>sho, do <u>vye</u>chyera.*

Ordering Заказ

Always check prices carefully before ordering, to avoid an
unpleasant surprise.

Waiter!/Waitress!	Официант!/Официантка! *ofeetsiant/ofeetsiantka*
May I see the wine list, please?	Можно посмотреть карту вин? *mozhna pasmatryet' kartoo veen*
Do you have a set menu?	У Вас есть меню? *oo vas yest' meenyoo*
Can you recommend some typical local dishes?	Что Вы рекомендуете типично местное? *shto vi reekameendooeetye teepeechna meestnaye*
Could you tell me what … is?	Скажите, что такое …? *skazhitye shto takoye …*
What's in it?	Что туда входит? *shto tooda fkhodeet*
What kind of … do you have?	Какой … у вас есть? *kakoy … oo vas yest'*
I'll have …	Я возьму … *ya vaz'moo …*
a bottle/glass/carafe of …	бутылку/стакан/графин … *booteelkoo/stakan/grafeen …*

Будете заказывать?	Are you ready to order?
Что Вы хотите?	What would you like?
Что будете пить?	Would you like to order drinks first?
Я бы рекомендовал(а) …	I recommend …
У нас нет …	We don't have …
Будет готово через … минут.	That will take … minutes.
Приятного аппетита!	Enjoy your meal.

– *boodeetye zakazivat'?*
– *shto vi rekamyendooeetye teepeechna meestnaye?*
– *ya bi rekamandaval(a) ….*
– *kharasho ya vaz'moo eta.*
– *pazhalsta a shto vi boodeetye peet'?*
– *grafeen krasnava veena pazhalsta.*
  kharasho.

DRINKS ➤ 50; MENU READER ➤ 52

Side dishes/Accompaniments
Салаты и гарниры

Could I have ... without ...?	Можно мне ... без ...? _mozhna_ mnye ... byez ...
With a side order of ...	С гарниром из ... z gar_nee_ram eez ...
Could I have salad instead of vegetables, please?	Можно мне салат вместо овощей? _mozhna_ mnye sa_lat_ vmyesta ava_shchyey_
Does the meal come with vegetables/potatoes?	Это блюдо с овощами/с картошкой? eta _blyooda_ s ava_shchya_mee/ s kar_toshkoy_
Do you have any sauces?	У вас есть соусы? oo vas yest' _so_-oosi
Would you like ... with that?	Вам с ...? vam s ...
vegetables/salad	овощами/салатом ava_shchya_mee/sa_la_tam
potatoes/fries	картофелем/жареным картофелем kar_to_feeleem/_zha_reenim kar_to_feeleem
rice	рисом _ree_sam
sauce	соусом _so_-oosam
ice	льдом l'dom
May I have some ...?	Можно мне ...? _mozhna_ mnye ...
bread	хлеба _khlye_ba
butter	масла _mas_la
lemon	лимон lee_mon_
mustard	горчицу gar_chyeet_sa
pepper	перец _pye_reets
salt	соль sol'
seasoning	приправы pree_pa_vi
sugar	сахар _sa_khar
artificial sweetener	сахарин sakha_reen_
blue cheese dressing	сырная заправка _sir_naya za_praf_ka
vinaigrette [French dressing]	уксусная заправка _ook_soosnaya za_praf_ka

General questions   Общие вопросы

Could I/we have a(n) (clean) …, please?	Можно (чистый) … , пожалуйста? _mozhna (chyeestiy) … pazhalsta_
ashtray	пепельницу _pyepeel'neetsoo_
cup/glass	чашку/стакан _chyashkoo/stakan_
fork/knife/spoon	вилку/нож/ложку _veelkoo/nosh/loshkoo_
serviette [napkin]	салфетку _salfyetkoo_
plate/spoon	тарелку _taryelkoo_
I'd like some more …, please.	Можно ещё … пожалуйста. _mozhna eeshchyo… pazhalsta_
Nothing more, thanks.	Ничего больше, спасибо. _neechyeevo bol'she spaseeba_
Where are the bathrooms [toilets]?	Где туалет? _gdye tooalyet_

Special requirements   Особые требования

I can't eat food containing …	Мне нельзя есть … _mnye neel'zya yest' …_
flour/fat	мучное/жирное _moochnoye/zheernaya_
salt/sugar	солёное/сладкое _salyonaye/slatkaye_
Do you have meals/drinks for diabetics?	Есть что-нибудь для диабетиков? _yest' shtoneebood' dlya deeabyeteekaf_
Do you have vegetarian dishes?	Есть что-нибудь для вегетарианцев? _yest' shtoneebood' dlya veegeetareeantsef_

For the children   Для детей

Do you have children's portions?	У вас есть детские порции? _oo vas yest' dyetskeeye portsiyee_
Could we have a child's seat, please?	Можно детский стульчик, пожалуйста. _mozhna dyetskeey stool'chyeek pazhalsta_
Where can I feed the baby?	Где можно покормить ребёнка? _gdye mozhna pakarmeet' reebyonka_
Where can I change the baby?	Где можно перепеленать ребёнка? _gdye mozhna peereepeeleenat' reebyonka_

CHILDREN ➤ 113

Fast food/Café Кафе

Something to drink Что-нибудь попить

I'd like …	Я хотел(а) бы … *ya khatyel(a) bi …*
beer	пиво *peeva*
(hot) chocolate	(горячий) шоколад *(garyacheey) shakalat*
tea/coffee	чай/кофе *chyay/kofye*
black/with milk	чёрный/с молоком *chyorniy/s malakom*
fruit juice	сок *sok*
mineral water	минеральную воду *meeneeral'nooyoo vodoo*
red/white wine	красное/белое вино *krasnaye/byelaye veeno*

And to eat … И поесть …

A piece of …, please.	Кусочек … , пожалуйста. *koosocheek … pazhalsta*
I'd like two of those.	Два кусочка вон того. *dva koosochka von tavo*
burger	гамбургер *gamboorgeer*
cake (small/large)	пирожное /торт *peerozhnaye/ tort*
fries/omelet	чипсы/омлет *cheepsi/amlyet*
sandwich	бутерброд *bootirbrot*
A … ice cream, please.	мороженое … *marozheenaye …*
vanilla/chocolate/strawberry	ванильное/шоколадное/клубничное *vaneel'naye/shakalatnaye/ kloobneechnaye*
A … portion, please.	Порцию …, пожалуйста. *portsiyoo … pazhalsta*
small/medium/large	маленькую/среднюю/большую *maleen'kooyoo/sryednyooyoo/ bal'shooyoo*
It's to go [take away].	Это с собой. *eta s saboy*
That's all, thanks.	Это всё, спасибо. *eta fsyo spaseeba*

– chto vi kha<u>tee</u>tye?
– dva <u>kof</u>ye pazha<u>lsta</u>.
– <u>chyor</u>niy <u>ee</u>lee s mala<u>kom</u>?
– s mala<u>kom</u> pazha<u>lsta</u>.
– shto <u>eesh</u>chyo?
– <u>e</u>ta fsyo spa<u>see</u>ba.

Complaints Жалобы

I don't have a knife/fork/spoon.	У меня нет ножа/вилки/ложки. *oo mee<u>nya</u> nyet na<u>zha</u>/<u>veel</u>kee/<u>losh</u>kee*
There must be some mistake.	Вы должно быть ошиблись. *vi dalzh<u>no</u> bit' a<u>shi</u>blees'*
That's not what I ordered.	Это не то, что я заказывал(а). *eta nee to shto ya za<u>ka</u>zival(a)*
I asked for …	Я просил(а)… *ya pra<u>seel</u>(a) …*
I can't eat this.	Это невозможно есть. *eta neeva<u>mozh</u>na yest'*
The meat is …	Мясо … *<u>mya</u>sa …*
overdone	пережарено *peeree<u>zha</u>reena*
underdone	недожарено *needa<u>zha</u>reena*
too tough	очень жёсткое *<u>ochyeen' zhost</u>kaye*
This is too …	Это очень … *eta ochyeen'…*
bitter/sour	горькое/кислое *<u>gor'</u>kaye/<u>kees</u>laye*
The food is cold.	Это холодное. *eta kha<u>lod</u>naye*
This isn't fresh.	Это несвежее. *eta neesvye<u>zhee</u>ye*
How much longer will our food be?	Сколько ещё ждать? *<u>skol'</u>ka eesh<u>chyo</u> zhdat'*
We can't wait any longer. We're leaving.	Мы не можем больше ждать. Мы уходим. *mi nee <u>mozh</u>em <u>bol'</u>she zhdat'. mi oo<u>kho</u>deem*
Have you forgotten our drinks?	Вы не забыли про наши напитки? *vi nee za<u>bi</u>lee pra <u>na</u>shi na<u>peet</u>kee*
This isn't clean.	Это грязное. *eta <u>gryaz</u>naye*
I'd like to speak to the head waiter/manager.	Я хочу поговорить с метр д'отелем/директором. *ya kha<u>chyoo</u> pagava<u>reet'</u> s myetr da<u>tye</u>leem/dee<u>rek</u>taram*

41

Paying Оплата

Remember to add 15% for service ➤ 32

The bill, please.	Можно счёт, пожалуйста? *mozhna shchyot pazhalsta*
I'd like to pay.	Я хотел(а) бы заплатить. *ya khatyel(a) bi zaplateet'*
We'd like to pay separately.	Мы будем платить отдельно. *mi boodeem plateet' addyel'na*
It's all together, please.	Всё вместе, пожалуйста. *fsyo vmyestye pazhalsta*
I think there's a mistake.	Мне кажется, Вы ошиблись. *mnye kazheetsa vi asheeblees'*
What is this amount for?	А это за что? *a eta za shto*
I didn't have that. I had …	Я это не заказывал(а). У меня было … *ya eta nee zakazival(a) oo meenya bila …*
Is service included?	Счёт включает обслуживание? *schyot fklyoochayeet apsloozhevaneeye*
Can I pay with this credit card?	Можно платить кредитной карточкой? *mozhna plateet' kreedeetnigh kartachkoy*
I forgot my wallet.	Я забыл(а) кошелёк. *ya zabil(a) kasheelyok*
I don't have enough money.	У меня не хватает денег. *oo meenya nee khvataeet dyeneek*
Could I have a receipt, please?	Можно отдельный чек? *mozhna addyel'niy chyek*
Can I have an itemized bill, please?	Можно счёт по пунктам? *mozhna shchyot pa poonktam*
That was a very good meal.	Всё было очень вкусно. *fsyo bila ochyeen' fkoosna*

– afitsyant schyot pazhalsta.
   – *pazhalsta. vot.*
– schyot fklyoochayeet apsloozhevaneeye?
   – *da.*
– mozhna plateet' kreedeetniy kartachkoy?
   – *kanyeshna.*
– spaseeba. fsyo bila ochyeen' fkoosna.

Course by course
Блюдо за блюдом

Breakfast Завтрак

A Russian breakfast can be quite hearty. You can either have tea
or coffee with bread, butter, and jam or, if you are feeling hungry, try hot
cereals, ham, eggs, sausages, and cheese.

I'd like to have breakfast.	Я хотел(a) бы позавтракать. *ya khatyel(a) bi pazaftrakat'*
I'd like …	Я бы хотел(a) … *ya bi khatyel(a)* …
a boiled egg	вареное яйцо *varyonaya yaytso*
fried eggs	яичницу *yaychneetsoo*
scrambled eggs	яичницу-болтунью *yaychneetsoo-baltoonyoo*
ham and eggs	яичницу с ветчиной *yaeechneetsoo c veechyeenoy*
oatmeal porridge/yogurt	овсянку/йогурт *avsyankoo/yagoort*
fruit juice	фруктовый сок *frooktoviy sok*
orange/grapefruit juice	апельсиновый/грейпфрутовый сок *apeel'seenoviy/greypfrootaviy sok*
jam/honey	джем/мёд *dzhem/myot*
bread/toast	хлеб/тост *khlyep/tost/*

Appetizers/Starters Закуски

These are often divided into "hot" and "cold." When ordering a starter,
just say На закуску … (**na zakooskoo**) and the name of the dish(es).

assorted meats/fish	ассорти мясное/рыбное *asartee myasnoye/ribnaye*
caviar	икра *eekra*
ham	ветчина *veetchyeena*
mushrooms	грибы *greebi*
spiced herring (sprats)	кильки *keel'kee*
sausage (mortadella)	колбаса *kalbasa*
shrimp [prawns]	креветки *kreevyetkee*
sturgeon	осетрина *asyertreena*
paté (mostly liver)	паштет *pashtyet*
herring	селёдка, сельдь *seelyotka, syel'd'*

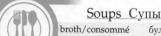

Soups Супы

broth/consommé	бульон *boolyon*
chicken soup	суп из курицы *eez kooreetsi*
fish soup	уха *ookha*
mushroom soup	грибной суп *greebnoy soop*
pea soup	гороховый суп *garokhaviy soop*
potato soup	картофельный *kartofeel'niy soop*
… with noodles/savory pastries/croutons	… с лапшой/пирожками/гренками … *s lapshoy/peerozhkamee/gryenkamee*

Борщ *borshch*
Borscht is a substantial dish made from beef, vegetables (chiefly beets), and sour cream. There are a number of regional varieties, including московский **maskofskee** (Moscow borscht with extra bacon); украинский **ookrayeenskee** (Ukrainian borscht with garlic); and холодный **khalodniy** (cold borscht).

Окрошка *akroshka*
A cold summer soup made from kvass (a Russian soft drink), cucumber, egg, onion, and sour cream.

Солянка *salyanka*
A soup made with salted cucumbers and olives, with either meat or fish.

Харчо *kharcho*
A spicy Georgian soup made with mutton and rice.

Шурпа *shoorpa*
Uzbek mutton soup with bacon and tomatoes.

Щи *shchyee*
Shchee is a thick Russian speciality soup made with cabbage or sauerkraut. There are a number of regional varieties, including зелёные с яйцом **zeelyonye s yeetsom** (flavored with sorrel and thickened with beaten egg); кислые **keesliye** (made with sauerkraut); and свежие **svyezhiye** (made with fresh cabbage).

Salads Салаты

зелёный салат	*zeelyoniy salat*	green salad
картофельный салат	*kartofeelniy salat*	potato salad
салат из крабов	*salat eez krabaf*	crabmeat salad
салат из редиски	*salat eez reedeeskee*	radish salad
салат из свежей капусты	*salat eez svyezhey kapoostee*	raw cabbage salad
салат с сельдью	*salat s syel'dyoo*	herring salad

Fish and seafood Рыба и дары моря

треска	*treeska*	cod
карп	*karp*	carp
краб	*krap*	crab
палтус	*paltoos*	halibut
сельдь, селёдка	*syel'd', seelyotka*	herring
омар	*amar*	lobster
макрель	*makryel'*	mackerel
устрицы	*oostreetsi*	oysters
креветки	*kreevyetkee*	shrimp [prawns]
сёмга	*syomga*	salmon
лососина	*lasaseena*	salmon
шпроты	*shproti*	sprats (herring)
форель	*faryel'*	trout
тунец	*toonyets*	tuna

Осетрина под белым соусом *aseetreena pad byelim sooosam*
Sturgeon served with a white sauce.

Осетрина паровая *aseetreena paravaya*
Steamed sturgeon served with a light sauce.

Осетрина по-русски *aseetreena parooskee*
Poached sturgeon served with a tomato sauce and vegetables.

Судак жареный в тесте *soodak zharyeniy v tyestee*
Pike perch fried in batter.

Судак отварной соус яичный *atvarnoy sooos yaeechnyi*
Pike perch poached and served with an egg sauce.

Meat/Poultry Мясо/Птица

говядина	*gavyadeena*	beef
молодая баранина	*maladaya baraneena*	lamb
печёнка	*peechyonka*	liver
свинина	*sveeneena*	pork
телятина	*teelyateena*	veal
кура	*koora*	chicken
утка	*ootka*	duck
гусь	*goos'*	goose
кролик	*kroleek*	rabbit
индейка	*eendyeyka*	turkey

Meat cuts Сорта мяса

грудинка/нога/крыло	*groodeenka/naga/krilo*	breast/leg/wing
антрекот/ромштекс/филе	*antreekot/ramshteks/feele*	entrecote/rump/fillet
биточки	*beetochbki*	rissoles
котлета	*katlyeta*	cutlet/chop
ростбиф	*rostbeef*	roast beef

Азу *azoo*
Chopped meat in a savory sauce.

Бефстроганов *beefstroganaf*
The famous Russian dish Beef Stroganoff. Fine strips of steak cooked in a cream and brandy sauce.

Говядина тушёная *gavyadeena tooshonaya*
Braised beef with aromatic vegetables.

Голубцы *galloopsi*
Cabbage stuffed with meat and rice.

Шашлык *shashlik*
Caucasian shashlik – pieces of lamb grilled on skewers.

Утка тушеная с яблоками *ootka tooshyonaya s yablakamee*
Duck roasted with apples.

Котлеты по-киевски *katlyeti pa keeyefskee*
Chicken Kiev – breast of chicken stuffed with butter and garlic.

Чахохбили из кур *chakhakhbeelee ees koor*
Caucasian chicken casserole, served with tomatoes and lots of onions.

Vegetables Овощи

фасоль	*fasol'*	beans
свёкла	*svyokla*	beetroot
капуста	*kapoosta*	cabbage
морковь	*markof'*	carrots
цветная капуста	*tsvyeetnaya kapoosta*	cauliflower
огурец	*agooryets*	cucumber
баклажан	*baklazhan*	eggplant [aubergine]
грибы	*greebi*	mushrooms
лук	*look*	onions
горох	*garokh*	peas
перец	*pyereets*	pepper
картофель	*kartofeel'*	potato
сладкая кукуруза	*slatkaya kookoorooza*	sweetcorn
помидоры	*pomeedori*	tomatoes
молодые кабачки	*maladiye kabachkee*	zucchini [courgettes]

Fruit Фрукты

яблоки	*yablaki*	apples
абрикосы	*abreekosi*	apricots
бананы	*banani*	bananas
черешня	*chyeeryeshnya*	cherries
виноград	*veenagrad*	grapes
лимоны	*leemoni*	lemons
дыня	*dinya*	melon
апельсины	*apeel'seeni*	oranges
персики	*pyerseeki*	peaches
груши	*grooshi*	pears
ананас	*ananas*	pineapple
сливы	*sleevi*	plums
клубника	*kloobneeka*	strawberries
арбуз	*arboos*	watermelon

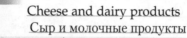

Cheese and dairy products
Сыр и молочные продукты

брынза	*brinza*	ewe's milk cheese (salty)
кефир	*keefeer*	kefir (butter milk)
ряженка	*ryazhinka*	baked sour milk, often served chilled
сливки	*sleefkee*	cream

сметана *smeetana*
Sour cream, an integral part of Russian cuisine, used in soups, salads, vegetable and meat dishes as well as in desserts.

сыр ... *sir ...* Cheeses come in many regional varieties:

латвийский	*latveeskeey*	Latvian
пошехонский	*pashyekhonskeey*	Poshekhonsky
российский	*rasseeyskee*	Russian

сырок *sirok*
Fresh white cheese (or spread).

творог *tvarok*
White unsalted cheese similar to cottage cheese – extremely popular and used in many dishes.

топлёное молоко *taplyonoye malako*
Baked milk, served chilled.

ватрушка *vatrooshka*
Cheese pastry (made from white cheese) often served as a savory with soups or as a sweet with tea, milk, etc.

Pies and dumplings Пирожки и пельмени

| пельмени | *peel'myenee* | stuffed dumplings |
| пирог/пирожки | *peerok/peerozhkee* | large pie/small pie |

пирог *peerok*
Large pie filled with meat, cabbage, mushroom, fish, etc. and topped with pastry.

пирожки *peerashkee*
Small pies with various fillings: meat, cabbage, mushrooms, onions, jam, etc.

хачапури *khachyapooree*
Georgian speciality: a kind of hot pancake filled with cheese (a popular snack).

вареники *varyeneekee*
Ukrainian dumplings filled with white cheese.

сырники со сметаной *sirneekee sa smeetanay*
White cheese fritters served with sour cream.

Dessert Сладкое

ватрушка	*vatrooshka*	cottage cheese pastry
кисель	*keesyel'*	fruit jelly
компот	*kampot*	fruit compote
оладьи с яблоками	*aladee c yablakamee*	small apple pancakes
рисовый пудинг	*reesaviy poodeeng*	rice pudding
ромовая баба	*romavaya baba*	rum baba
рулет	*roolyet*	sponge roll
яблоко в тесте	*yablaka v tyestye*	apple baked in pastry
взбитые сливки	*vzbeetiye sleefkee*	whipped cream

блинчики с вареньем **bleenchyeekee s varyeneeyam**
Small pancakes served with jam.

мороженое **marozhyenaye**
Ice cream – very popular everywhere and available in many flavors, including vanilla (ванильное **vaneel'naye**); fruit (фруктовое **frooktovaye**); and chocolate (шоколадное **shakalatnaye**).

пирог **peerok**
Pies or tarts served with a variety of fruit or cheese fillings, including lemon (с лимоном **s leemonam**); cottage cheese (творогом **tvaragom**); and fruit (фруктами **frooktamee**).

Pancakes Блины

Russian pancakes are made with yeast and served with different fillings. Smaller and thicker than Western pancakes, they are usually served with sour cream (сметана) and/or butter.

блины с икрой	*bleeni s eekroy*	pancakes with caviar
блины с сёмгой	*bleeni s syomgoy*	pancakes with salmon
блины со сметаной	*bleeni so smetanay*	pancakes with sour cream
блины с вареньем	*bleeni s varyenyem*	pancakes with jam
блины с брынзой	*bleeni s brinzoy*	pancakes with ewe's milk cheese

Drinks Напитки

Wine Вино

Wines from many countries are available throughout Russia. And it is sometimes easier to find French, California, and Italian wines than to find old favorites from Georgia such as **Tsinandali** (a dry, white wine), **Mukuzani** (a red table wine), and **Kindzmaraooli** (Stalin's favorite – red, a little sweet).

Russian champagne or sparkling wine is a popular drink. Dry, it can accompany almost any meal; sweet, it is usually enjoyed after meals or with dessert. Quality and price vary for wine with the same label. In general it is better to buy any drink from a liquor store than from a street kiosk.

I'd like a bottle of…	Я хотел(а) бы бутылку… *ya khatyel(a) bi bootilkoo…*
red wine	красного вина *krasnava veena*
white wine	белого вина *byelava veena*
champagne	шампанского *shampanskava*
blush [rosé] wine	розового вина *rozavava veena*
dry/sweet/sparkling wine	сухое/сладкое/шипучее вино *sookhoye/slatkaye/sheepoochyeeye veeno*

Beer Пиво

It is often easier to buy imported beer than milk. There is no shortage of the former, from all over the world. Many Russian beers taste weak to the Western palate, but it is worthwhile trying some while you are in Russia. **Zhigulyovskoye** and **Stolichnoye** are reliable brands.

Russian beer	жигулёвское *zheegoolyevskaye*
Riga beer	рижское *rishskaye*
Moscow beer	московское *maskofskaye*
Please bring me a bottle of beer.	Принесите мне, пожалуйста, бутылку пива. *preeneeseetye mne pazhalsta bootilkoo peeva*
Lager, please.	Светлого пива, пожалуйста. *svyetlava peeva pazhalsta*

Vodka Водка

Vodka is served chilled and always neat in small glasses. The etiquette of vodka drinking is as follows: drain the glass in one gulp, then chase it down with a morsel of food (usually a piece of black bread or salted cucumber). It is common to propose a toast when raising your glass. The smallest measure of vodka you can order is 50 grams (equal to a single), the next measure being 100 grams (equal to a double).

Please give me 50 grams of vodka.	Дайте мне, пожалуйста, 50 грамм водки. *daytye mnye pazhalsta peedeesyat' gram votkee*
I would like …	Я хотел(а) бы… *ya khatyel(a) bi…*
brandy (cognac)/sherry	коньяк/херес *kanyak/khyeres*
whisky/gin/rum	виски/джин/ром *veeskee/dzhin/rom*
liqueur	ликёр *leekyor*
To your good health!	За ваше здоровье! *za vashe zdarov'ye*

Non-alcoholic drinks Безалкогольные напитки

Stores and kiosks in big towns and cities are full of imported and locally produced soft drinks, fruit juices, and mineral water. The drink called a "cocktail" (коктейль **kakteyl'**), offered in ice-cream parlors, is a non-alcohol soft drink made from fruit juice or lemonade, to which ice cream and sometimes whipped cream is added – an ice-cream soda. Elsewhere this drink is called a "milk cocktail" (молочный коктейль **malochniy kakteyl'**) – a milk shake.

Kvass (квас) is a popular soft drink and a good thirst quencher in the summer when it is sold from small stalls in the street. Kvass, which looks like beer, is made from black bread and yeast.

Coffee Кофе

Coffee is not a traditional Russian drink. If you want strong coffee, ask for "eastern-style coffee" (кофе по-восточному **kofee pa vastochynamoo**), similar to Turkish coffee. If you order coffee with milk, you'll often get a glass of very sweet coffee with condensed milk.

coffee	кофе *kofye*
black/with milk	чёрный/с молоком *chyorniy/s malakom*
decaffeinated	без кафеина *bees kafeyna*

Tea Чай

Tea is the most popular Russian beverage. During your stay you will probably see one of the traditional Russian samovars (самовар **samavar**) used to heat the water for tea making. Tea is usually served in glasses, and it is often sweetened with honey or jam rather than sugar.

tea	чай *chyay*
black/with milk	чёрный/с молоком *chyorniy/s malakom*
with lemon	с лимоном *s leemonam*
iced tea	чай со льдом *chyay so l'dom*

Menu Reader

This Menu Reader gives listings under main food group headings. You will see that the Russian words are shown in large type. This is to help you to identify, from a menu that has no English, at least the basic ingredients making up a dish.

Meat, fish, and poultry

мясо	myasa	meat (general)
говядина	gavyadeena	beef
свинина	sveeneena	pork
телятина	talyateena	veal
молодая баранина	maladaya baraneena	lamb
кура	koora	chicken
утка	ootka	duck
рыба	riba	fish (general)
дары моря	dari morya	seafood (general)
икра	eekra	caviar
яйца	yaytsa	eggs (general)

Vegetables

овощи	_ovashchee_	vegetable(s) (general)
бобы/ фасоль	_babi/fasol'_	beans
шпинат	_shpeenat_	spinach
картофель	_kartofeel'_	pototoes
помидоры	_pameedori_	tomatoes
салат	_salat_	lettuce
огурец	_agooryets_	cucumber
морковь	_markof'_	carrrots
лук	_look_	onions
брокколи	_brakolee_	broccoli
капуста	_kapoosta_	cabbage
свёкла	_svyokla_	beetroot

Fruit

фрукты	*frookti*	fruit (general)
яблоко	*yablako*	apple
апельсин	*apeel'seen*	orange
банан	*banan*	banana
дыня	*dinya*	melon
арбуз	*arboos*	watermelon
груша	*groosha*	pear
слива	*sleeva*	plum
клубника	*kloobneeka*	strawberries
киви	*keevee*	kiwi fruit
ананас	*ananas*	pineapple

Staples: bread, rice, pasta, etc.

хлеб	*khlyep*	bread
рис	*rees*	rice
лапша	*lap<u>sha</u>*	noodles
каша	*<u>ka</u>sha*	porridge
макароны	*maka<u>ro</u>ni*	pasta
спагетти	*spa<u>gye</u>tee*	spaghetti
бобовые	*ba<u>bo</u>viye*	beans [pulses]

Basics

соль	*sol'*	salt
перец	*<u>pye</u>reets*	pepper
горчица	*gar<u>chee</u>tsa*	mustard
сахар	*<u>sa</u>khar*	sugar
уксусная заправка	*<u>ook</u>soosnaya za<u>pra</u>fka*	vinaigrette [French dressing]

Basic styles

варёный	*varyoniy*	boiled
жареный	*zhareeniy*	fried
жареный на гриле	*zhareeniy na greelee*	grilled
жаркое	*zharkoye*	roasted
копчёный	*kapchyoniy*	smoked
паровой	*paravoy*	steamed
отварной	*atavarnoy*	poached
тушёный	*tooshoniy*	stewed
соте	*sate*	sautéed
фарширо-ванный	*farsheerovaniy*	stuffed
маринованный	*mareenovaniy*	marinated

Classic dishes

азу	*azoo*	chopped meat in a savory sauce
бефстроганов	*beefstroganaf*	Beef Stroganoff *strips of beef fillet cooked with shallots in cream and brandy*
говядина тушёная с кореньями	*gavyadeena toshonaya s karyenyami*	braised beef with aromatic vegetables
жаркое из свинины с черносливом	*zharkoyl ees sveeneeni cheernasleevam*	roast pork with plums
утка тушёная с яблоками	*ootka tooshonaya s yablakamee*	roast duck with apples
котлеты по-киевски	*katlyeti pa keeyefskee*	Chicken Kiev *breast of chicken stuffed with butter and garlic*

Classic dishes (continued)

чахохбили из кур	*chakhakhbeelee ees koor*	Caucasian chicken casserole *served with tomatoes and lots of onions*
голубцы	*galooptsi*	cabbage stuffed with rice and meat
пельмени	*peel'myenee*	stuffed dumplings
шашлык	*shashlik*	Caucasian shashlik *pieces of lamb grilled on skewers*
осетрина под белым соусом	*aseetreena pat byelim sooosam*	steamed sturgeon in white sauce
осетрина по-русски	*aseetreena pa rooskee*	poached sturgeon served with tomato sauce and vegetables
судак жареный в тесте	*soodak zhareeniy f tyestye*	battered pike perch deep fried in batter
судак отварной соус яичный	*soodak atvarnoy sooos yaeechniy*	poached pike perch in an egg sauce

Drinks

вода	_vada_	water
молоко	_malako_	milk
чай	_chay_	tea
кофе	_kofye_	coffee
шоколад	_shakalat_	chocolate
водка	_votka_	vodka
виски	_veeskee_	whisky
джин	_dzheen_	gin
пиво	_peeva_	beer
вино	_veeno_	wine
шампанское	_shampanskaya_	champagne
фруктовый сок	_frooktoviy sok_	(fruit) juice

Drinks (continued)

апельсиновый сок	*apeel'seenavay sok*	orange juice
сок из грейпфрута	*sek ees greypfroota*	grapefruit juice
лимонад	*leemanat*	lemonade
кока-кола	*kola*	cola
содовая вода	*sodavaya vada*	soda water
тоник	*toneek*	tonic water
молочный коктейль	*malochniy kakteyl'*	milk shake
минеральная вода	*meeneeral'naya vada*	mineral water
квас	*kvas*	soft drink

жареный картофель	_zhareeniy kartofeel'_	French fries [chips]
гамбургер	_gamboorgeer_	hamburger
колбаса	_kalbasa_	sausage
омлет	_amlyet_	omelet
бутерброд	_bootirbrot_	sandwich
чипсы	_cheepsi_	potato chips [crisps]
мороженое	_marozheenaya_	ice cream
блины	_bleeni_	pancakes
печенье	_peechyenye_	cookie [biscuit]
пирожное	_peerozhnaya_	cake (small)
торт	_tort_	cake (large)

Soups/soup-based dishes

борщ	*borshch*	borscht *a substantial soup made with beef and vegetables, chiefly beet, served with sour cream*
щи	*shchee*	shchee *cabbage soup with many regional varieties*
бульон	*boolyon*	broth or consommé made from a variety of ingredients
бульон из куры	*boolyon ees koori*	chicken soup
окрошка	*akroshka*	summer soup *cold soup made with cucumber, egg, onion, and sour cream*
суп	*soop*	thick soup usually made with either peas, mushrooms, or potatoes
уха	*ookha*	fish soup

Soups/soup-based dishes (continued)

| харчо | kharcho | mutton soup – spicy Georgian soup made with mutton and rice |
| шурпа | shoorpa | an Uzbek soup made with mutton, bacon, and tomato |

Dairy/soy products

сыр	sir	cheese
йогурт	yogoort	yogurt
сливки	sleeftee	cream
масло	masla	butter
молоко	malako	milk
соевый творог	soyeviy tvarok	tofu
кефир	keefeer	kefir *sour milk, similar to thinner types of plain yogurt*
топлёное молоко	taplyonaye malako	baked milk served chilled, similar to junket
сырок	sirok	fresh white cheese

63

Desserts

ватрушка	*vatrooshka*	cottage cheese tart
кисель	*keesyel'*	fruit jelly topped with sugar, milk or cream
компот	*kampot*	fruit compote
оладьи с яблоками	*aladyee s yablakamee*	small apple pancakes
рисовый пудинг	*reesavay poodeeng*	rice pudding
ромовая баба	*romavaya baba*	rum baba
рулет	*roolyet*	sponge roll
яблоко в тесте	*yablaka b tyestye*	apple baked in pastry
блинчики с вареньем	*bleencheekee s varyenyem*	pancakes with jam
пирог	*peerok*	pie or tart served with a variety of fruit or cheese fillings

Travel

ESSENTIAL

1/2/3 ticket(s) to …	один билет/два/три билета в... *adeen beelyet/dva/tree beelyeta v …*
To …, please.	В ..., пожалуйста *v … pazhalsta*
one-way [single]	в один конец *v adeen kanyets*
round-trip [return]	туда и обратно *tooda ee abratna*
How much …?	Сколько стоит ...? *skol'ka stoeet*

Safety Безопасность

Beware of pickpockets in crowded places. It is a good idea to keep your money in a money belt.

Would you accompany me to the bus stop?	Проводите меня до автобусной остановки, пожалуйста. *pravadeetye meenya da aftoboosnay astanofkee pazhalsta*
I don't want to … on my own.	Я не хочу ... один/одна. *ya nee khachyoo … adeen/adna*
stay here	оставаться здесь *astavat'sa zdyes'*
walk home	идти домой *eettee damoy*
I don't feel safe here.	Я не чувствую себя здесь в безопасности. *ya nee choofsvooyoo seebya zdyes' f beezapasnastee*

Arrival Прибытие

As well as a valid passport, you will need a visa to visit Russia. You can obtain one from the Russian Embassy, or, perhaps, your travel agent.

Some international airports in Russia now have red and green custom's channels. The red channels often have long lines, due to "shuttle" traders. However, if you need to have currency and customs declaration forms stamped to avoid being detained upon leaving Russia because of any valuable items, such as photographic equipment and jewelry, which you brought with you, you need to go through the red channel. Currently, declaration forms are not stamped if you go through the green channel. Check on current regulations before setting off.

If you intend to stay in Russia for more than three months, you must produce a medical certificate showing that you are not HIV positive. Keep your passport with you at all times, especially if you have a dark complexion. People who look as if they are from the Caucuses/Chechnya are frequently stopped by the police.

The chart below shows what duty-free items you can bring into the country.

Cigarettes	Cigars	Tobacco	Spirits	Wine
250	250	250g.	1l.	2l.

Passport control Паспортный контроль

Ваш паспорт, пожалуйста	Can I see your passport, please?
Цель Вашего визита?	What's the purpose of your visit?
С кем Вы здесь?	Who are you here with?

We have a joint passport.	У нас двойной паспорт. *oo nas dvaynoy pasport*
The children are on this passport.	Дети вписаны в паспорт. *dyetee fpeesani f pasport*
I'm here on vacation [holiday]/business.	Я здесь в отпуске/по делу. *ya zdyes' v otpooskye/pa dyeloo*
I'm just passing through.	Я проездом. *ya prayezdam*
I'm going to ...	Я еду в ... *ya yedoo v ...*
I'm on my own.	Я один(одна). *ya adeen (adna)*
I'm with my family.	Я с семьёй. *ya s seemyey*
I'm with a group.	Я с группой. *ya s groopay*

Customs Таможня

I have only the normal allowances.

У меня только то, что разрешается. *oo meenya tol'ka to shto rasreeshayetsa*

It's a gift/for my personal use.

Это подарок/для личного пользования. *eta padarak/dlya leechnava pol'zavaneeya*

У Вас есть что-нибудь предъявить таможне? — Do you have anything to declare?

Вам надо платить пошлину. — You must pay duty on this.

Где Вы это купили? — Where did you buy this?

Откройте эту сумку. — Please open this bag.

У Вас есть ещё багаж? — Do you have any more luggage?

I would like to declare …

Я хочу предъявить … таможне. *ya khachyoo preedyaveet' … tamozhnye*

I don't understand.

Я не понимаю. *ya nee paneemayoo*

Does anyone here speak English?

Здесь кто-нибудь говорит по-английски? *zdyes' ktoneebood' gavareet pa angleeyskee*

ПАСПОРТНЫЙ КОНТРОЛЬ	passport control
СВОБОДНЫЙ КОРИДОР	nothing to declare
ГРАНИЦА	border crossing
ТАМОЖНЯ	customs
ТАМОЖЕННЫЙ ДОСМОТР	goods to declare
МИЛИЦИЯ	police
ТОВАРЫ БЕЗ ПОШЛИНЫ	duty-free goods

Duty-free shopping Покупка товаров без пошлины

What currency is this in?

В какой это валюте? *f kakoy eta valyootye*

Can I pay in …

Можно платить в … *mozhna plateet' v …*

dollars/rubles/pounds

долларах/рублях/фунтах *dollarakh/rooblyakh/foontakh*

Plane Самолёт

The former national airline, Aeroflot, has been broken up into many different companies, producing a confusing array of domestic carriers. International flights with an internal stopover are generally more realiable.

Tickets and reservations Заказ билетов

When is the … flight to Moscow?	Когда … рейс в Москву? *kagda … reys v maskvoo*
first/next/last	первый/следующий/последний *pyerviy/slyedooyooshchyeey/paslyedneey*
I'd like two … tickets to Moscow.	Мне надо два билета … в Москву? *mnye nada dva beelyeta … v maskvoo*
one-way [single]	в один конец *v adeen kanyets*
round-trip [return]	туда и обратно *tooda ee abratna*
first class	первый класс *pyerviy klass*
business class	бизнес класс *beeznees klass*
economy class	пассажирский класс *passazhirskeey klass*
How much is a flight to …?	Сколько стоит билет в …? *skol'ka stoeet beelyet v …*
Are there any supplements/discounts?	Есть какая-нибудь доплата/скидка? *yest' kakaya-neebood' daplata/skeetka*
I'd like to … my reservation for flight number …	Я хотел(а) бы … мой заказ на рейс номер … *ya khatyel(a) bi … moy zakas na reys nomeer …*
cancel	отменить *atmeeneet'*
change	поменять *pameenyat'*
confirm	подтвердить *pattveerdeet'*

Inquiries about the flight Справки о полётах

How long is the flight?	Сколько длится полёт? *skol'ka dleetsa palyot*
What time does the plane leave?	Во сколько вылетает самолёт? *va skol'ka vileetayet samalyot*
What time will we arrive?	Во сколько мы прилетаем? *va skol'ka mi preeleetayem*
What time do I have to check in?	Во сколько регистрация? *va skol'ka reegeestratsiya*

NUMBERS ➤ 216; TIME ➤ 220

Checking in Регистрация

Where is the check-in desk for flight …?	Где регистрация на рейс в …? *gdye reegeestratsiya na reys v …*
I have …	У меня … *oo meenya …*
three cases to check in	три чемодана *tree chyeemadana*
two pieces of hand luggage	два места ручной клади *dva myesta roochnoy kladee*
How much luggage is allowed free?	Сколько багажа можно провести бесплатно? *skol'ka bagazha mozhna praveestee beesplatna*

Ваш билет/паспорт, пожалуйста.	Your ticket/passport, please.
Вам место у окна или боковое?	Would you like a window or an aisle seat?
Курящий или некурящий?	Smoking or non-smoking?
Проходите в зал ожидания.	Please go through to the departure lounge.
Сколько у Вас мест багажа?	How many pieces of baggage do you have?
У Вас перевес багажа.	You have excess baggage.
Вы должны заплатить … рублей.	You'll have to pay a supplement of … rubles.
Этот слишком тяжёлый/большой для ручной клади.	That's too heavy/large for hand baggage.
Вы сами упаковывали багаж?	Did you pack these bags yourself?
Там есть острые или электрические предметы?	Do they contain any sharp or electronic items?

ПРИБЫТИЕ	arrivals
ОТПРАВЛЕНИЕ	departures
СЛУЖБА КОНТРОЛЯ	security check
НЕ ОСТАВЛЯЙТЕ БАГАЖ БЕЗ ПРИСМОТРА	do not leave bags unattended

BAGGAGE ➤ 71

Information Справки

Is there any delay on flight …?	Рейс в … задерживается? *reys v … zadyerzhivaeetsa*
How late will it be?	На сколько задерживается? *na skol'ka zadyerzhivaeetsa*
Has the flight from … landed?	Самолёт из … прибыл? *samalyot eez … preebil*
Which gate does flight … leave from?	С какого выхода посадка на рейс …? *s kakova vikhada pasatka na reys*

Boarding/In-flight Посадка/В полёте

Your boarding card, please.	Ваш посадочный талон, пожалуйста. *vash pasadachniy talon pazhalsta*
Could I have a drink/ something to eat, please?	Можно что-нибудь попить/поесть? *mozhna shtoneebood' papeet'/payest'*
Please wake me for the meal.	Разбудите меня, когда принесут еду. *razboodeetye meenya kagda preeneesoot eedoo*
What time will we arrive?	Во сколько мы прилетаем? *va skol'ka mi preeleetayem*
An air sickness bag, please.	Дайте гигиенический пакет, пожалуйста. *daytye geegeeyeeneechyeeskeey pakyet pazhalsta*

Arrival Прибытие

Where is/are the …?	Где …? *gdye …*
currency exchange	обмен валюты *abmyen valyooti*
buses	автобусы *aftoboosi*
car rental [hire]	прокат автомобилей *prakat aftamabeeleey*
exit	выход *vikhat*
taxis	такси *taksee*
telephone	телефон *teeleefon*
Is there a bus into town?	Есть автобус в город? *yest' aftoboos v gorat*
How do I get to the … hotel?	Как мне добраться до отеля …? *kak mnye dabrat'sa da atyelya*

BAGGAGE ➤ 71; CUSTOMS ➤ 67

Baggage Багаж

Porter! Excuse me!

Носильщик! Можно вас!
naseel'shchyeek
mozhna vas

Could you take my
luggage to …?

Подвезите мой багаж до …
padveezeetye moy bagash da …

a taxi/bus

такси/автобуса *taksee/aftoboosa*

Where is/are the …?

Где …? *gdye …*

luggage carts [trolleys]

багажные тележки
bagazhniye teelyeshkee

luggage lockers

камеры хранения
kameeri khranyeneeya

luggage check [left-luggage
office]

багажное отделение
bagazhnaye addeelyeneeye

baggage reclaim

выдача багажа *vidachya bagazha*

Where is the baggage
from flight …?

Где багаж рейса из …?
gdye bagash reysa eez …

Loss, damage, and theft Потеря, повреждение и кража

My luggage has been lost/
stolen.

У меня пропал/украли багаж.
oo meenya prapal/ookralee bagazh

My suitcase was damaged

Мне повредили чемодан.
mnye pavreedeelee chyeemadan

Our luggage has not arrived.

Наш багаж не прибыл.
nash bagash nee preebil

Do you have claim forms?

У Вас есть бланки?
oo vas yest' blankee

Как выглядит Ваш багаж?	What does your baggage look like?
У Вас есть багажный талон?	Do you have the claim check [reclaim tag]?
Ваш багаж …	Your baggage …
могли отправить в …	may have been sent to …
может прибыть сегодня позднее	may arrive later today
Пожалуйста, приходите завтра.	Please come back tomorrow.
Позвоните по этому номеру . подтвердить, прибыл ли багаж	Call this number to check if your baggage has arrived.

POLICE ➤ 152; COLOR ➤ 143

Train Поезд

The Russian writer Nikolay Gogol (1809–1852) wrote that the roads in Russia were bad. They still are. But a very comprehensive rail network was built during the Soviet era. Sadly, train stations can be frequented by drunks and homeless people, and are not the exciting and animated places they were a few years ago. Overnight trains – while remaining a wonderful way to travel around Russia – are not as safe as they used to be. So, check with your embassy or travel agent before traveling.

For long journeys make your reservations in advance. For short trips out to the suburbs check with your Intourist representative or ask at you hotel beforehand to see if there are any travel limits.

Экспресс *ehkspryes*
Long-distance express with luxury coaches; stops only at main stations.

Скорый поезд *skorriy poeezd*
Standard long-distance train; stopping at main stations.

Пассажирский поезд *passazhirskeey*
Inter-city train; doesn't stop at very small stations; regular fare. This type of train is seldom available for tourist travel.

Электричка *eeleektreechka*
Local train stopping at almost every station.

Международный вагон *meezhdoonarodniy vagon*
Sleeper with individual compartments (usually double) and washing facilities.

Купированный вагон *koopeeravanniy vagon*
Car with compartments for four people; berths with blankets and pillows. You can choose between "soft" (first) class, and "hard" (second) class.

Мякий вагон *myakhkeey vagon*
"Soft" (first) class; individual compartments for two or four people.

Жёсткий вагон *zhostkeey vagon*
"Hard" (second) class.

Плацкартный вагон *platskartniy vagon*
Second class only; no individual compartments, but with sleeping places.

To the station На вокзал

How do I get to the train station?	Как мне добраться до вокзала? *kak mnye dabrat'sa da vagzala*
Do trains to Moscow leave from … station?	Поезда на Москву отправляются с … вокзала? *paeezda na maskvoo atpravlyayootsa s … vagzala*
Is it far?	Это далеко? *eta daleeko*
Can I leave my car here?	Можно здесь оставить машину? *mozhna zdyes' astaveet' mashinoo*

At the station На вокзале

Where is/are the …?	Где …? *gdye …*
baggage check [left-luggage office]	багажное отделение *bagazhnaye addeelyeneeye*
currency exchange office	обмен валюты *abmyen valyooti*
information desk	справочное бюро *spravachnaye byooro*
lost-and-found office [lost-property office]	бюро находок *byooro nakhodak*
luggage lockers	камеры хранения *kameeri khranyeneeya*
platforms	платформы *platformi*
snack bar	буфет *boofyet*
ticket office	билетные кассы *beelyetniye kassi*
waiting room	зал ожидания *zal azhidaneeya*

ВХОД	entrance
ВЫХОД	exit
К ПЛАТФОРМАМ	to platforms
ИНФОРМАЦИЯ	information
ЗАКАЗ БИЛЕТОВ	reservations
ПРИБЫТИЕ	arrivals
ОТПРАВЛЕНИЕ	departures

DIRECTIONS ➤ *94*

Tickets Билеты

There are now many travel agencies in Russia where you can buy train tickets. Many hotels can also obtain tickets for you. Tickets purchased at a train station may be cheaper, but will probably cost you more in time and nervous energy.

I'd like a ... ticket to St. Petersburg.	Я хотел(а) бы билет ... до Санкт Петербурга. *ya khatyel(a) bi beelyet ... da sankt peeteerboorga*
one-way [single]	туда *tooda*
round-trip [return]	туда и обратно *tooda ee abratna*
first/second class	мягкий/купейный вагон *myakhkeey/koopyeyniy vagon*
concessionary	плацкарта *platskarta*
I'd like to reserve a(n) ...	Я хотел(а) бы заказать ... *ya khatyel(a) bi zakazat' ...*
seat	место *myesta*
window seat	у окна *oo akna*
berth	полку *polkoo*
Is there a sleeping car [sleeper]?	Это купейный/плацкартный вагон? *eta koopyeyniy/platskartniy vagon*
I'd like a(n) ... berth.	Я хотел(а) бы ... полку. *ya khatyel(a) bi ... polkoo*
upper/lower	верхнюю/нижнюю *vyerkhnyooyoo/neezhnyooyoo*
Can I buy a ticket on board?	Можно купить билет в поезде? *mozhna koopeet' beelyet v poyezdye*

Price Цена

How much is that?	Сколько стоит? *skol'ka stoeet*
Is there a discount for ...?	Есть скидка на ...? *yest' skeetka na ...*
children/families	детей/семейные группы *deetyey/seemyeyniye groopi*
senior citizens	пенсионерам *peenseeanyeram*
students	студентам *stoodyentam*
Do you offer a cheap same-day round-trip [return] fare?	Можно купить дешёвый билет туда и обратно? *mozhna koopeet' deeshoviy beelyet tooda ee abratna*

NUMBERS ➤ 216; DAYS OF THE WEEK ➤ 218

Queries Справки

Do I have to change trains?	Мне надо делать пересадку? *mnye nada dyelat' peereesatkoo*
Is it a direct train?	Это прямой поезд? *eta preemoy poeest*
You have to change at …	Вам надо делать пересадку в … *vam nada dyelat' peereesatkoo v …*
How long is this ticket valid for?	Сколько действителен этот билет? *skol'ka deestveeteeleen etat beelyet*
Can I take my bicycle on to the train?	Можно провезти велосипед в поезде? *mozhna praveestee veelaseepyet f poeezdye*
Can I return on the same ticket?	Это обратный билет? *eta abratniy beelyet*
In which car [coach] is my seat?	В каком вагоне моё место? *f kakom vagonye mayo myesta*
Is there a dining car on the train?	В поезде есть ресторан? *f poeezdye yest' reestaran*

– ya khatyel(a) bi beelyet da vladeemeera, pazhalsta.
— *tol'ka tooda eelee tooda ee abratna?*
— tooda ee abratna pazhalsta.
— *s vas peedeesyat rooblyey.*
— mnye nada dyelat' peereesatkoo?
— *da eta s peereesatkay v maskvye.*
— spaseeba. da sveedaneeya.

Train times Расписание поездов

Could I have a timetable, please?	Можно расписание, пожалуйста? *mozhna raspeesaneeye pazhalsta*
When is the … train to Vladimir?	Когда … поезд до Владимира? *kagda … poeezd da vladeemeera*
first/next/last	первый/следующий/последний *pyerviy /slyedooyooshchyeey /paslyedneey*
There's a train to Vladimir at …	Есть поезд до Владимира в … *yest' poeezd da vladeemeera v …*

	How frequent are the trains to …?	Как часто идут поезда до …? *kak chyasta eedoot paeezda da …*
	once/twice a day	один раз/два раза в день *adeen ras/dva raza v dyen'*
five times a day		пять раз в день *pyat' ras v dyen'*
every hour		каждый час *kazhdiy chyas*
What time do they leave?		Во сколько они отправляются? *va skol'ka anee atpravlyayootsa*
on the hour		каждый час *kazhdiy chyas*
20 minutes past the hour		каждые 20 минут *kazhdiye dvatsat' meenoot*
What time does the train stop at …?		Во сколько поезд останавливается в …? *va skol'ka poeezd astanavleevaeetsa v …*
What time does the train arrive in …?		Во сколько поезд прибывает в …? *va skol'ka poeezd preebivayet v …*
How long is the trip [journey]?		Сколько длится поездка? *skol'ka dleetsa payestka*
Is the train on time?		Поезд прибывает во время? *poeest preebivayet vovreemya*

Departures Отправление

Which platform does the train to … leave from?	С какой платформы отходит поезд до …? *s kakoy platformi atkhodeet poeezd da …*
Where is platform 4?	Где платформа номер четыре? *gdye platforma nomeer chyeetiree*
over there	вон там *von tam*
on the left/right	налево/направо *nalyeva/naprava*
under the underpass	через подземный переход *chyeereez padzyemniy peereekhot*
Where do I change for …?	Где мне делать пересадку на …? *gdye mnye dyelat' peereesatkoo na …*
How long will I have to wait for a connection?	Сколько нужно ждать поезда на пересадку? *skol'ka noozhna zhdat' poeezda na peereesatkoo*

Boarding Посадка

Is this the right platform for …?	Поезд до … отходит с этой платформы? *poeezd da … atkhodeet s etiy platformi*
Is this the train to …?	Это поезд до …? *eta poeezd da …*
Is this seat taken?	Это место занято? *eta myesta zaneeta*
I think that's my seat.	Мне кажется, это моё место. *mnye kazhetsa eta mayo myesta*
Here's my reservation.	Вот мой билет. *vot moy beelyet*
Are there any seats/berths available?	Есть свободные места/полки? *yest' svabodniye meesta/polkee*
Do you mind if …?	Не возражаете если…? *nee vazrazhaeetye yeslee …*
I sit here	я сяду здесь *ya syadoo zdyes'*
I open the window	я открою окно *ya atkroyoo akno*

On the journey В дороге

On long distance trains the attendant (проводник **pravadneek**) will check your ticket and may offer you some tea. There is often a dining car, but even if one is advertised it is still a good idea to bring food with you. And take plenty of soft drinks or mineral water. Trains can be very hot and stuffy. If you are in a separate compartment, secure the door from inside before you go to sleep. Take some strong string with you for this.

How long are we stopping here for?	Сколько мы здесь стоим? *skol'ka mi zdyes' staeem*
When do we get to …?	Когда мы будем в …? *kagda mi boodyem v …*
Have we passed …?	Мы проехали…? *mi prayekhalee …*
Where is the dining/sleeping car?	В каком вагоне ресторан? *f kakom vagonye reestaran*
Where is my berth?	Где моя полка? *gdye maya polka*
I've lost my ticket.	Я потерял(а) билет. *ya pateeryal(a) beelyet*

СТОП КРАН	emergency brake
АВТОМАТИЧЕСКИЕ ДВЕРИ	automatic doors
ВЫЗОВ ПРОВОДНИКА	alarm

TIME ➤ 220

Long-distance bus [Coach]
Междугородний автобус

There are long-distance buses between towns in Russia, but the network is not as accessible as the rail network – you will need to ask around to find out where the terminus is for a particular destination.

Where is the bus [coach] station? Где автобусная станция?
gdye aftoboosnaya stantsiya

When's the next bus [coach] to …? Когда следующий автобус до …?
kagda slyedooyooshchyeey aftoboos da …

Which bus stop [bay] does it leave from? С какой стоянки отправляется?
s kakoy stayankee atpravlyaeeetsa

Where are the bus stops [coach bays]? Где стоянка автобусов?
gdye stayanka aftoboosaf

Does the bus [coach] stop at …? Этот автобус останавливается в …?
etat aftoboos astanavleevaeeetsa v …

How long does the trip [journey] take? Сколько длится поездка?
skol'ka dleetsa payestka

Bus/Streetcar [Tram] Автобус/Трамвай

Buses are not as fast as the subway [metro], and run less frequently; on the other hand, you see more of the city. The fare is standard, regardless of the distance (but you can't change buses on the same ticket). It is a good idea to buy a booklet of tickets at a newsstand or subway station, although you can also get one on the bus, from the driver.

Where is the terminal [bus station]? Где автобусная станция/кольцо?
gdye aftoboosnaya stantsiya/kal'tso

Where can I get a bus/ streetcar [tram] to …? Где я могу сесть на автобус/трамвай до …?
gdye ya magoo syest' na aftoboos/

Остановка вон там/ вниз по улице	You need that stop over there/ down the road.
Вам нужен автобус номер …	You need bus number …
Вам нужно делать пересадку в …	You must change buses at …

АВТОБУСНАЯ ОСТАНОВКА	bus stop
ПО ТРЕБОВАНИЮ	request stop
НЕ КУРИТЬ	no smoking
(ЗАПАСНЫЙ) ВЫХОД	(emergency) exit

Buying tickets Покупка билетов

Where can I buy tickets?	Где можно купить билеты? *gdye mozhna koopeet' beelyeti*
A ... ticket to the center, please.	Билет ... до центра, пожалуйста. *beelyet ... da tsyentra pazhalasta*
one-way [single]	в один конец *v adeen kanyets*
round-trip [return]	туда и обратно *tooda ee abratna*
day/weekly/monthly	на день/на неделю/ на месяц *na dyen'/na needyelyoo/na myeseets*
A booklet of tickets, please.	Книжку талонов, пожалуйста. *kneeshkoo talonaf pazhalasta*
How much is it to ...?	Сколько стоит билет до ...? *skol'ka stoeet beelyet da ...*

Traveling Поездка

Is this the right bus/streetcar [tram] to ...?	Этот автобус/трамвай идёт до ...? *etat aftoboos/tramvay eedyot da ...*
Could you tell me when to get off?	Вы скажите мне где выходить? *vi skazhitye mnye gdye vikhadeet'*
Do I have to change buses?	Мне нужно делать пересадку? *mnye noozhna dyelat' peereesatkoo*
How many stops are there to ...?	Сколько остановок до ...? *skol'ka astanovak da ...*
Next stop, please!	На следующей, пожалуйста. *na slyedooyooshchyee pazhalsta*

– *eezveeneetye etat avtoboos eedyot da garsavyeta?*
– *da.*
– *adeen da garsavyeta pazhalsta.*
– *s vas adeen roobl'.*
– *vi skazheetye mnye gdye vikhadeet'?*
– *eta chyeetiree astanofkee atsyooda.*

NUMBERS ➤ 216; DIRECTIONS ➤ 94

Subway [Metro] Метро

The subway [metro] is the fastest and most convenient way of getting around in town. There are good networks in Moscow, St. Petersburg, and some other big cities. Moscow has the most extensive subway system, which is worth a visit for its fabulous décor alone. It runs from 6 a.m. to 1 a.m. The fare is standard, regardless of the distance traveled. You'll need to buy some tokens (жетоны **zhetoni**) at the counter and drop one in the token machine at the entrance. If you plan to travel around the city a lot, you may decide to buy a pass (единый билет **yedeeniy beelyet**), valid for 8 days, 16 days, or monthly, for travel on the subway, bus, trolleybus, and streetcar [tram].

General inquiries Общие вопросы

Where's the nearest subway [metro] station?
Где ближайшая станция метро?
gdye bleezhayshaya stantsiya meetro

Where can I buy a ticket?
Где можно купить билет?
gdye mozhna koopeet' beelyet

Could I have a map of the subway [metro], please?
Где можно посмотреть схему метро?
gdye mozhna pasmatryet' skhyemoo meetro

Traveling Поездка

Which line should I take for ...?
По какой линии ехать до ...?
pa kakoy leeneeyee yekhat' da ...

Is this the right train for ...?
Этот поезд идёт до ...?
etat poeest eedyot da ...

Which stop do I get off at for ...?
Где мне выходить у ...?
gdye mnye vikhadeet' oo ...

How many stops is it to ...?
Сколько остановок до ...?
skol'ka astanovak da ...

Is the next stop ...?
Следующая ...? *slyedooyooshchyaya ...*

Where are we?
Где мы находимся? *gdye mi nakhodeemsa*

Where do I change for ...?
Где делать пересадку до ...?
gdye dyelat' peereesatkoo da ...

What time is the last train to ...?
Когда отправляется последний поезд до ...?
kagda atpravlyaeetsya paslyedneey poyeezd da ...

ПЕРЕСАДКА НА ... to other lines/transfer

NUMBERS ➤ 216; BUYING TICKETS ➤ 74, 79

Ferry Паром

There are many rivers and lakes in Russia which have
regular ferry services. This is especially important in Siberia
where there are few roads.

When is the … car ferry to Volgograd?	Когда … паром до Волгограда? *kagda … param da Volgagrada*
first/next/last	первый/следующий/последний *pyerviy/slyedooyooshchyeey/paslyedneey*
hovercraft/ship	ракета/пароход *rakyeta/parakhot*
A round-trip [return] ticket for …	Билет до … туда и обрано. *beelyet da … tooda ee abratna*
one car and one trailer [caravan]	одна машина и один трейлер *adna mashina ee adeen tryeyleer*
two adults and three children	двое взрослых и трое детей *dvoye vzroslikh ee troye deetyey*
I want to reserve a … cabin.	Я хочу заказать … каюту. *ya khachyoo zakazat' … kayootoo*
single/double	одноместную/двухместную *adnamyestnooyoo/dvookhmyestnooyoo*

СПАСАТЕЛЬНЫЙ КРУГ	life preserver [life belt]
СПАСАТЕЛЬНАЯ ШЛЮПКА	lifeboat
МЕСТО СБОРА	muster station
ПРОХОД ЗАПРЕЩЁН!	no access

Boat trips Водные экскурсии

Is there a …?	У вас есть…? *oo vas yest' …*
boat trip	водная экскурсия *vodnaya ekskoorseeya*
river cruise	речной круиз *reechnoy krooeez*
What time does it leave/return?	Когда она начинается/кончается? *kagda ana nacheenayeetsya/ kanchayeetsya*
Where can we buy tickets?	Где можно купить билеты? *gdye mozhna koopeet' beelyeti*

TIME ➤ 220; BUYING TICKETS ➤ 74, 79

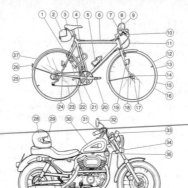

1 brake pad тормозная колодка f *tarmaznaya kalotka*
2 bicycle bag подседельная сумка f *patseedyel'naya soomka*
3 saddle седло n *seedlo*
4 pump насос m *nasos*
5 water bottle бутылка с водой f *bootilka s vadoy*
6 frame рама f *rama*
7 handlebars руль m *rool'*
8 bell звонок m *zvanok*
9 brake cable тросик тормоза m *troseek tormaza*
10 gear shift переключатель скоростей m *peereeklyoochateel' skarastyey*
11 gear cable тросик переключателя скоростей m *troseek peereeklyoochateelya skarastyey*
12 inner tube камера f *kameera*
13 front/back wheel переднее/заднее колесо n *peeryedneeye/zadneeye kaleeso*
14 axle ось f *os'*
15 tire протектор m *pratyektar*
16 wheel колесо n *kaleeso*
17 spokes спицы fpl *speetsi*
18 bulb лампа f *lampa*
19 headlight [headlamp] фара f *fara*
20 pedal педаль f *peedal'*
21 lock замок m *zamok*

22 generator генератор m *geeneeratar*
23 chain цепь f *tsyep'*
24 rear light задняя фара f *zadnyaya fara*
25 rim обод m *obat*
26 reflector отражатель m *atrazhateel'*
27 fender фартук m *fartook*
28 helmet шлем m *shlyem*
29 visor щиток m *shcheetok*
30 fuel tank топливный бак m *topleevniy bak*
31 clutch lever рычаг сцепления m *richak stseeplyeneeya*
32 mirror зеркало n *zyerkala*
33 ignition switch зажигание n *zazheeganeeya*
34 turn signal [indicator] указатель поворота m *ookazateel' pavarota*
35 horn звуковой сигнал m *zvookavoy seegnal*
36 engine двигатель m *dveegateel'*
37 gear shift [lever] рычаг переключения передач m *richak peereeklyoochateelya peereedach*
38 kick stand упор m *oopor*
39 exhaust pipe выхлопная труба f *vikhlapnaya trooba*
40 chain guard щиток цепи m s *hcheetok tsepee*

Bicycle/Motorbike
Велосипеды/Мотоциклы

I'd like to rent [hire] a ...	Я хотел(а) бы взять напрокат ... *ya khatyel(a) bi vzyat' naprakat ...*
3-/10-speed bicycle	3/10-скоростной велосипед *tryokh/deesateeskarastnoy veelaseepyet*
moped	мопед *mapyet*
motorbike	мотоцикл *matatseekal*
How much does it cost per day/week?	Сколько это стоит в день/неделю? *skol'ka eta stoeet v dyen'/needyelyoo*
Do you require a deposit?	Нужно платить аванс? *noozhna plateet' avans*
The brakes don't work.	Тормоза не работают. *tarmaza nee rabotayoot*
There are no lights.	Нет фар. *nyet far*
The front/rear tire [tyre] has a flat [puncture].	Передняя/задняя шина проколота. *peeryednyaya/zadnyaya shina prakolota*

Hitchhiking Голосовать на дороге.

Hitchhiking in Russia can be dangerous and is not recommended for foreigners, except in cases of extreme emergency.

Where are you heading?	Куда Вы едете? *kooda vi yedeetye*
I'm heading for ...	Я еду в ... *ya yedoo v ...*
Can you give me/us a lift?	Вы можете меня/нас подвезти? *vi mozhetye meenya/nas padveestee*
Is that on the way to ...?	Это по пути в ...? *eta pa pootee ...*
Could you drop me off ...?	Высадите меня ..., пожалуйста. *visadeetye meenya ... pazhalsta*
here	здесь *zdyes'*
at the ... exit	у поворота *oo pavarota*
downtown	в центре *f tsentrye*
Thanks for the lift.	Спасибо, что подвезли. *spaseeba shto padveezlee*

DIRECTIONS ➤ 94; NUMBERS ➤ 216

Taxi/Cab Такси

In the early 1990s taxis, which were all state owned, almost disappeared. Now more and more private taxi companies are being set up. Despite this there are still few taxis on the streets.

Most people hail private cars in the street. If you do this, make sure that the driver understands where you want to go. In addition, fix the price before getting in. Warning: Never get into a car if somebody else is in it with the driver. Be especially careful after dark.

Where can I get a taxi?	Где можно взять такси?
	kak vizvat' taksee pa teeleefonoo
Do you have the number for a taxi?	Как вызвать такси по телефону?
	kak vizvat' taksee pa teeleefonoo
I'd like a taxi …	Мне нужно такси ...
	mnye noozhna taksee …
now	сейчас *seechyas*
in an hour	через час *chyeereez chyas*
for tomorrow at 9:00	на завтра на 9:00 *na zaftra na devyat*
The pick-up address is …, going to …	Заберите по адресу ..., и езжайте по адресу ... *zabeereetye pa adreesoo …, ee eezhzhaytye pa adreesoo …*

	СВОБОДНО	for hire	

Please take me to (the) …	Пожалуйста, отвезите меня ...
	pazhalsta atveezeetye meenya …
airport	в аэропорт *v aeraport*
train station	на вокзал *na vagzal*
this address	по этому адресу *pa etamu adreesoo*
How much will it cost?	Сколько это будет стоить?
	skol'ka eta boodeet stoeet'
How much is that?	Сколько с меня? *skol'ka s meenya*
You said … rubles	Вы сказали ... рублей
	vi skazalee … rooblyey
Keep the change.	Оставьте сдачу. *astaf'tye zdachyoo*

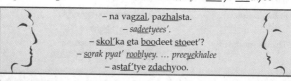

– na vagzal, pazhalsta.
  – sadeetyees'.
  – skol'ka eta boodeet stoeet'?
– sorak pyat' rooblyey. … preeyekhalee
  – astaf'tye zdachyoo.

84

NUMBERS ➤ 216; DIRECTIONS ➤ 94

Car/Automobile Машина

If you want to rent a car you must be 21 and have an international driver's license ➤ 86. If you are coming from Europe and want to take your car, you will need an international driving license, car registration papers, and insurance. It is essential to obtain up-to-date information on precisely what documents you need, so check with your travel agent or with the Russian Embassy. In both cases, however, be aware that car theft is big business in Russia, and that anything left unattended in the car is likely to be stolen. If you have a removable radio-cassette player, take it with you. It is also a good idea to take the windshield [windscreen] wipers!

When driving you must have an international driver's license and the car's registration papers. You should also check with your travel agent or the Russian Embassy as to what other documents you may need.

Russian drivers do not give way to pedestrians at pedestrian crossings. So if you are on foot, beware! And if you are driving, remember that the trucks and cars behind you will not stop!

Be especially careful at traffic-light controled intersections. Some drivers go through red lights well after they have changed. Others set off before their lights have turned to green.

In addition, you should observe speed limits as there are lots of radar traps. And always wear a seat belt – it is compulsory.

Conversion chart

km	1	10	20	30	40	50	60	70	80	90	100	110	120	130
miles	0.62	6	12	19	25	31	37	44	50	56	62	68	74	81

Speed limits

Speed limits	Cars	Motorbikes
Residential/ Built-up areas	60 km/h	60 km/h

Fuel

Gasoline	Premium [super]/Regular	Diesel
бензин	бензин А-93/бензин А-98	дизельное топливо
beenzeen	*beenzeen a deeveenosta tree/ beenzeen a deeveenosta voseem*	*deezeel'naya topleeva*

Car rental Прокат автомобилей

If you plan on renting a car, try to make arrangements in advance via your travel agent. Cars can be rented on the spot through Intourist and at some hotels. Locally published English-language newspapers, available free from many hotels and foreign-currency stores (Берёзка **beeryoska**), advertise car rental companies. Credit cards are accepted by the large car rental companies. To rent a car you must be 21 and have an international driver's license.

Where can I rent a car?	Где можно взять машину напрокат? *gdye mozhna vzyat' mashinoo naprakat*
I'd like to rent a(n) …	Я хотел(а) бы взять машину … напрокат. *ya khatyel(a) bi vzyat' mashinoo … naprakat*
2-/4-door car	с двумя/четырьмя дверями *z dvoomya/chyeetir'mya dveeryamee*
automatic	с автоматической трансмиссией *s aftamateecheeskay transmeeseeyey*
car with 4-wheel drive	с полным приводом *s polnim preevadam*
car with air conditioning	с кондиционером *s kandeetsianyeram*
I'd like it for a day/week.	Я хотел(а) бы на день/неделю. *ya khatyel(a) bi na dyeny/needyelyoo*
How much does it cost per day/week?	Сколько стоит на день/неделю? *skol'ka stoeet na dyen'/needyelyoo*
Is mileage/insurance included?	Километраж/страховка входит? *keelameetrash/strakhofka fkhodeet*
Are there special weekend rates?	Есть особый тариф по выходным? *yest' asobiy tareef pa vikhadnim*
Can I leave the car at …?	Можно возвратить машину в …? *mozhna vazvrateet' mashinoo v …*
What kind of fuel does it take?	Какой бензин нужен? *kakoy beenzeen noozheen*
Where is high [full]/ low [dipped] beam?	Где дальний/ближний свет? *gdye dal'neey/bleezhneey svyet*
Could I have full insurance, please?	Можно полную страховку, пожалуйста? *mozhna polnooyoo strakhofkoo pazhalsta*

Gas [Petrol] station Автосервис

New gas [petrol] stations are springing up like mushrooms, and gas is now usually available in urban areas. However, many Russians keep a full 20-liter gas container on board when going on long trips, just in case.

Where's the next gas [petrol] station?	Где ближайшая заправочная станция? *gdye bleezhayshaya zapravachnaya stantsiya*
Is it self-service?	Здесь самообслуживание? *zdyes' samaaps̲loozhivaneeye*
Fill it up, please.	Полный бак, пожалуйста. *polniy bak pazhalsta*
… liters, please.	… литров бензина, пожалуйста. *… leetraf beenzeena pazhalsta*
premium [super]/regular	бензин 98/бензин 93 *beenzeen nomeer deeveenosta voseem'/ beenzeen nomeer deeveenosta tree*
unleaded/diesel	очищенный/дизельное топливо *achyeeshchyeeniy/deezeel'naye topleeva*
Where is the air pump/water?	Где воздух/вода? *gdye vozdookh/vada*

ЦЕНА ЗА ЛИТР   price per liter

Parking Автостоянка

Parking is usually unrestricted, except in central areas in Moscow and St. Petersburg where one can now encounter not only parking meters and restricted zones but also booting [clamping] and tow-away vehicles.

Is there a parking lot [car park] nearby?	Здесь рядом есть автостоянка? *zdyes' ryadam yest' aftastayanka*
What's the charge per hour/day?	Сколько стоит в час/день? *skol'ka stoeet f chyas/dyen'*
Do you have some change for the parking meter?	Разменяйте для автомата, пожалуйста. *razmeenyaytye dlya aftamata pazhalsta*
My car has been booted [clamped]. Who do I call?	Моя машина заблокирована. Кого нужно вызвать? *Maya mashina zablakeerovana. Kavo noozhna vizbat'*

NUMBERS ➤ 216; DIRECTIONS ➤ 94

Breakdown Поломка

The state vehicle inspection authority patrols the traffic on highways [motorways] and gives roadside assistance.

Where is the nearest garage?	Где ближайшая станция обслуживания? *gdye bleezhayshaya stantsiya apsloozhivaneeya*
My car broke down.	У меня сломалась машина. *oo meenya slamalas' mashina*
Can you send a mechanic/ tow [breakdown] truck?	Можно прислать механика/буксир? *mozhna preeslat' meekhaneeka/bookseer*
I belong to a recovery service.	Я из службы технической помощи. *ya ees sloozhbi teekhneecheeskay pomashchee*
My registration number is …	Мой номер … *moy nomeer …*
The car is …	Машина … *mashina …*
on the highway [motorway]	на шоссе *na shasse*
2 km from …	2 км от … *dva keelamyetra at …*
How long will you be?	Как долго Вы будете? *kak dolga vi boodeetye*

What's wrong? Что случилось?

I don't know what's wrong.	Я не знаю, что-то не в порядке. *ya nee znayoo shtoto nee f paryatkee*
My car won't start.	Мотор не заводится. *mator nee zavodeetsa*
The battery is dead.	Аккумулятор сел. *akkoomoolyatar syel*
I've run out of gas [petrol].	Бензин кончился. *beenzeen konchyeelsa*
I have a flat [puncture].	Шина проколота. *shina prakolota*
There is something wrong with …	Что-то не в порядке с … *shtoto nee f paryatkye s …*
I've locked the keys in the car.	Я закрыл(а) ключи в машине. *ya zakril(a) klyoochyee v mashinye*

TELEPHONING ➤ 127; CAR PARTS ➤ 90–91

Repairs Ремонт

Do you do repairs?	Вы ремонтируете машины? *vi reemanteerooeetye mashini*
Could you take a look at my car?	Посмотрите мою машину, пожалуйста. *pasmatreetye mayoo mashinoo pazhalsta*
Can you repair it?	Можно починить? *mozhna pachyeeneet'*
Please make only essential repairs.	Пожалуйста, сделайте только основной ремонт. *pazhalsta zdyelaytye tol'ka asnavnoy reemont*
Can I wait for it?	Мне подождать? *mnye padazhdat'*
Can you repair it today?	Вы отремонтируете её сегодня? *vi atreemanteerooeetye yeyo seevodnya*
When will it be ready?	Когда будет готово? *kagda boodyet gatova*
How much will it cost?	Сколько это будет стоить? *skol'ka eta boodyet stoeet'*
That's outrageous!	Это возмутительно! *eta vazmooteeteel'na*
Can I have a receipt for my insurance?	Можно квитанцию для страховки? *mozhna kveetantsiyoo dlya strakhofkee*

... не работает.	The ... isn't working.
У меня нет запасных частей.	I don't have the necessary parts.
Нужно будет заказать части.	I will have to order the parts.
Это можно починить только временно.	I can only repair it temporarily.
Вашу машину можно списать.	Your car is beyond repair.
Это нельзя починить.	It can't be repaired.
Будет готово ...	It will be ready ...
сегодня попозже	later today
завтра	tomorrow
через ... дня(дней).	in ... days

DAYS OF THE WEEK ➤ 218; NUMBERS ➤ 216

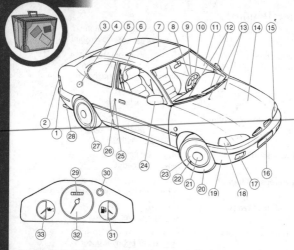

1 tail lights [back lights] задние огни mpl _zadnee agnee_

2 brakelights тормозные огни mpl _tarmazniye agnee_

3 trunk [boot] багажник m _bagazhneek_

4 gas tank door [petrol cap] крышка бензобака f _krishka beenzabaka_

5 window окно n _akno_

6 seat belt привязной ремень m _preevyaznoy reemyen'_

7 sunroof люк m _lyook_

8 steering wheel рулевое колесо n _rooleevoye kaleeso_

9 ignition зажигание n _zazheeganeeye_

10 ignition key ключ зажигания m _klyooch zazheeganeeya_

11 windshield [windscreen] ветровое стекло n _veetrovaye steeklo_

12 windshield [windscreen] wipers очистители ветрового стекла mpl _acheesteeteelee veetravova steekla_

13 windshield [windscreen] washer омыватель ветрового стекла m _amiyatel' veetravova steekla_

14 hood [bonnet] капот m _kapot_

15 headlights фары переднего света fpl _fari peeryedneeva svyeta_

16 license [number] plate номерной знак m _nameernoy znak_

17 fog lamp туманная фара f _toomanaya fara_

18 turn signals [indicators] указатели поворота mpl _ookazateelee pavarota_

19 bumper бампер m _bampeer_

20 tires [tyres] шины fpl _sheeni_

21 wheel cover [hubcap] колпак m _kalpak_

22 valve клапан m _klapan_

23 wheels колеса npl _kalyosa_

24 outside [wing] mirror боковое зеркало n _bakavoye zyerkala_

25 cental locking центральный замок m _tseetral'niy zamok_

26 lock замок двери m _zamok dvyeree_

27 wheel rim обод m _obat_

28 exhaust pipe выхлопная труба f _vikhlapnaya trooba_

29 odometer [milometer] одометр m _adomeetar_

30 warning light контрольная лампа f _kantrol'naya lampa_

31 fuel gauge расход топлива m _raskhot topleeva_

32 speedometer спидометр m _speedomeetar_

33 oil gauge расход масла m _raskhot masla_

34 backup [reversing] lights фара заднего хода f _fara zadneeva khoda_

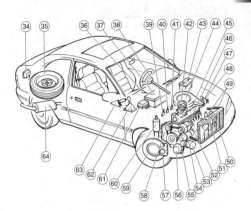

35 spare wheel запасное колесо n
   zapasnoye kaleso
36 choke воздушная заслонка f
   vazdooshnaya zaslonka
37 heater обогреватель m
   abagreevatel'
38 steering column рулевая колонка f
   rooleevaya kalonka
39 accelerator акселератор m
   akseeleerator
40 pedal педаль f *peedal'*
41 clutch сцепление n *stseeplyeneeye*
42 carburetor карбюратор m
   karbyooratar
43 battery аккамулятор m
   akamoolyatar
44 alternator генератор m *geeneeratar*
45 camshaft распределительный вал
   m *raspreedeeleeteel'niy val*
46 air filter воздушный фильтр m
   vazdooshniy feel'tar
47 distributor распределитель m
   raspreedeleeteel'
48 points контакты mpl *kantakti*
49 radiator hose (top/bottom) шланг
   радиатора (верхний, нижний) m
   shlang radeeatara (verkhneey, neezhneey)

50 radiator радиатор m *radeeatar*
51 fan вентилятор m *veenteelyatar*
52 engine двигатель m *dveegateel'*
53 oil filter масляный фильтр m
   maslyaniy feel'tar
54 starter [motor] стартер m *startyor*
55 fan belt ремень вентилятора m
   reemyen' veenteelyatara
56 horn звуковой сигнал m
   zvookavoy seegnal
57 brake pads тормозные колодки fpl
   tarmazniye kalotkee
58 transmission [gearbox] коробка
   передач f *karopka peereedach*
59 brakes тормоза mpl
   tarmaza
60 shock absorbers амортизаторы mpl
   amarteezatari
61 fuses предохранители mpl
   preedakhraneeteelee
62 gear shift [lever] рычаг
   переключения передач m *richak
   peereeklyoochyeneeya peereedach*
63 handbrake ручной тормоз m
   roochnoy tormas
64 muffler [silencer] глушитель m
   gloosheeteel'

REPAIRS ➤ 89

Accidents Авария

Insurance is not obligatory, but it is advisable to make sure that you, your passengers, any third party, and the car are covered. Try to arrange insurance before setting off for Russia. It may be possible to do so via agents of the state insurance agency **Ingosstrakh** (Ингосстрах).

There has been an accident.	Произошла авария. *praeezashla avareeya*
It's …	Это *eta* …
on the highway [motorway]	на шоссе *na shasse*
near …	около … *okala*
Where's the nearest telephone?	Где ближайший телефон? *gdye bleezhayshiy teeleefon*
Call …	Вызовите … *vizaveetee*
an ambulance	скорую помощь *skorooyoo pomashch'*
a doctor	врача *vrachya*
the fire department [brigade]	пожарная команда *pazharnaya kamanda*
the police	милицию *meeleetseeyoo*
Can you help me, please?	Помогите, пожалуйста. *pamageetee pazhalsta*

Injuries Травмы

There are people injured.	Люди получили травмы. *lyoodee paloochyeelee travmi*
He's seriously injured/bleeding.	У него серьёзная травма/кровотечение. *oo neevo seeryoznaya travma/ kravateechyeneeya*
She's unconscious.	Она без сознания. *ana byes saznaneeya*
He can't breathe.	Он не может дышать. *on nee mozheet dishat'*
He can't breathe/move.	Он не двигается. *on nee dveegayetsa*
Don't move him.	Не трогайте его. *nee trogaytye eevo*

ACCIDENT & INJURY ➤ 162; DIRECTIONS ➤ 94

Legal matters Юридические вопросы

What's your insurance company?	Кто ваш страхователь? *kto vash strakhavateel'*
What's your name and address?	Ваша фамилия и адрес? *vasha fameeleeya ee adrees*
He ran into me.	Он врезался в меня. *on vryezalsa v meenya*
She was driving too fast/too close.	Она ехала слишком быстро/близко. *ana yekhala sleeshkam bistra/bleeska*
I had the right of way.	У меня было право проезда. *oo meenya bila prava prayezda*
I was (only) driving at … kmph.	Я ехал(а) со скоростью (всего) … км в час. *ya yekhal(a) sa skorastyoo (fsyevo) … keelamyetraf f chyas*
I'd like an interpreter.	Мне нужен переводчик. *mnye noozhen peereevotchyeek*
I didn't see the sign.	Я не видел(а) знака. *ya nee veedyel(a) znaka*
He/She saw it happen.	Он/она видел(а) как это случилось. *on/ana veedyel(a) kak eta sloochyeelas'*
The registration number was …	Номер … *nomeer*

Ваш(и) …. пожалуйста?	Can I see your …, please?
водительские права	driver's license [licence]
страховое свидетельство	insurance card
регистрационные документы	vehicle registration document
Во сколько это случилось?	What time did it happen?
Где это случилось.	Where did it happen?
Кто-нибудь ещё был там?	Was anyone else involved?
Есть свидетели?	Are there any witnesses?
Вы превышали скорость.	You were speeding.
Фары не работают	Your lights aren't working.
Вы должны заплатить штраф.	You'll have to pay a fine (on the spot).
Вам придётся дать показания в отделении.	We need you to make a statement at the station.

TIME ➤ 220

Asking directions Как проехать

Excuse me, please.	Извините, пожалуйста. *eezvee<u>nee</u>tye pa<u>zhal</u>sta*
How do I get to …?	Как мне доехать до …? *kak mnye da<u>ye</u>khat' da …*
Where is …?	Где …? *gdye …*
Can you show me on the map where I am?	Покажите на карте, где я? *paka<u>zhi</u>tye na <u>kar</u>tye gdye ya*
I've lost my way.	Я заблудился(лась). *ya zabloo<u>dee</u>lsa(las')*
Can you repeat that, please?	Повторите, пожалуйста. *paf<u>ta</u>reetye pa<u>zhal</u>sta*
More slowly, please.	Помедленнее, пожалуйста. *pa<u>mye</u>dleennee pa<u>zhal</u>sta*
Thanks for your help.	Спасибо за помощь. *spa<u>see</u>ba za <u>po</u>mashch'*

Traveling by car На машине

Is this the right road for …?	Это дорога на …? *eta da<u>ro</u>ga na …*
How far is it to … from here?	Далеко до … отсюда? *da<u>lee</u>ko da … at<u>syoo</u>da*
Where does this road lead?	Куда ведёт эта дорога? *koo<u>da</u> vee<u>dyot</u> eta da<u>ro</u>ga*
How do I get onto the highway [motorway]?	Как мне выехать на шоссе? *kak mnye <u>vi</u>yekhat' na sha<u>sse</u>*
What's the next town called?	Как называется следующий город? *kak nazi<u>va</u>eetsa <u>slye</u>dooyooshchyeey <u>go</u>rat*
How long does it take by car?	Сколько времени ехать туда на машине? *<u>skol'</u>ka <u>vrye</u>meenee <u>ye</u>khat' too<u>da</u> na ma<u>shi</u>nye*

– eezvee<u>nee</u>tye pa<u>zhal</u>sta. kag mnye
da<u>ye</u>khat' da vag<u>za</u>la?
– <u>trye</u>teey pava<u>rot</u> na<u>lye</u>va ee pa<u>tom</u> pree<u>ya</u>ma.
– <u>trye</u>teey pava<u>rot</u> na<u>lye</u>va. eta da<u>lye</u>eko?
– da nyet, <u>dye</u>seet' mee<u>noot</u> khad'<u>bi</u>.
– spa<u>see</u>ba za <u>po</u>mashch'.
– pa<u>zhal</u>sta.

Location Как искать дорогу

Это ...	It's ...
прямо	straight ahead
налево	on the left
направо	on the right
на другой стороне улицы	on the other side of the street
на углу/за углом	on the corner/around the corner
по направлению к ...	in the direction of ...
напротив .../позади ...	opposite .../behind ...
рядом с .../после ...	next to .../after ...
Езжайте вниз по ...	Go down the ...
боковой улице/главной улице	side street/main street
Езжайте через площадь/мост.	Cross the square/bridge.
Поверните третий поворот направо.	Take the third right.
Поверните налево ...	Turn left ...
после первого светофора	after the first traffic light
у второго перекрёстка	at the second intersection [crossroad]

By car На машине

Это к ... от сюда.	It's ... here.
северу/югу/востоку/западу	north/south/east/west
Езжайте по дороге на ...	Take the road for ...
Это не та дорога.	You're on the wrong road.
Езжайте назад до ...	You'll have to go back to ...
Следуйте за дорожными знаками на ...	Follow the signs for ...

How far? Это далеко?

Это ...	It's ...
близко/недалеко/очень далеко	close/not far/a long way
5 минут ходьбы	5 minutes on foot
10 минут на машине	10 minutes by car
около 100 м вниз по дороге	about 100 meters down the road
примерно в 10 километрах	about 10 kilometers away

TIME ➤ 220; NUMBERS ➤ 216

Road signs Дорожные знаки

ПРОЕЗД	access only
ВАРИАНТ МАРШРУТА	alternative route
ОБЪЕЗД	detour [diversion]
УСТУПИ ДОРОГУ	yield [give way]
ОСТОРОЖНО, НИЗКИЙ ПРОЛЕТ	low bridge
ОДНОСТОРОННЕЕ ДВИЖЕНИЕ	one-way street
ДОРОГА ЗАКРЫТА	road closed

Town plans План города

аэропорт	airport
автобусный маршрут	bus route
автобусная остановка	bus stop
церковь	church
справочное бюро	information office
главная/центральная улица	main [high] street
кинотеатр	movie theater [cinema]
старый город	old town
парк	park
автостоянка	parking lot [car park]
переход	pedestrian crossing
пешеходная зона	pedestrian zone [precinct]
спортплощадка	playing field [sports ground]
отделение милиции	police station
почта	post office
стадион	stadium
вокзал	station
станция метро	subway [metro] station
стоянка такси	taxi stand [rank]
театр	theater
подземный переход	underpass
Вы вот здесь.	You are here.

Sightseeing

Intourist hotels have service bureaus (бюро обслуживания **byooro apsloozheevaneeya**) manned by multilingual staff who provide information, arrange outings and excursions, make reservations, and give general assistance. Other useful sources of information are the English-language newspapers, *Moscow Times* and *Where in St. Petersburg?*, found in many hotels and at kiosks.

Tourist information office
Туристическое бюро

Where's the tourist office?	Где справки? *gdye sprafkee*
What are the main attractions?	Какие главные достопримечательности? *kakeeye glavniye dastapreemeechyateelnastee*
We're here for …	Мы здесь на … *mi zdyes' na …*
only a few hours	несколько часов *nyeskal'ka chyasof*
a day	на один день *na adeen dyen'*
a week	на неделю *na needyelyoo*
Can you recommend …?	Вы можете порекомендовать …? *vi mozheetye pareekameendavat' …*
a sightseeing tour	обзорную экскурсию *abzornooyoo ekskoorseeyoo*
an excursion	экскурсию *ekskoorseeyoo*
a boat trip	водную экскурсию *vodnooyoo ekskoorseeyoo*
Are these leaflets free?	Эти брошюры бесплатно? *etee brashyoori beesplatna*
Do you have any information on …?	У Вас есть информация по …? *oo vas yest' eenfarmatsiya pa …*
Are there any trips to …?	Есть экскурсии в …? *yest' ekskoorseeyee v …*

Excursions Экскурсии

How much does the tour cost?	Сколько стоит эта экскурсия? *skol'ka stoeet eta ekskoorseeya*
Is lunch included?	Цена включает обед? *tseena fklyoochayeet abyet*
Where do we leave from?	Откуда мы отправляемся? *atkooda mi atpravlyayemsa*
What time does the tour start?	Во сколько начинается экскурсия? *va skol'ka nachyeenayetsa ekskoorseeya*
What time do we get back?	Во сколько мы возвращаемся? *va skol'ka mi vazvrashchyayemsa*
Do we have free time in ...?	У нас будет свободное время в ...? *oo nas boodyet svabodnaye vryemya v ...*
Is there an English-speaking guide?	У вас есть говорящий по-английски гид? *oo vas yest' gavaryashcheey pa angleeyskee geet*

On tour На экскурсии

Public lavatories are rare and horrible. If you must go, try a supermarket, a large store, or a pharmacy. Toilet paper is not to be found in most toilets, so carry some tissues with you.

Are we going to see ...?	Мы увидим ...? *mi ooveedeem ...*
We'd like to have a look at the ...	Нам хотелось бы посмотреть ...? *nam khatyelas' bi pasmatryet' ...*
Can we stop here ...?	Можно здесь остановиться, чтобы ...? *mozhna zdyes' astanaveet'sa shtobi ...*
to take photographs	фотографировать *fatagrafeeravat'*
to buy souvenirs	купить сувениры *koopeet' sooveeneeri*
to use the bathrooms [toilets]	сходить в туалет *skhadeet' f tooalyet*
Would you take a photo of us, please?	Фотографируйте нас, пожалуйста. *fatagrafeerooeetye nas pazhalta*
How long do we have here/in ...?	Сколько времени у нас здесь/в ...? *skol'ka vryemeenee oo nas zdyes'/v ...*
Wait! ... isn't back yet.	Подождите! ... ещё не пришёл(пришла). *padazhdeetye ... eeshcho nee preeshol (preeshla)*
Stop the bus! My child is feeling sick.	Остановите автобус – ребёнка тошнит. *astanaveetye aftoboos – reebyonka tashneet*

Sights Достопримечательности

Probably the best maps are the *New City Map and Guide* range, which sell for around $7. Maps in Cyrillic are cheaper, but the transliterated versions tend to be more up to date. (Maps printed before 1992 will have outdated street names.)

Where is the …	Где находится ...? *gdye nakhodeetsa …*
art gallery	картинная галерея *karteennaya galeeryeya*
battle site	место сражения *myesta srazheneeya*
botanical garden	ботанический сад *bataneechyeeskee sat*
castle	замок *zamak*
cathedral/church	собор/церковь *sabor/tserkaf'*
downtown area	центр города *tsentr gorada*
fountain	фонтан *fantan*
library	библиотека *beebleeatyeka*
market	рынок *rinak*
(war) memorial	мемориал *meemareeal*
monastery	монастырь *manastir'*
museum	музей *moozyay*
old town	старый город *stariy gorat*
opera house	оперный театр *opeerniy teeatr*
palace	дворец *dvaryets*
park	парк *park*
parliament building	здание парламента *zdaneeye parlameenta*
ruins	развалины *razvaleeni*
shopping area	торговый центр *targoviy tsentr*
statue/tower	статуя/башня *statooya/bashnya*
theater	театр *teeatr*
town hall	горсовет *garsavyet*
viewpoint	смотровая площадка *smatravaya plashchyatka*
Can you show me on the map?	Покажите мне на карте. *pakazhitye mnye na kartye*

DIRECTIONS ➤ 94

Admission Вход

Museums are usually open from 9 – 10 a.m. to 5 – 6 p.m. You'll find that they are invariably closed at least one day a week (usually Monday) and, in addition, one day a month will be set aside as "cleaning day."

Is the … open to the public?	… открыт(а) для всех? *atkrit (a) dlya fsyekh*
Can we look around?	Можно посмотреть? *mozhna pasmatryet'*
What are the opening hours?	В какие часы работает? *f kakeeye chyasi rabotayet*
When does it close?	Когда закрывается? *kagda zakrivayetsa*
Is … open on Sundays?	… открыт(а) по воскресеньям? *atkrit (a) pa vaskreesyenyeem*
When's the next guided tour?	Во сколько следующая экскурсия? *va skol'ka slyedooyooshchaya*
Do you have a guidebook (in English)?	У Вас есть путеводитель (на английском)? *oo vas yest' pooteevadeeteel' (na angleeskam)*
Can I take photos?	Можно фотографировать? *mozhna fatagrafeeravat'*
Is there access for the disabled?	Инвалидам можно? *eenvaleedam mozhna*
Is there an audioguide in English?	Есть запись экскурсии на английском? *yest' zapees' ekskoorseeyee na angleeskam*

Paying/Tickets Оплата/Билеты

How much is the entrance fee?	Сколько стоит входной билет? *skol'ka stoeet fkhadnoy beelyet*
Are there discounts for …?	Есть скидка для …? *yest' skeetka dlya* …
children/students	детей/студентов *deetyey/ stoodyentaf*
disabled/groups	инвалидов/групп *eenvaleedaf/groop*
senior citizens	пенсионеров *peenseeanyeraf*
1 adult and 2 children, please.	1 взрослый и 2 детских, пожалуйста. *adeen vzrosli ee dva dyetskeek pazhalsta*
I've lost my ticket.	Я потерял(а) билет. *ya pateeryal(a) beelyet*

– pyat' bee*lyet*af pa*zhal*sta. oo vas yest' *skeet*ka?
– *da yest'. dlya deetyey ee peenseeyanyeraf cheetiree rooblya.*
– dva *vzros*likh ee tree *dyets*keekh pa*zhal*sta.
– *s vas dvattsat' voseem' rooblyey pazhal*sta.

ВХОД СВОБОДНЫЙ	free admission
ЗАКРЫТО	closed
СУВЕНИРЫ	gift shop
ПОСЛЕДИЙ ВПУСК В 5 ЧАСОВ	latest entry at 5 p.m.
СЛЕДУЮЩАЯ ЭКСКУРСИЯ В ...	next tour at …
ВХОДА НЕТ	no entry
ФОТОГРАФИРОВАТЬ СО ВСПЫШКОЙ ЗАПРЕЩАЕТСЯ	no flash photography
НЕ ФОТОГРАФИРОВАТЬ!	no photography
ОТКРЫТО	open
ЧАСЫ РАБОТЫ	visiting hours

Impressions Впечатления

It's …	Это ... *eta* …
amazing	поразительно *parazeeteel'na*
beautiful	прекрасно *preekrasna*
bizarre	причудливо *preechoodleeva*
incredible	невероятно *neeveerayatna*
interesting/boring	интересно/скучно *eenteeryesna/skoochna*
magnificent	великолепно *veeleekalyepna*
romantic	романтично *ramanteechna*
strange/superb	странно/превосходно *stranna/preevaskhodna*
terrible/ugly	ужасно/безобразно *oozhasna/ beezabrazna*
It's good value.	Это стоит того. *eto stoeet tavo*
It's a rip-off.	Это слишком дорого. *eta sleeshkam doraga*
I like/don't like it.	Мне нравится/не нравится. *mnye nraveetsa/nee nraveetsa*

101

Tourist glossary
Словарь туриста

церковь/храм	*tsyerkaf'/khram*	church/temple
собор	*sabor*	cathedral
дворец	*dvar'yets*	palace
купол	*koopal*	dome
купол-луковка	*koopal-lookafka*	onion dome
английский парк	*angleeyskeey park*	formal garden
склеп	*sklyep*	crypt
икона/образ	*eekona/obraz*	icon
старинные вещи	*stareeniye vyeshchee*	antiquities
мавзолей	*mavzolyey*	mausoleum
башня	*bashnya*	tower

архитектура	*arkheeteektoora*	architecture
искусство	*eeskoostva*	art
керамика/фарфор	*keerameeka/farfor*	ceramics/porcelain
гончарные изделия	*gancharniye eezdyeleeya*	pottery
коллекция	*kalyektseeya*	collection
выставка	*vistafka*	exhibition
картина	*karteena*	painting
акварель	*akvaryel'*	watercolor painting
рукопись	*rookapees'*	manuscript
скульптура	*skool'ptoora*	sculpture
гобелен	*gabeelyen*	tapestry
ремёсла	*reemyosla*	crafts

Who/What/When?
Кто/Что/Когда?

What's that building?	Что это за здание? *shto eta za zdaneeye*
Who was the architect/artist/sculptor?	Кто архитектор/художник/скульптор? *kto arkheetyektar/khoodozhneek/skool'ptar*
When was it built/painted?	Когда это было построено/написано? *kagda eta bila pastroyeena/napeesana*
What style is that?	Какой это стиль? *kakoy eta steel'*
What period is that?	Какой это период? *kakoy eta peereeat*

Moscow Москва

The city of Moscow covers an area of 900 square kilometers. However, despite its size, the layout of the city is easily grasped – a series of concentric circles and radial lines, emanating from the Kremlin. The center of the city is compact enough to explore on foot.

Red Square and the **Kremlin** are the nucleus of the city. Here you'll find Lenin's Mausoleum and St. Basil's Cathedral, the famous GUM department store, and the Kremlin itself, whose splendid cathedrals and Armory museum head the list of attractions. The Kremlin is surrounded by two quarters, **Beliy Gorod** and **Zemlyanoy Gorod,** which are defined by circular boulevards built over the original medieval ramparts. In both quarters there are museums and art galleries. Beyond the historic core of the city, to the southwest of the Kremlin, there is the area called **Krasnaya Presnya** where the White House (the Russian Parliament building) is situated. South across the river from the Kremlin is **Zamoskvareche**, the home of the Tretyakov Gallery of Russian art, and Gorky Park.

St. Petersburg Санкт-Петербург

Founded by Peter the Great in 1703, the city has been known as St. Petersburg, Petrograd, Leningrad, and now again, St. Petersburg. It is a city built on a grand scale in keeping with its original status as the capital of the Tsarist Empire. The **River Neva** and its tributaries divide the city. The center lies on the south bank with its southern boundary marked by the **River Fontanka**. Some of the greatest sights and monuments are in and around **Nevsky Prospekt**. Here you will find the **Winter Palace** and the art collections of the **Hermitage**, the Mikhailovsky Palace and Russian Museum, the Summer Palace and Garden, and the cathedrals of St. Isaac and Kazan. Across the **Palace Bridge** from the Winter Palace, on Vasilevsky Island in the area called the **Strelka**, are some of the city's oldest institutions and a number of fascinating museums.

On the north side of the River Neva is the **St. Peter and Paul Fortress**, whose construction anticipated the foundation of the city. Besides its strategic and military significance, it housed St. Petersburg's first prison and cathedral.

Rulers Правители

Ivan III, Ivan the Great   1462–1505
Ruler of Muscovy, the first clear emergence of a nation-state.

Ivan IV, Ivan the Terrible   1547–1584
The first Muscovite ruler to make official and regular use of the title **tsar**, a Slavonic form of "Caesar."

The Time of Troubles   1598–1682
Peasant wars and foreign intervention; reign of Boris Godunov. Nominally ending with the first Romanov tsar.

Peter 1, Peter the Great   1682–1725
Foundation of St. Petersburg.

Catherine 11, Catherine the Great   1762–1796

Alexander I   1801–1825
1812 invasion of Russia by Napoleon.

Nicholas I   1825–1855
Crimean War.

Alexander II   1855–1881
Sale of Alaska to the United States. Serfs emancipated. Tsar assassinated.

Alexander III   1881–1894
Industrialization of Russia. *Communist Manifesto* translated into Russian.

Nicholas II   1894–1917
War with Japan. 1905 revolution. First World War. Abdication of the Tsar (1917). Tsar executed (1918).

1917–1991
Two revolutions in 1917 culminating in the *October Revolution* lead to the establishment of the Soviet government under Lenin.

1991–present
Breakup of the U.S.S.R. Establishment of the Russian Federation under Boris Yeltsin.

Places of worship Храмы

Russian Orthodox churches are being restored all over the country. Most are open to the public during services only. You will also find Protestant and Catholic churches.

Orthodox/Catholic/ Protestant church	православная/католическая/ протестанская церковь *pravaslavnaya/ kataleechyeeskaya/prateestantskaya tserkaf'*
mosque/synagogue	мечеть/синагога *meechyet'/seenagoga*
What time is …?	Когда будет…? *kagda boodeet …*
the mass/service	месса/служба *myessa/sloozhba*

105

In the countryside За городом

I'd like a map of …	Я хотел(а) бы карту … *ya khatyel(a) bi kartoo …*
this region	этого района *etava rayona*
walking routes	пешеходных маршрутов *peesheekhodnikh marshrootaf*
cycle routes	велосипедных маршрутов *veelaseepyedneekh marshrootaf*
How far is it to …?	Сколько километров до ...? *skol'ka keelamyetraf da …*
Can I walk there?	Можно пройти туда пешком? *mozhna praytee tooda peeshkom*
Is there a trail/scenic route to …?	Есть просёлочная дорога/живописный маршрут до ...? *yest' prasyolachnaya daroga/zhivapeesniy marshroot da …*
Can you show me on the map?	Покажите мне на карте. *pakazhitye mnye na kartye*
I'm lost.	Я заблудился(ась). *ya zabloodeelsa(as')*

Organized walks/hikes Походы

When does the guided walk start?	Когда будет поход? *kagda boodyet pakhot*
When will we return?	Когда мы вернёмся? *kagda mi veernyomsa*
What's the walk/hike like?	Какой это поход? *kakoy eta pakhot*
gentle/medium/tough	лёгкий/средний/трудный *lyokhkeey/sryeneey/troodniy*
Where do we meet?	Где мы встречаемся? *gdye mi fstreechyayemsa*
I'm exhausted.	Я устал(а). *ya oostal(a)*
How high is that mountain?	Какая высота этой горы? *kakaya visata etay gari*
What kind of … is that?	Что это за ...? *shto eta za …*
animal/bird	животное/птица *zhivotnaye/pteetsa*
flower/tree	цветок/дерево *tsveetok/dyereeva*

Geographic features
Географические особенности

bridge	мост *most*
cave	пещера *peeshchyera*
cliff	обрыв *abriv*
farm	ферма *fyerma*
field	поле *polye*
footpath	тропинка *trapeenka*
forest	лес *lyes*
hill	холм *kholm*
lake	озеро *ozeera*
mountain	гора *gara*
mountain pass	перевал *peereeval*
mountain range	хребет *khreebyet*
nature reserve	заповедник *zapavyedneek*
panorama	панорама *panarama*
park	парк *park*
pass	проход *prakhot*
path	тропинка *trapeenka*
peak	пик *peek*
picnic area	площадка для привала *plashchyatka dlya preevala*
pond	пруд *proot*
rapids	пороги *parogee*
ravine	овраг *avrak*
river	река *reeka*
sea	море *morye*
spa	минеральные воды *meeneeral'niye vodi*
stream	ручей *roochyey*
valley	долина *daleena*
viewpoint	смотровая площадка *smatravaya plashchyatka*
village	деревня *deeryevnya*
vineyard/winery	виноградник *veenagradneek*
waterfall	водопад *vadapat*
wood	лес *lyes*

Leisure

Events Развлечения

Intourist hotels have service bureaus manned by multilingual staff who provide information, arrange outings and excursions, make reservations, and give general assistance. You can also find listings of events in the various English-language entertainment guides available ➤ 97

During your stay, try to get tickets to the circus цирк (**tseerk**), especially the Moscow Circus or the Circus on Ice.

Do you have a program of events?	У Вас есть программа? *oo vas yest' pragramma*
Can you recommend a …?	Вы можете порекомендовать …? *vi mozheetye pareekameendavat'* …
ballet/concert	балет/концерт *balyet/kantsert*
movie [film]	фильм *feel'm*
opera	оперу *opeeroo*
play	спектакль *speektakal'*

Availability В продаже

When does it start/end?	Когда начинается/кончается? *kagda nachyeenayetsa/kanchyayetsa*
Where can I get tickets?	Где можно купить билеты? *gdye mozhna koopeet' beelyeti*
Are there any seats for tonight?	Есть билеты сегодня на вечер? *yest' beelyeti seevodnya na vyechyeer*
There are … of us.	Нас … *nas* …

Tickets Билеты

How much are the seats?	Сколько стоят эти места? *skol'ka stoyet etee meesta*
Do you have anything cheaper?	Есть что-нибудь подешевле? *yest' shtoneebood' padeeshevlye*
I'd like to reserve …	Я хотел(а) бы заказать … *ya khatyel(a) bi zakazat' …*
three tickets for Sunday evening	3 на воскресенье вечером *tree na vaskreesyenye vyecheeram*
one ticket for the Friday matinée	1 на пятницу на дневное представление *adno na pyatneetsoo na dnevnoye predstavlyeneeye*

Какой ... кредитной карточки?	What's your credit card …?
номер	number
тип	type
срок действия	expiration [expiry] date
Пожалуйста, выкупите билеты ...	Please pick up the tickets …
к ... часам	by … p.m.
в кассе	at the reservations desk

May I have a program, please?	Можно программу, пожалуйста? *mozhna pragramoo pazhalsta*
Where's the coatcheck [cloakroom]?	Где гардероб? *gdye gardeerop*

– ya vas slooshayoo?
– ya khatyel bi dva beelyeta na seevodnyashneey kantsert.
– pazhalsta.
– ya magoo zaplateet' kreedeetnay kartachkay?
– da.
– tagda ya vaspol'zooyoos' veezay.
– spaseeba … raspeesheetees' pazhalsta?

ЗАКАЗ БИЛЕТОВ	advance reservations
БИЛЕТЫ ПРОДАНЫ	sold out
БИЛЕТЫ НА СЕГОДНЯ	tickets for today

NUMBERS ➤ 216

Movies [Cinema] В кино

You should be able to find several movie theaters [cinemas] showing films in their original language.

Is there a multiplex cinema near here?	Здесь есть многозальный кинотеатр поблизости? *zdyes' yest' mnaga<u>zal</u>niy keenatee<u>atr pablee</u>zastee*
What's playing at the movies [on at the cinema] tonight?	Что идёт в кинотеатре сегодня вечером? *shto ee<u>dyot</u> f keenatee<u>a</u>trye see<u>vo</u>dnya <u>vye</u>chyeeram*
Is the film dubbed/subtitled?	Этот фильм дублирован/с субтитрами? *etat feel'm doo<u>blee</u>ravan/s soop<u>tee</u>tramee*
Is the film in the original English?	Этот фильм на английском? *etat feel'm na an<u>glee</u>skam*
Who's the main actor/actress?	Кто играет главную роль? *kto ee<u>gra</u>yet <u>gla</u>vnooyoo rol'*
A ..., please.	..., пожалуйста. *pa<u>zhal</u>sta*
box [carton] of popcorn	пакет воздушной кукурузы *pa<u>kyet</u> vaz<u>doosh</u>niy kookoo<u>roo</u>zi*
chocolate ice cream [choc-ice]	шоколадное мороженое *shaka<u>lad</u>naye ma<u>ro</u>zzhenaye*
hot dog	хот-дог *khot dok*
soft drink	напиток/газированную воду *na<u>pee</u>tak/gazee<u>ro</u>vannooyoo <u>vo</u>doo*
small/regular/large	маленький/средний/большой *ma<u>leen'</u>keey/<u>sryed</u>neey/bal'<u>shoy</u>*

Theater Театр

What's playing at the ... theater?	Что идёт в ... театре? *shto ee<u>dyot</u> v ... tee<u>a</u>tree*
Who's the playwright?	Чья постановка? *chya pasta<u>nof</u>ka*
Do you think I'd enjoy it?	Вы думаете, мне понравится? *vi <u>doo</u>mayetye mnye pan<u>ra</u>veetsa?*
I don't know much Russian.	Я плохо понимаю по-русски. *ya plokha panee<u>ma</u>yoo pa <u>roo</u>skee*

Opera/Ballet/Dance
Опера/Балет/Танец

Where's the opera house?	Где находится оперный театр? *gdye nakhodeetsa opeerniy teeatar*
Who's the composer/soloist?	Кто композитор/солист? *kto kampazeetar/saleest*
Is formal dress required?	Вечернее платье обязательно? *veechyerneeye platye abeezateel'na*
Who's dancing?	Кто танцует? *kto tantsooyet*
I'm interested in contemporary dance.	Меня интересует современный балет. *meenya eenteereesooyet savreemyenniy balyet*

Music/Concerts Музыка/Концерты

Where's the concert hall?	Где находится концертный зал? *gdye nakhodeetsa kantsertniy zal*
Which orchestra/band is playing?	Какой(ая) оркестр/группа играет? *kakoy(aya) arkyestr/groopa eegrayet*
What are they playing?	Что они исполняют? *shto anee eespalnyayoot*
Who is the conductor/soloist?	Кто дирижёр/солист? *kto deereezhor/saleest*
Who is the support band?	В сопровождении какого оркестра? *f sapravazhdyeneeye kakova arkyestra*
I really like …	Мне нравится ... *mnye nraveetsa …*
country music	музыка кантри *moozika kantree*
folk music	народная музыка *narodnaya moozika*
jazz	джаз *dzhas*
music of the sixties	музыка 60-х *moozika shesteedeesatikh*
pop	поп-музыка *popmoozika*
rock music	рок-музыка *rok moozika*
soul music	музыка сол *moozika sol*
Have you ever heard of her/him?	Вы слышали о ней/нём? *vi slishalee a nyey/nyom*
Are they popular?	Они популярны? *anee papoolyarniy*

Nightlife Ночная жизнь

You'll find nightclubs and discos mainly in hotels. You can also join in with the locals enjoying a dinner-dance at most restaurants.

What is there to do in the evenings?	Что здесь можно делать по вечерам? *shto zdyes' mozhna dyelat' pa veercheeram*
Can you recommend a …?	Вы можете порекомендовать …? *vi mozhetye pareekameendavat' …*
Is there a … in town?	В городе есть …? *v gorodye yest' …*
bar	бар *bar*
casino	казино *kazeeno*
discotheque	дискотека *deeskatyeka*
gay club	клуб гомосексуалистов *kloob gamaseeksooaleestaf*
nightclub	ночной клуб *nachnoy kloop*
restaurant	ресторан *reestaran*
Is there a floor show/cabaret?	Здесь есть кабаре? *zdyes' yest' kabare*
What type of music do they play?	Какую музыку они играют? *kakooyoo moozikoo anee eegrayoot*
How do I get there?	Как туда попасть? *kak tooda papast'*

Admission Вход

What time does the show start?	Во сколько начинается представление? *va skol'ka nachyeenayetsa preedstavlyeneeye*
Is evening dress required?	Вечернее платье обязательно? *veechyerneeye platye abyazateel'na*
Is there a cover charge?	Есть наценка? *Yest' natsyenka*
Is a reservation necessary?	Нужно заказывать заранее? *noozhna zakazivat' zaraneeye*
Do we need to be members?	Нужно быть членами клуба? *noozhna bit' chlyenamee klooba*
How long will we have to stand in line [queue]?	Как долго стоять в очереди? *kak dolga stayat' v ocheereedee*
I'd like a good table.	Я хотел(а) бы хороший столик. *ya khatye(l)a bi kharoshiy stoleek*

Children Дети

Can you recommend something for the children?	Что Вы рекомендуете для детей? *shto vi reekameendooyetye dlya deetyey*
Are there changing facilities here for babies?	Где можно перепеленать ребёнка? *gdye mozhna peereepeeleenat' reebyonka*
Where are the bathrooms [toilets]?	Где здесь туалет? *gdye zdyes' tooalyet*
amusement arcade	зал аттракционов *zal atraktseeonaf*
fairground	луна-парк *loonapark*
kiddie [paddling] pool	детский бассейн *dyetskeey bassyeyn*
playground	детская площадка *dyetskaya plashchyatka*
play group	детская группа *dyetskaya grooppa*
zoo	зоопарк *zapark*

Baby-sitting Присмотр за ребёнком

Can you recommend a reliable baby-sitter?	Вы можете порекомендовать хорошую няню? *vi mozhetye pareekamendavat' kharoshooyoo nyanyoo*
Is there constant supervision?	Дети постоянно под присмотром? *dyetee pastayanna pad preesmotram*
Are the staff properly trained?	Няни специально обучены? *nyanee speetsial'na aboochyeeni*
When can I drop them off?	Когда я могу их привести? *kagda ya magoo eekh preeveestee*
I'll pick them up at …	Я заберу их в … *ya zabeeroo eekh v …*
We'll be back by …	Мы вернёмся к … *mi veernyomsa k …*
What age is he/she?	Какой возраст? *kakoy vozrast*
She's 3 and he's 18 months.	Ей 3, а ему 18 месяцев. *yey tree a eemoo vaseemnatsat' myeseetseef*

Sports Спорт

Most of the sports common in the West are also played in Russia. The most popular in winter are ice hockey, skiing, and skating; in summer soccer, volleyball, and riding. Water sports, especially swimming, are very popular all year round, as are hunting and fishing.

Turkish-style public baths баня (**banya**) are a very popular form of relaxation and are a good way to meet people.

Spectating Спортивные зрелища

Is there a soccer [football] game [match] this Saturday?	Есть футбол в это воскресенье? *yest' foodbol' v eta vaskreesyeneeye*
Which teams are playing?	Какие команды играют? *kakeeye kamandi eegrayoot*
Can you get me a ticket?	Вы можете достать мне билет? *vi mozhetye dastat' mnye beelyet*
What's the admission charge?	Сколько стоит входной билет? *skol'ka stoeet fkhadnoy beelyet*
Where's the racetrack [race course]?	Где находится ипподром? *gdye nakhodeetsa eeppadrom*
Where can I place a bet?	Где я могу сделать ставку? *gdye ya magoo sdyelat' stafkoo*
What are the odds on ...?	Какие шансы на ...? *kakeeye shansi na ...*
athletics	атлетика *atlyeteeka*
basketball	баскетбол *baskeedbol*
cycling	велоспорт *veelasport*
golf	гольф *gol'f*
horse racing	скачки *skachkee*
soccer [football]	футбол *foodbol*
swimming	плавание *plavaneeye*
tennis	теннис *tyenees*
volleyball	волейбол *valeebol*

Playing Спортивные игры

Where's the nearest …?	Где здесь поблизости …? *gdye zdyes' pableezastee …*
golf course	корт для гольфа *kort dlya gol'fa*
sports club	спортклуб *spartkloop*
Where are the tennis courts?	Где теннисные корты? *gdye tyenneesniye korti*
What's the charge per …?	Сколько стоит билет на …? *skol'ka stoeet beelyet na*
day/hour	день/час *dyeny/chyas*
game/round (golf)	партия/раунд *parteeya/raoont*
Do I need to be a member?	Обязательно быть членом клуба? *abeezateel'na bit' chlyenam klooba*
Where can I rent [hire] …?	Где можно взять напрокат …? *gdye mozhna vzyat' naprakat*
boots	спортивную обувь *sparteevnooyoo oboof'*
clubs	клюшки *klyoopkee*
equipment	снаряжение *snareezheneeye*
a racket	ракетку *rakyetkoo*
Can I get lessons?	Можно брать уроки? *mozhna brat' oorokee*
Is there an aerobic class?	Здесь есть класс аэробики? *zdyes' yest' klass ayerobeekee*
Do you have a fitness room?	У Вас есть тренажёрный зал? *oo vas yest' reenazhorniy zal*
Can I join in?	Можно мне вступить? *mozhna mnye fstoopeet'*

Извините, всё занято.	I'm sorry, we're booked up.
Нужен залог …	There is a deposit of …
Какой у Вас размер?	What size are you?
Нужна фотография размером на паспорт.	You need a passport-size photo.

РАЗДЕВАЛКА	changing room
РЫБНАЯ ЛОВЛЯ ЗАПРЕЩЕНА	no fishing
ТОЛЬКО ПО СПЕЦИАЛЬНОМУ РАЗРЕШЕНИЮ	permit holders only

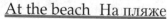

At the beach На пляже

Although the Russian summer is short, it can be hot, and there are a number of popular resorts on the Black Sea.

Is the beach …?	На пляже … *na plyazhee* …
pebbly/sandy	галька/песок *gal'ka/peesok*
Is there a … here?	Здесь есть …? *zdyes' yest'* …
children's pool	детский бассейн *dyetskeey bassyeyn*
swimming pool	бассейн *bassyeyn*
indoor/open-air	закрытый/открытый *zakritiy/atkritiy*
Is it safe to swim/dive here?	Здесь неопасно плавать/нырять? *zdyes' neeapasna plavat'/niryat'*
Is it safe for children?	Здесь неопасно для детей? *zdyes' neeapasna dlya deetyey*
Is there a lifeguard?	Здесь есть спасатели? *zdyes' yest' spasateelee*
I want to rent [hire] a/some …	Я хочу взять … напрокат. *ya khachyoo vzyat' … naprakat*
deck chair	шезлонг *shezlonk*
jet-ski	водный мотоцикл *vodniy matatseekal*
motorboat	моторную лодку *matornooyoo lotkoo*
rowboat	лодку *lotkoo*
sailboat	яхту *yakhtoo*
diving equipment	акваланг *akvalank*
umbrella [sunshade]	зонт *zont*
surfboard	доску *doskoo*
water skis	водные лыжи *vodniye lizhi*
windsurfer	виндсерфинг *veentsyorfeenk*
For … hours.	На … час(-а, -ов). *na … chyas(-a, -of)*

Skiing Лыжи

Skiing, particularly cross-country, is a popular sport in Russia. The *Russian Ski Club* can be a source of detailed information (http://www.poseidon.aha.ru/~ski/). Skating is also very popular. There are ice rinks in large parks and squares. Russians also love traditional horse-driven sleighs.

Is there much snow?	Сегодня много снега? *seevodnya mnoga snyega*
What's the snow like?	Какой сегодня снег? *kakoy seevodnya snyeg*
heavy/icy	тяжелый/со льдом *tyazholiy/sa l'dom*
powdery/wet	жесткий/влажный *zhyoskeey/vlazhniy*
I'd like to hire …	Я хотел(а) бы взять ... напрокат. *ya khatyel(a) bi vzyat' … naprakat*
poles	лыжные палки *lizhniye palkee*
skates	коньки *kan'kee*
ski boots/skis	лыжные ботинки/лыжи *lizhniye bateenkee/lizhi*
These are too …	Это слишком ... *eta sleeshkam …*
big/small	велико/мало *veeleeko/mala*
A lift pass for a day/ five days, please.	Проездной на день/пять дней, пожалуйста. *praeezdnoy na dyen'/ pyat' dnyey pazhalsta*
I'd like to join the ski school.	Я хотел(а) бы записаться в лыжную школу. *ya khatyel(a) bi zapeesat'sa v lizhnooyoo shkoloo*
I'm a beginner.	Я новичок. *ya naveechyok*
I'm experienced.	Я опытный лыжник. *ya opitniy lizhneek*

ВАГОН ПОДВЕСНОЙ ДОРОГИ	cable car/gondola
ПОДВЕСНОЙ ПОДЪЁМНИК	chair lift

117

Making Friends

Introductions Знакомство

You can use the Russian equivalent of Mr. (господин **gaspadeen**) and Mrs. or Miss/Ms. (госпожа **gaspazha**) along with the person's surname. However, these were not used during the communist era, when "comrade" (товарищ **tavareeshch**) was used for both men and women. As a result, today Russian people often don't know how to address each other!

It is polite to address people you know by their first name and patronymic, derived from the father's name. So, Nikolay, whose father's name is Ivan, would be called *Nikolay Ivanovich*; Natalia, whose father's name is Alexander, would be called *Natalia Alexandrovna*.

In Russian there are two forms of "you" (taking different forms of the verb): ты (**ti**) is used between members of the same family, close friends, and when talking to young children; вы (**vi**) is the polite form of address when you are talking to a person you do not know or to an acquaintance. When you are addressing more than one person, вы must always be used.

Hello, we haven't met.	Здравствуйте, мы не знакомы? *zdrastvooytye mi nee znakomi*
My name is …	Меня зовут … *meenya zavoot* …
May I introduce …?	Познакомьтесь … *paznakomtees'* …
John, this is …	Джон, это … *Dzhon eta* …
Pleased to meet you.	Очень приятно. *ochyeen' preeyatna*
What's your name?	Как Вас зовут? *kak vas zavoot*
How are you?	Как дела? *kak deela*
Fine, thanks. And you?	Спасибо, хорошо. А как вы?* *spaseeba kharasho a kak vi*

* The question "And you?" is given here in the polite form with "вы." In the dialog you will see the same question in the familiar form with "ты."

– *preevyet. kag deela?*
– spas<u>ee</u>ba *kharasho.* a kak ti?
– spas<u>ee</u>ba *kharasho.*

Where are you from? Откуда Вы?

Where do you come from?	Откуда Вы приехали? *atkooda vi preeyekhalee*
Where were you born?	Где Вы родились? *gdye vi radeelees'*
I'm from (the) …	Я из … *ya eez …*
Australia	Австралии *afstraleeyee*
Britain	Великобритании *veeleekabreetaneeyee*
Canada	Канады *kanadi*
England	Англии *angleeyee*
Ireland	Ирландии *eerlandeeyee*
Scotland	Шотландии *shatlandeeyee*
United States	Соединенных Штатов *sayeedeenyonikh shtataf*
Wales	Уэльса *ooel'sa*
Where do you live?	Где Вы живёте? *gdye vi zhivyotye*
What part of … are you from?	В каком районе … Вы живёте? *f kakom rayonye … vi zhivyotye*
Russia	России *rasseeyee*
Ukraine	Украины *ookraeeni*
Belarus	Белоруссии *beelarooseeyee*
We come here every year.	Мы приезжаем сюда каждый год. *mi pree eezzhzhayem syooda kazhdiy got*
It's my/our first visit.	Это мой/наш первый приезд. *eta moy/nash pyerviy preeyest.*
Have you ever been to …?	Вы бывали …? *vi bivalee …*
Britain/the United States	Великобритании/из Соединенных Штатов *veeleekabreetaneeyee/eez sayeedeenyonikh shtataf*
Do you like it here?	Вам нравится здесь? *vam nraveetsa zdyes'*
What do you think of the …?	Что Вы думаете о …? *shto vi doomayetye a …*
I love the … here.	Мне очень нравится … здесь. *mnye ochyeen' nraveetsa … zdyes'*
I don't care for the … here.	Мне не нравится … здесь. *mnye nee nraveetsa … zdyes'*
food/people	кухня/люди *kookhnya/lyoodee*

Who are you with? С кем Вы?

Who are you with?	С кем Вы? *s kyem vi*
I'm on my own.	Я один (одна). *ya adeen (adna)*
I'm with a friend.	Я с другом. *ya z droogam*
I'm with …	Я с … *ya s …*
my wife	моей женой *mayey zheenoy*
my husband	моим мужем *mayeem moozhem*
my family	моей семьёй *mayey seemyoy*
my children	моими детьми *mayeemee deet'mee*
my parents	моими родителями *mayeemee radeeteelyamee*
my boyfriend/my girlfriend	моей подругой *mayey padroogay*
my father/my mother	моим отцом/моей матерью *mayeem atsom/mayey mateeryoo*
my son/my daughter	моим сыном/моей дочерью *mayeem sinam/mayey docheeryoo*
my brother/my sister	моим братом/моей сестрой *mayeem bratam/mayey seestroy*
my uncle/my aunt	моим дядей/моей тетей *mayeem dyadeey/mayey tyoteey*
What's your son's/ wife's name?	Как зовут Вашего сына/Вашу жену? *kak zavoot vasheva sina/vashoo zheenoo*
Are you married?	Вы женаты? (to a man)/Вы замужем? (to a woman) *vi zhenati/vi zamoozhem*
I'm married.	Я женат (man)/замужем (woman). *ya zhenat /zamoozhem*
I'm single.	Я холост(а). *kholast (khalasta)*
I'm divorced/separated.	Я разведён(а)/не живу с мужем(женой). *razveedyon (razveedeena)/nee zhivoo s moozhem (zhenoy)*
I'm engaged.	Я обручён(а). *abroochyon (abroochyeena)*
We live together.	Мы живём вместе. *mi zhivyom vmyestye*
Do you have any children?	У вас есть дети? *oo vas yest' dyetee*
Two boys and a girl.	Два мальчика и девочка. *dva mal'cheeka ee dyevachka*
How old are they?	Сколько им лет? *skol'ka eem lyet*
They're ten and twelve.	Им десять и двенадцать. *eem dyeseet' ee dveenattsat'*

What do you do? Ваша профессия?

What do you do?	Ваша профессия? *vasha prafyeseeya*
What are you studying?	Что вы изучаете? *shto vi eezoochayeetye*
I'm studying ...	Я изучаю ... *ya eezoochyayoo*
I'm in business.	Я занимаюсь бизнесом. *ya zaneemayoos' beezneesam*
I'm in sales.	Я занимаюсь торговлей. *ya zaneemayoos' targovleey*
Who do you work for?	Где вы работаете? *gdye vi rabotayetye*
I work for ...	Я работаю в/на ... *ya rabotayoo v/na ...*
I'm a(n) ...	Я ... *ya ...*
accountant	бухгалтер *bookhgalteer*
engineer	инженер *eenzhenyer*
housewife	домохозяйка *damakhazyayka*
student	студент *stoodyent*
I'm ...	Я ... *ya ...*
retired	на пенсии *na pyenseeyee*
self-employed	работаю на себя *rabotayoo na seebya*
between jobs	временно не работаю *vryemeenna nee rabotayoo*
What are your interests/ hobbies?	Какие у вас интересы/хобби? *kakeeye oo vas eenteeryesi/khobbee*
I like ...	Я люблю ... *ya lyooblyoo*
music	музыку *moozikoo*
reading	читать *chyeetat'*
sports	спорт *sport*
I play ...	Я играю в ... *ya eegrayoo v ...*
Would you like to play ...?	Хотите сыграть в ...? *khateetye sigrat' v ...*
cards	карты *karti*
chess	шахматы *shakhmati*

What weather! Какая хорошая погода!

What a lovely day!	Какой прекрасный день! *ka<u>koy</u> pree<u>kras</u>niy dyen'*
What terrible weather!	Какая ужасная погода! *ka<u>ka</u>ya oo<u>zhas</u>naya pa<u>go</u>da*
It's cold/hot today.	Как холодно/жарко сегодня. *kak <u>kho</u>ladna/<u>zhar</u>ka see<u>vod</u>nya*
Is it usually this warm?	Здесь обычно такая тёплая погода? *zdyes' a<u>bich</u>na ta<u>ka</u>ya <u>tyo</u>playa see<u>vod</u>nya*
Do you think it's going to ... tomorrow?	Как вы думаете, завтра будет ...? *kak vi <u>doo</u>mayetye <u>zaf</u>tra <u>boo</u>dyet ...*
be a nice day	хороший день *kha<u>ro</u>shiy dyen'*
rain	дождь *dozhd'*
snow	снег *snyek*
What is the weather forecast?	Какой прогноз погоды? *ka<u>koy</u> prag<u>nos</u> pa<u>go</u>di*
It's ... today.	Сегодня ... *see<u>vod</u>nya ...*
cloudy	облачно *<u>ob</u>lachna*
foggy	туман *too<u>man</u>*
frosty	мороз *ma<u>ros</u>*
icy	гололёд *gala<u>lyot</u>*
rainy	дождь *dozhd'*
snowy	снег *snyek*
stormy	гроза *gra<u>za</u>*
windy	ветер *<u>vye</u>teer*
Has the weather been like this for long?	Давно стоит такая погода? *dav<u>no</u> sta<u>eet</u> ta<u>ka</u>ya pa<u>go</u>da*
What's the water temperature?	Как температура воды? *Kak teempeera<u>too</u>ra va<u>di</u>*
hot/warm/cold	горячая/тёплая/холодная *ga<u>rya</u>chyaya/<u>tyo</u>playa/<u>kho</u>ladnaya*
Will it be good weather for skiing?	Какой прогноз для лыжных прогулок? *ka<u>koy</u> prag<u>nos</u> dlya <u>lizh</u>nikh pra<u>goo</u>lok*

ПРОГНОЗ ПОГОДЫ   weather forecast

Enjoying your trip?
Вам здесь нравится?

Вы в отпуске?	Are you on vacation?
На чём Вы приехали сюда?	How did you get here?
Как прошла поездка?	How was your trip?
Где Вы остановились?	Where are you staying?
Сколько Вы уже здесь?	How long have you been here?
Сколько Вы пробудете здесь?	How long are you staying?
Что удалось посмотреть?	What have you done so far?
Какие у Вас планы?	Where are you going next?
Вам здесь нравится?	Are you enjoying your vacation?

I'm here on …	Я здесь … *ya zdyes'* …
business	в командировке *f kamandeerofkye*
vacation [holiday]	в отпуске/на каникулах *v otpooskye/na kaneekoolakh*
We came by …	Мы приехали на … *mi preeyekhalee na* …
train/bus/plane	поезде/автобусе/самолёте *poeezdye/aftoboosye/samalyotye*
car/ferry	машине/пароме *mashinye/paromye*
I have a rental [hire] car.	Я взял(а) машину напрокат. *ya vzyal(a) mashinoo naprakat*
We're staying …	Мы остановились …. *mi astanaveelees'* …
in an apartment	на квартире *na kvarteerye*
at a hotel/campsite	в отеле/кемпинге *vatyelye/kyempeengye*
with friends	у друзей *oo droozyey*
Can you suggest …?	Посоветуйте …? *pasavyetooytye* …
things to do	что здесь можно делать *shto zdyes' mozhna dyelat'*
places to eat	где можно поесть *gdye mozhna payest'*
places to visit	куда можно поехать *kooda mozhna payekhat'*
We're having a great/ terrible time.	Нам здесь очень нравится/совсем не нравится. *nam zdyes' ochyeen' nraveetsa/savsyem nee nraveetsa*

Invitations Приглашения

Would you like to have dinner with us on …?	Можно пригласить вас к нам на ужин в …? *mozhna preeglaseet' vas k nam na oozhin v …*
Are you free for lunch?	Можно пригласить вас на обед? *mozhna preeglaseet' vas na abyet*
Can you come for a drink this evening?	Может быть посидим где-нибудь сегодня вечером? *mozhet bit' paseedeem gdye neebood' seevodnya*
We are having a party. Can you come?	У нас вечеринка. Придёте? *oo nas veechyeereenka preedyotye*
May we join you?	Можно к вам присоединиться? *mozhna k vam preesaeedeeneet'sa*
Would you like to join us?	Не хотите к нам присоединиться? *nee khateetye k nam preesaeedeeneet'sa*

Going out Прогулка

What are your plans for …?	Какие у вас планы на …? *kakeeye oo vas plani na …*
today/tonight	сегодня/сегодня вечером *seevodnya/seevodnya vyechyeeram*
tomorrow	завтра *zaftra*
Are you free this evening?	Вы свободны сегодня вечером? *vi sfabodni seevodnya vyechyeeram*
Would you like to …?	Хотите …? *khateetye …*
go dancing	пойти потанцевать *paytee patantsevat'*
go for a drink/meal	пойти в ресторан *paytee v reestaran*
go for a walk	пойти погулять *paytee pagoolyat'*
go shopping	пойти по магазинам *paytee pa magazeenam*
Where would you like to go?	Куда вы хотите пойти? *kooda vi khateetye paytee*
I'd like to go to …	Я хотел(а) бы пойти в … *ya khatyel(a) bi paytee v …*
I'd like to see …	Я хотел(а) бы посмотреть … *ya khatyel(a) bi pasmatryet' …*
Do you enjoy …?	Вам понравилось …? *vam panraveelas' …*

Accepting/Declining
Принять/Отказать

Thank you. I'd love to.	Спасибо. Я с удовольствием. *spaseeba. ya s oodavol'stveeyem*
Thank you, but I'm busy.	Спасибо, но я занят(а) *spaseeba no ya zanyat(a)*
May I bring a friend?	Можно с другом? *mozhna z droogam*
Where shall we meet?	Где встретимся? *gdye fstryeteemsa*
I'll meet you …	Я буду ждать вас …. *ya boodoo zhdat' vas …*
in the bar	в баре *v barye*
in front of your hotel	перед входом в отель *pyereet fkhodam v atyel'*
I'll call for you at 8.	я зайду за вами в 8. *ya zaydoo za vamee v voseem'*
Could we make it a bit later/earlier?	Можно чуть позже/раньше? *mozhna chyoot' pozhzhe/ran'she*
How about another day?	Как-нибудь в другой раз. *kakneebood' v droogoy ras*
That will be fine.	Договорились. *dagavareelees'*

Dining out/in Ужин в ресторане/дома

If you are invited to a person's home for a visit or a meal, it will be much appreciated if you take a gift – flowers, chocolates, wine – or perhaps a small souvenir from your own country.

Let me buy you a drink.	Позвольте вам предложить что-нибудь выпить. *pazvol'tee vam preedlazheet' shto-neebood' vipeet'*
Do you like …?	Вы любите ...? *vi lyoobeetye …*
What are you going to have?	Что вы будете? *shto vi boodyetye*
That was a lovely meal.	Это был прекрасный ужин. *eta bil preekrasniy oozhin*

TIME ➤ 220

Encounters В гостях

Are you waiting for someone?	Вы ждёте кого-нибудь? *vi zhdyotye kavoneebood'*
Do you mind if I ...?	Вы не возражаете, если я ...? *vi nee vazrazhayetye yeslee ya ...*
sit here/smoke	сяду здесь/закурю *syadoo zdyes' zakooryoo*
Can I get you a drink?	Вам принести что-нибудь пить? *vam preeneestee shtoneebood' peet'*
I'd love to have some company.	Я люблю быть в компании. *ya lyooblyoo bit' f kampaneeyee*
Why are you laughing?	Почему Вы смеётесь? *pachyeemoo vi smeeyotyes'*
Is my Russian that bad?	Что мой русский так плох? *shto moy roosskeey tak plokh*
Shall we go somewhere quieter?	Давайте пойдём куда-нибудь где потише. *davaytye paydyom koodaneebood'*
Leave me alone, please!	Оставьте меня в покое, пожалуйста. *astaf'tye meenya f pakoye pazhalsta*
You look great!	Ты прекрасно выглядишь! *ti preekrasna vigleedeesh*
May I kiss you?	Можно тебя поцеловать? *mozhna teebya patselavat'*
I'm not ready for that.	Я не готов(а) к этому. *ya nee gotof(va) k etamoo*
I'm afraid we have to leave now.	Боюсь, что нам пора идти. *bayoos' shto nam para eettee*
Thanks for the evening.	Спасибо за вечер. *spaseeba za vyechyeer*
It was great.	Всё было прекрасно. *fsyo bila preekrasna*
Can I see you again tomorrow?	Может увидимся завтра? *mozhet ooveedeemsa zaftra*
See you soon.	Пока. *paka*
Can I have your address?	Можно твой адрес? *mozhna tvoy adrees*

Telephoning Телефон

One of the biggest changes in the "New Russia" has been in internal and international telecommunications. It is now possible to dial direct to almost anywhere in the world from a private or hotel phone.

The public telephone system is changing rapidly in the big towns and cities. However, public telephones can only be used for local calls. There are two types of public phone – those requiring brown plastic tokens (жетоны **zhetoni**) and those requiring telephone cards (карточки **kartochkee**). Both can be bought at subway [metro] stations. There are small telephone directories available in Moscow and St. Petersburg, listing numbers of organizations, shops, restaurants, and hotels. However, there are still no telephone directories listing numbers of private individuals.

Can I have your telephone number?
Можно Ваш номер телефона?
mozhna vash nomeer teeleefona

Here's my number.
Вот мой телефон. *vot moy teeleefon*

Please call me.
Пожалуйста, звоните.
pazhalsta zvaneetye

I'll give you a call.
Я позвоню Вам. *ya pazvanyoo vam*

Where's the nearest telephone booth?
Где здесь телефон-автомат?
gdye zdyes' teeleefon aftamat

May I use your phone?
Можно от Вас позвонить?
mozhna at vas pazvaneet'

It's an emergency.
Это срочно. *eta srochna*

I'd like to call someone in England.
Я хочу позвонить в Англию.
ya khachyoo pazvaneet' v angleeyoo

What's the area [dialling] code for …?
Какой код в …? *kakoy kod v …*

What's the number for Information [Directory Enquiries]?
Какой номер справочной службы?
kakoy nomeer spravachniy sloozhb

I'd like the number for …
Мне нужен номер …
mnye noozhen nomeer …

I'd like to call collect [reverse the charges].
Я хочу позвонить с оплатой вызываемого. *ya khachyoo pazvaneet' s aplatay vizivayeemava*

127

Speaking Разговор по телефону

Hello. This is …	Алло. Это … *allo eta …*
I'd like to speak to …	Можно .... к телефону. *mozhna … k teeleefonoo*
Extension …	Добавочный номер ... *dabavachniy nomeer …*
Speak louder, please.	Говорите громче, пожалуйста. *gavareetye gromchye pazhalsta*
Speak more slowly, please?	Говорите медленнее, пожалуйста. *gavareetye myedleennyeye pazhalsta*
Could you repeat that, please.	Повторите, пожалуйста. *paftareetye pazhalsta*
I'm afraid he's/she's not in.	Боюсь, что его/её нет. *bayoos' shto eevo/eeyo nyet*
You have the wrong number.	Вы неправильно набрали номер. *vi neepraveel'na nabralee nomeer*
Just a moment.	Минуточку. *meenootachkoo*
Hold on, please.	Подождите, пожалуйста. *padazhdeetye pazhalsta*
When will he/she be back?	Когда он/она будет? *kagda on/ana boodyet*
Will you tell him/her that I called?	Передайте ему/ей что я звонил(а). *peereedaytye eemoo/yey shto ya zvaneel(a)*
My name is …	Моя фамилия … *maya fameeleeya …*
Would you ask him/her to phone me?	Попросите его/её позвонить мне. *papraseetye eevo/eeyo pazvaneet' mnye*
Would you take a message, please?	Что передать? *shto peereedat'*
I must go now.	Мне пора. *mnye para*
Nice to speak to you.	Приятно было поговорить. *preeyatna bila pagavareet'*
I'll be in touch.	Я еще позвоню. *ya eshchyo pazvanyoo*
Bye.	Пока. *Paka*

128

Stores & Services

All stores used to be state owned. Now privatization is in full swing. However, there are still long lines [queues] in state-owned food stores, where prices tend to be lower. You can buy almost anything in Moscow and St. Petersburg, although imported goods are more expensive. Street markets are fun places to shop – and don't be afraid to bargain! Ask at your hotel about the nearest, or best, street market. Foreign-currency stores (Берёзка **beeryoska**) were set up in Soviet times to profit from tourist hard currency, and to offer a selection of luxury goods not generally available. And they are still good places to find souvenirs and gifts.

ESSENTIAL

I'd like …	Я хотел(а) бы … *ya khatyel(a) bi …*
Do you have …?	У Вас есть …? *oo vas yest' …*
How much is that?	Сколько стоит? *skol'ka stoeet*
Thank you.	Спасибо. *spaseeba*

ОТКРЫТО	open
ЗАКРЫТО	closed
РАСПРОДАЖА	sale

Stores and services
Товары и услуги

Where is ...? Где ...?

Where's the nearest ...?	Где ближайший ...? *gdye bleezhayshiy* ...
Where's there a good ...?	Где здесь есть хороший ...? *gdye zdyes' yest' kharoshiy* ...
Where's the main shopping mall [centre]?	Где здесь торговый центр? *gdye zdyes' targoviy tsentr*
Is it far from here?	Это далеко отсюда? *eta daleeko atsyooda*
How do I get there?	Как туда добраться? *kak tooda dabrat'sa*

Stores Товары

Most stores just carry the name of the article sold, e.g., ХЛЕБ (bread), РЫБА (fish), ОБУВЬ (shoes), ЦВЕТЫ (flowers), etc.

antique store	антикварный магазин *anteekvarniy magazeen*
bakery	булочная *boolachnaya*
bank	банк *bank*
bookstore	книжный магазин *kneezhniy magazeen*
butcher	мясной магазин *meesnoy magazeen*
camera store	фототовары *fatatavari*
cigarette kiosk [tobacconist]	табачный киоск *tabachniy keeosk*
clothing store	одежда *adyezhda*
delicatessen	магазин деликатесов *magazeen deeleekatyessaf*
department store	универмаг *ooneeveermak*
drugstore	аптека *aptyeka*
fish store [fishmonger]	рыба *riba*
florist	цветы *tsveeti*
gift store	подарки *padarkee*
greengrocer	овощи и фрукты *ovashchyee ee frookti*
health food store	диетические продукты *deeeeteechyeeskeeye pradookti*

liquor store [off-licence]	винный магазин *veenniy magazeen*
market	рынок *rinak*
pastry store	кондитерская *kandeeteerskaya*
pharmacy [chemist]	аптека *aptyeka*
produce [grocery] store	бакалея *bakalyeya*
record [music] store	пластинки *plasteenkee*
shoe store	обувь *oboof'*
shopping mall [centre]	торговый центр *targoviy tsentar*
souvenir store	сувениры *sooveeneeri*
sporting goods store	спорттовары *sparttavari*
supermarket	универсам *ooneeveersam*
toy store	игрушки *eegrooshkee*

Services Обслуживание

clinic	поликлиника *paleekleeneeka*
dentist	зубной врач *zoobnoy vrach'*
doctor	врач *vrach'*
dry cleaner	химчистка *kheemcheestka*
hairdresser/barber	парикмахерская *pareekmakheerskaya*
hospital	больница *bal'neetsa*
laundromat	прачечная *prachyeechnaya*
library	библиотека *beebleeatyeka*
optician	оптика *opteeka*
police station	отделение милиции *atdeelyeneeye meeleetsiyee*
post office	почта *pochta*
travel agency	бюро путешествий *byooro pooteeshestveey*

Opening hours Часы работы

State-owned stores are usually open from 8 a.m. – 8 p.m. with a lunch break from 1 p.m. – 2 p.m. Monday to Saturday, with shorter hours on Sundays. Most privately owned stores keep similar hours, but do not close for lunch.

When does the ... open/shut?	Когда ... открывается/закрывается? *kagda ... atkrivaeetsa/zakrivaeetsa*
Are you open in the evening?	Вы вечером работаете? *vi vyecheeram rabotaeetye*
Do you close for lunch?	Вы закрываетесь на обед? *vi zakrivaeetyes' na abyet*
Where is the ...	Где ... *gdye ...*
cashier [cash desk]	касса *kassa*
elevator [lift]	лифт *leeft*
escalator	эскалатор *eskalatar*
store directory [guide]	перечень отделов *pyereechyeen' atdyelaf*
It's in the basement.	Это в подвале. *eta f padvalye*
It's on the ... floor.	Это на ... этаже. *eta na ... etazhe*
first [ground (Brit.)] floor	первом *pyervam*
second [first (Brit.)] floor	втором *ftarom*
Where's the ... department?	Где ... отдел? *gdye ... atdyel*

ЗАКРЫТО НА ОБЕД	closed for lunch
БЕЗ ПЕРЕРЫВА НА ОБЕД	open all day
ЧАСЫ РАБОТЫ	business hours
ВХОД	entrance
ВЫХОД	exit
ЗАПАСНЫЙ ВЫХОД	emergency exit
ПОЖАРНЫЙ ВЫХОД	fire exit
ЛЕСТНИЦА	stairs

Service Обслуживание

Can you help me?	Помогите мне, пожалуйста. *pamageetye mnye pazhalsta*
I'm looking for …	Я ищу … *ya eeshchyoo* …
I'm just browsing.	Я просто смотрю. *ya prosta smatryoo*
It's my turn.	Это моя очередь. *eta maya ochyeereed'*
Do you have any …?	У Вас есть …? *oo vas yest'* …
I'd like to buy …	Я хочу купить … *ya khachyoo koopeet'* …
Could you show me …?	Покажите мне …, пожалуйста. *pakazhitye mnye … pazhalsta*
How much is this/that?	Сколько это/то стоит? *skol'ka eta/to stoeet*
That's all, thanks.	Это всё, спасибо. *eta fsyo spaseeba*

Доброе утро/Добрый день госпожа/господин.	Good morning/afternoon, madam/sir.
Я вас слушаю?	Can I help you?
Что Вы хотите?	What would you like?
Я сейчас посмотрю.	I'll just check that for you.
Это всё?	Is that everything?
Что ещё?	Anything else?

– *shto vi khateetye?*
– *spaseeba neechyeevo. ya prosta smatryoo.*
– *kharasho.*
– *eezveeneetye.*
– *da slooshayoo vas.*
– *skol'ka eta stoeet?*
– *ya seechyas pasmatryoo … deeveenosta voseem rooblyey.*

ОБСЛУЖИВАНИЕ	customer service
САМООБСЛУЖИВАНИЕ	self-service
РАСПРОДАЖА	clearance

Preference Выбор

I want something …	Я хочу что-нибудь … *ya kha<u>chyoo</u> shto-neebood'*…
It must be …	Это должно быть … *<u>e</u>ta dolzh<u>no</u> bit'*…
big/small	большой/маленький *bal'<u>shoy</u>/ma<u>leen'keey</u>*
cheap/expensive	дешёвый/дорогой *dee<u>sho</u>viy/dara<u>goy</u>*
dark/light	тёмный/светлый *<u>tyo</u>mniy/<u>svyetliy</u>*
light/heavy	лёгкий/тяжелый *<u>lyokh</u>keey/teezh<u>oliy</u>*
oval/round/square	овальный/круглый/квадратный *a<u>val'</u>niy/<u>kroo</u>gliy/kvad<u>ra</u>tniy*
I don't want anything too expensive.	Я не хочу ничего дорогого. *ya nee kha<u>chyoo</u> neechyee<u>vo</u> dara<u>go</u>va*
In the region of … rubles.	Примерно … рублей. *pree<u>myer</u>na … roo<u>blyey</u>*

Какого … Вы хотите?	What … would you like?
цвета/покроя	color/shape
качества/количества	quality/quantity
Какого плана Вы хотите?	What sort would you like?
За какую цену?	What price range are you thinking of?

Do you have anything …?	У Вас есть …? *oo vas yest'* …
larger	побольше *pa<u>bol'</u>she*
better quality	лучшего качества *<u>looch</u>sheva*
cheaper	подешевле *padee<u>shev</u>lye*
smaller	поменьше *pa<u>myen'</u>she*
Can you show me …?	Покажите мне …? *paka<u>zhi</u>tye mnye* …
that/this one	то/это *to/<u>e</u>ta*
these/those ones	эти/те *<u>e</u>tee/tye*
the one in the window/ display case	то, что в витрине/ в горке *to shto v vee<u>treen</u>ye/f <u>gor</u>kee*
some others	другие *droo<u>gee</u>ye*

COLOR ➤ 143

Conditions of purchase
Условия покупки

Is there a guarantee?

Есть гарантия?
yest' garanteeya

Are there any instructions with it?

Есть инструкция?
yest' eenstrooktsiya

Out of stock Продано

Извините, у нас нет.	I'm sorry, we don't have any.
Извините, продано.	We're out of stock.
Показать Вам что-нибудь ещё?	Can I show you something else/ a different sort?
Хотите это заказать?	Shall we order it for you?

Decision Решение

That's not quite what I want.

Это не совсем то, что я хочу.
eta nee safsyem to shto ya khachyoo

No, I don't like it.

Нет, это мне не нравится.
nyet eta mnye nee nraveetsa

That's too expensive.

Это очень дорого.
eta ochyeen' doraga

I'd like to think about it.

Надо подумать.
nada padoomat'

I'll take it.

Я возьму это.
ya vaz'moo eta

– *zdrastvooytye. ya khachyoo koopeet' roobashkoo pazhalsta.*

– *kakooyoo roobashkoo vi khateetye?*

– *aranzhiviyoo pazhalsta. ee safsyem bal'shova razmyera.*

– *vot. eta sto dvattsat' rooblyey.*

– *hmm. eta nee safsyem to shto ya khachyoo. spaseeba.*

Paying Оплата

When shopping in foreign-currency stores, you pay in the normal way. In other stores, however, you have to memorize the price of the item you want to buy, pay that amount at the cash desk, and then using the receipt you have obtained, pick up the item you want from the counter.

International credit cards are accepted in many stores. However, it is illegal to pay in foreign currency, although prices are often given in U.S. dollars and converted to rubles at the current exchange rate.

Where do I pay?	Куда платить? *kooda plateet'*
How much is that?	Сколько это стоит? *skol'ka eta stoeet*
Could you write it down, please?	Напишите, пожалуйста. *napeeshitye pazhalsta*
Do you accept ...?	Вы принимаете ...? *vi preeneemaeetye ...*
traveler's checks [cheques]	аккредитивы *akreedeeteevi*
I'll pay ...	Я заплачу ... *ya zaplachoo ...*
by cash/by credit card	наличными/по кредитной карточке *naleechnimee/pa kreedeetniy kartachkee*
I don't have any smaller change.	У меня нет сдачи. *oo meenya nyet zdachyee*
Sorry, I don't have enough money.	Извините, у меня не хватает денег. *eezveeneetee oo meenya nee khvatayeet dyeneek*
Could I have a receipt, please?	Можно чек, пожалуйста? *mozhna chyek pazhalsta*
I think you've given me the wrong change.	Мне кажется, что вы неправильно дали сдачу. *mnye kazhetsa shto vi neepraveel'na dalee zdachyoo*

Как будете платить?	How are you paying?
... рублей, пожалуйста.	That's ... rubles, please.
Это мы не принимаем.	This transaction has not been approved/accepted.
Эта карточка недействительна.	This card is not valid.
Можно Ваше удостоверение?	May I have additional identification?
У Вас есть деньги мельче?	Do you have any smaller change?

ПЛАТИТЬ ЗДЕСЬ.	Please pay here.
КРАЖА ТОВАРОВ ПРЕСЛЕДУЕТСЯ ПО ЗАКОНУ.	Shoplifters will be prosecuted.

Complaints Жалобы

This doesn't work.	Это с браком. *eta z brakam*
Where can I make a complaint?	Куда я могу пожаловаться? *kooda ya magoo pazhalavat'sa*
Can I exchange this, please?	Можно это поменять? *mozhna eta pameenyat'*
I'd like a refund.	Я хотел(а) бы получить деньги назад. *ya khatyel(a) bi paloocheet' dyen'gee nazat*
Here's the receipt.	Вот чек. *vot chyek*
I don't have the receipt.	У меня нет чека. *oo meenya nyet chyeka*
I'd like to see the manager.	Я хотел(а) бы видеть администратора. *ya khatyel(a) bi veedyet' admeeneestratara*

Repairs/Cleaning Ремонт/Химчистка

This is broken. Can you repair it?	Это сломано. Можно это починить? *eta slomana. mozhna eta pachyeeneet'*
Do you have … for this?	У Вас есть ...? *oo vas yest'* …
a battery	батарейка *bataryeyka*
replacement parts	запасные части *zapasniye chyastee*
There's something wrong with …	Что-то не в порядке с ... *shtoto nee f paryatkye s* …
Can you … this?	Вы можете это ...? *vi mozhetye eta* …
clean	почистить *pachyeesteet'*
press	погладить *pagladeet'*
alter	переделать *peereedyelat'*
patch	заштопать *zashtopat'*
When will it/they be ready?	Когда будет готово? *kagda boodyet gatova*
Can I collect it …?	Я заберу это ... *ya zabeeroo eta* …
later today/tomorrow	сегодня позже/завтра *seevodnya pozhzhe/zaftra*
on Friday/next week	в пятницу/на следующей неделе *f pyatneetsoo/na slyedooyooshchyee needyelye*
This isn't mine.	Это не моё. *eta nee mayo*
There's … missing.	Здесь ... не хватает. *zdyes' … nee khvatayet*

TIME ➤ 220; DATES ➤ 218

Bank/Currency exchange
Банк/Обмен валюты

Check with your travel agent or the Russian embassy before your trip on the latest regulations regarding how much foreign currency you can bring in.

In big towns and cities there are many currency exchange offices in banks, hotels, stores, and even street kiosks. Some work non-stop, 24 hours a day. Others are open from early morning to late evening, with a break for lunch. You may be required to show your passport.

All currency exchange offices accept U.S. dollars. However, they will not take dirty notes or notes with writing on them. You may have difficulty changing notes issued before 1993, so try to obtain clean, post-1993 notes. Some currency exhange offices also accept clean German marks. For other currencies and traveler's checks use the banks and big hotels. But remember: U.S. dollars are your best bet!

Where's the nearest …?	Где ближайший ...? *gdye bleezhayshiy* …
bank	банк *bank*
currency exchange office [bureau de change]	обмен валюты *abmyen valyooti*

Changing money Обмен денег

Warning: You may be approached by someone on the street offering normal or slightly better rates. It is easy to be cheated, so stick to the official places.

Can I exchange foreign currency here?	Можно обменять валюту здесь? *mozhna abmeenyat' valyootoo zdyes'*
I'd like to change some dollars/ pounds into rubles.	Я хотел(а) бы обменять доллары/фунты на рубли. *ya khatyel(a) bi abmeenyat' dollari/foonti na rooblee*
I want to cash some traveler's checks [cheques].	Я хочу обменять аккредитивы. *ya khachyoo abmeenyat' akreedeeteevi*
What's the exchange rate?	Какой курс? *kakoy koors*
How much commission do you charge?	Сколько процентов комиссионный сбор? *skol'ka pratsentaf kameesseeonniy zbor*
I've lost my traveler's checks. These are the numbers.	Я потерял(а) аккредитивы. Вот номера. *ya pateeryal(a) akreedeeteevi. vot nameera*

КАССЫ	cashiers
ВСЕ ОПЕРАЦИИ	all transactions
ОТ СЕБЯ/НА СЕБЯ/НАЖМИТЕ	push/pull/press

Security Служба безопасности

Можно ...?	Could I see ...?
Ваш паспорт	your passport
удостоверение	some identification
Вашу кредитную карточку	your bank card
Ваш адрес?	What's your address?
Где вы остановились?	Where are you staying?
Заполните этот бланк, пожалуйста.	Fill in this form, please.
Распишитесь здесь.	Please sign here.

ATMs [Cash machines] Банкоматы

Can I withdraw money on my credit card here?

Можно здесь снять деньги по кредитной карточке? *mozhna zdyes' snyat' dyen'gee pa kreedeetniy kartachkye*

Where are the ATMs [cash machines]?

Где здесь банкоматы? *gdye zdyes' bankamati*

Can I use my ... card in the cash machine?

Можно мне использовать мою ... карточку в этом автомате? *mozhna mnye eespol'zavat' mayoo ... kartachkoo v etam aftamatye*

The cash machine has eaten my card.

У меня застряла карточка в автомате. *oo meenya zastryala kartachka v aftomatye*

КОМИССИОННЫЙ СБОР	bank charges
ИНОСТРАННАЯ ВАЛЮТА	foreign currency
БАНКОМАТ	automated teller (ATM) [cash machine]

The monetary unit is the ruble (рубль), which until recently was divided into 100 kopecks. Due to recent mass inflation, however, the kopeck is now worthless. To cope with this inflation, the Russian currency was "denominated," i.e., divided by 1,000. Hence 1,000 rubles (about 20 cents U.S./10 pence Sterling) are now worth 1 ruble. At the moment, both prices are being quoted to give Russians a chance to adapt.

Pharmacy Аптека

You can buy medicine at a pharmacy (аптека **aptyeka**) or from private foreign/joint-venture hospitals. Although medical treatment is free in Russian state hospitals, it is customary to give the doctor a present – a box of chocolates or a bottle of wine, for example. However, you will have to pay for medicine. Also, be sure to get medical insurance before you go.

For toiletries, you have to go to a парфюмерия (**parfyoomyereeya**). You can find a wide range of toiletries and cosmetics in big towns and cities. But prices are high, so stock up before going.

Where's the nearest (all-night) pharmacy?	Где ближайшая (ночная) аптека? *gdye bleezhayshaya (nachnaya) aptyeka*
What time does the pharmacy open/close?	Во сколько аптека открывается/ закрывается? *va skol'ka aptyeka atkrivaeetsa/zakrivaeetsa*
Can you make up this prescription for me?	Вы можете приготовить это лекарство? *vi mozhetye preegatoveet' eta leekarstva*
Shall I wait?	Мне подождать? *mnye padazhdat'*
I'll come back for it.	Я приду за ним. *ya preedoo za neem*

Dosage instructions Дозы и инструкции

How much should I take?	Сколько нужно принимать? *skol'ka noozhna preeneemat'*
How often should I take it?	Как часто нужно принимать? *kak chyasta noozhna preeneemat'*
Is it suitable for children?	Это можно детям? *eta mozhna dyeteem*

Принимайте ... таблетки/ ... ложки ...	Take ... tablets/... teaspoons ...
перед едой/после еды	before/after meals
с водой	with water
целые	whole
утром/вечером	in the morning/at night
в течение ... дней	for ... days

ЯД	poison
НАРУЖНОЕ	for external use only
НЕ ДЛЯ ВНУТРЕННЕГО УПОТРЕБЛЕНИЯ	not to be taken internally

DOCTOR ➤ 161

Asking advice Лекарства

What would you recommend for …?	Что Вы рекомендуете от …? *shto vi reekameendooeetye at …*
a cold	простуды *prastoodi*
a cough	кашля *kashlya*
diarrhea	поноса *panosa*
a hangover	похмелья *pakhmyelya*
hay fever	сенной лихорадки *seenoy leekharatkee*
insect bites	укусов насекомых *ookoosaf naseekomikh*
a sore throat	воспаления горла *vaspalyeneeye gorla*
sunburn	солнечного ожёга *solneechnava azhoga*
motion [travel] sickness	морской болезни *marskoy balyeznee*
an upset stomach	расстройства желудка *rasstroystva zheelootka*
Can I get it without a prescription?	Можно это получить без рецепта? *mozhna eta paloochyeet' byez reetsepta*
Can I have a(n)/some …?	Дайте, пожалуйста, … *daytye pazhalsta …*
antiseptic cream	антисептическую мазь *anteeseepteechyeeskooyoo maz'*
aspirin	аспирин *aspeereen*
gauze [bandages]	бинт *beent*
adhesive bandages [plasters]	пластыри *plastiree*
condoms	презервативы *preezeervateevi*
cotton [cotton wool]	вату *vatoo*
insect repellent	средство от комаров *sryetstva at kamaraf*
painkillers	болеутоляющее *baleeootalyayooshchyeye*
vitamin tablets	витамины в таблетках *veetameeni f tablyetkakh*

Toiletries Туалетные принадлежности

I'd like a(n)/some ... Дайте, пожалуйта ...
daytye pazhalsta ...

after shave	лосьон после бритья *las'on poslye breetya*
deodorant	дезодорант *deezadarant*
razor blades	лезвия *lyezveeya*
sanitary napkins [towels]	гигиенические салфетки *geegeeeeneechyeeskeeye salfyetkee*
sunscreen	крем для загара *kryem dlya zagara*
soap	мыло *mila*
tampons	тампоны *tamponi*
tissues	бумажные салфетки *boomazhniye salfyetkee*
toilet paper	туалетную бумагу *tooalyetnooyoo boomagoo*
toothpaste	зубную пасту *zoobnooyoo pastoo*

Haircare Уход за волосами

comb	расчёска *rashchyoska*
conditioner	кондиционер *kandeetsianyer*
hair brush	щётка для волос *shchyotka dlya valos*
hair mousse	мусс для волос *mooss dlya valos*
hair spray	лак для волос *lak dlya valos*
shampoo	шампунь *shampoon'*

For the baby Для ребёнка

baby food	детское питание *dyetskaye peetaneeye*
baby wipes	гигиенические салфетки *geegeeneecheskeeye salfyetkee*
diapers [nappies]	пелёнки *peelyonkee*
sterilizing solution	стерализующий раствор *steeraleezooyooshchyeey rastvor*

Clothing Одежда

Street markets are cheaper than stores. Don't be afraid to bargain – it's part of the fun.

Duty-free shopping is found at the airports and large hotels.

General Общие вопросы

I'd like …	Я хотел(а) бы … *ya khatyel(a) bi …*
Do you have any …?	У Вас есть…? *oo vas yest' …*

ЖЕНСКАЯ ОДЕЖДА	ladieswear
МУЖСКАЯ ОДЕЖДА	menswear
ДЕТСКАЯ ОДЕЖДА	childrenswear

Color Цвет

I'm looking for something in …	Я ищу что-нибудь … *ya eeshchyo shtoneebood' …*
beige	бежевое *byezhevaye*
black	чёрное *chyornaye*
blue	синее *seenyeeye*
brown	коричневое *kareechneevaye*
green	зелёное *zeelyonaye*
gray [grey]	серое *syeraye*
orange	оранжевое *aranzhevaye*
pink	розовое *rozavaye*
purple	алое *alaye*
red	красное *krasnaye*
white	белое *byelaye*
yellow	жёлтое *zholtaye*
light …	светло-… *svyetla-…*
dark …	тёмно-… *tyomna-…*
I want a darker/lighter shade.	Я хочу темнее/светлее. *ya khachyoo teemnyeye/sveetlyeye*
Do you have the same in …?	У Вас есть такое же по …? *oo vas yest' takoye zhe pa …*

Clothes and accessories
Одежда и аксессуары

belt	ремень/пояс	_reemyen'_/_poees_
bikini	бикини	_beekeenee_
blouse	блузка	_blooska_
bra	бюстгальтер	_byoostgal'teer_
briefs	трусики	_trooseekee_
coat	пальто	_pal'to_
dress	платье	_plat'e_
handbag	сумка	_soomka_
hat	шапка	_shapka_
jacket	пиджак	_peedzhak_
jeans	джинсы	_dzheensi_
leggings	лосины	_laseeni_
pants (U.S.)	брюки	_bryookee_
pantyhose [tights]	колготки	_kalgotkee_
raincoat	плащ	_plashch_
scarf	шарф	_sharf_
shirt	рубашка	_roobashka_
shorts	шорты	_shorti_
skirt	юбка	_yoopka_
socks	носки	_naskee_
stockings	чулки	_chyoolkee_
suit	костюм	_kastyoom_
sunglasses	солнечные очки	_solneechniye achkee_
sweater	пуловер	_pooloveer_
sweatshirt	рубашка (футболка)	_roobashka (footbolka)_
swimming trunks/swimsuit	плавки/купальник	_plafkee/koopal'neek_
T-shirt	майка	_mayka_
tie	галстук	_galstook_
trousers	брюки	_bryookee_
underpants	трусы	_troosi_
with long/short sleeves	с длинными/короткими рукавами	_z dleennimee/karotkeemee rookavamee_
with a V-/round neck	с вырезом/круглым воротом	_s vireezam/krooglim voratam_

Shoes Обувь

a pair of …	пара … _para_ …
boots	сапоги _sapagee_
flip-flops	шлёпанцы _shlyopantsi_
running [training] shoes	кроссовки _krassofkee_
sandals	сандалии _sandaleeyee_
shoes	туфли _tooflee_
slippers	тапочки _tapachkee_

Walking/Hiking gear В походе

hiking boots	ботинки _bateenkee_
knapsack	рюкзак _ryoogzak_
waterproof jacket/anorak	дождевик _dazhdeeveek_
windbreaker [cagoule]	куртка _koortka_

Fabric Ткани

I want something in …	Я хочу что-нибудь из … _ya khachyoo shtoneebood' eez_ …
cotton	хлопка _khlopka_
denim	джинсовой ткани _dzheensoviy tkanee_
lace	кружев _kroozhef_
leather	кожи _kozhi_
linen	льна _l'na_
wool	шерсти _sherstee_
Is this …?	Это …? _eta_ …
pure cotton	чистый хлопок _chyeestiy khlopak_
synthetic	синтетика _seentyeteeka_
Is it hand washable/ machine washable?	Это стирать в ручную/в машине? _eta steerat' v roochnooyoo/v mashinye_

ХИМЧИСТКА ТОЛЬКО	dry clean only
РУЧНАЯ СТИРКА	handwash only
НЕ ГЛАДИТЬ	do not iron
СТИРАТЬ ОТДЕЛЬНО	colorfast

145

Does it fit? Подходит?

Can I try this on?	Можно это примерить? *mozhna eta preemyereet'*
Where's the fitting room?	Где примерочная? *gdye preemyerachnaya*
It fits well. I'll take it.	Подходит. Я возьму. *patkhodeet. ya vaz'moo*
It doesn't fit.	Не подходит. *nee patkhodeet*
It's too …	Слишком … *sleeshkam …*
short/long	коротко/длинно *koratka/dleenna*
tight/loose	тесно/свободно *tyesna/sfabodna*
Do you have this in size …?	У Вас есть … размера? *oo vas yest' … razmyera*
What size is this?	Какой это размер? *kakoy eta razmyer*
Could you measure me, please?	Вы можете снять мерку? *vi mozhetye snyat' myerkoo*
What size do you take?	Какой у Вас размер? *kakoy oo vas razmyer*
I don't know Russian sizes.	Я не знаю русских размеров. *ya nee znayoo roosskeekh razmyeraf*

Size Размер

	Dresses/Suits						Women's shoes			
American	8	10	12	14	16	18	6	7	8	9
British	10	12	14	16	18	20	$4^{1/2}$	$5^{1/2}$	$6^{1/2}$	$7^{1/2}$
Russian	36	38	40	42	44	46	36	37	38	40

	Shirts				Men's shoes									
American } British	15	16	17	18	5	6	7	8	$8^{1/2}$	9	$9^{1/2}$	10	11	
Russian	38	41	43	45	38	39	41	42	43	43	44	44	45	

очень большой	extra large (XL)
большой	large (L)
средний	medium (M)
малый	small (S)

1 centimeter (cm.) = 0.39 in.	1 inch = 2.54 cm.
1 meter (m.) = 39.37 in.	1 foot = 30.5 cm.
10 meters = 32.81 ft.	1 yard = 0.91 m.

Health and beauty
Здоровье и красота

I'd like a …	Я хотела бы сделать … *ya khatyel(a) bi zdyelat'* …
facial	чистку лица *cheestkoo leetsa*
manicure	маникюр *maneekyoor*
massage	массаж *massash*
waxing	восковую ванну *vaskavooyoo vannoo*

Hairdresser/Hairstylist В парикмахерской

I'd like to make an appointment for …	Я хотел(а) бы записаться на … *ya khatyel(a) bi zapeesat'sa na* …
Can you make it a bit earlier/later?	Можно пораньше/попозже? *mozhna paran'she/papozhzhe*
I'd like a …	Я хочу … *ya khachyoo* …
cut and blow-dry	стрижку и посушить феном *streeshkoo ee pasooshit' fyenam*
shampoo and set	вымыть и уложить *vimit' ee oolazhit'*
trim	подстричься *padstreeh'sa*
I'd like my hair …	Я хотел(а) бы волосы *ya khatyel(a) bi volasi*
colored/tinted	покрасить/тонировать *pakraseet'/taneeravat'*
highlighted	осветлить *asveetleet'*
permed	сделать химическую завивку *zdyelat' kheemeecheeskooyoo zaveefkoo*
Don't cut it too short.	Не слишком коротко, пожалуйста. *nee sleeshkam koratka pazhalsta*
A little more off the …	Снимите ещё немного с … *sneemeetye eeshchyo neemnoga s* …
back/front	сзади/спереди *zzadee/spyereedee*
neck/sides	шеи/боков *sheyee/bakof*
top	затылка *zatilka*
That's fine, thanks.	Очень хорошо, спасибо. *ochyeen' kharasho spaseeba*

Household articles
Хозяйственные товары

I'd like a(n)/ some …	Мне нужен(а) ... *mnye noozhen (noozhna) ...*
adapter	адаптер *adapteer*
alumin(i)um foil	фольга *fol'ga*
bottle opener	открывалка *atkrivalka*
can [tin] opener	открывалка *atkrivalka*
candles	свечи *svyechyee*
clothes pins [pegs]	прищепки *preeshchyepkee*
corkscrew	штопор *shtopar*
light bulb	лампочка *lampachka*
matches	спички *speechkee*
paper napkins	бумажные салфетки *boomazhniye salfyetkee*
plastic wrap [cling film]	продуктовая плёнка *pradooktovaya plyonka*
plug	штепсель *shtyepseel'*
scissors	ножницы *nozhneetsi*
screwdriver	отвёртка *atvyortka*

Cleaning items Уборка

bleach	отбеливатель *atbyeleevateel'*
dish cloth	тряпка *tryapka*
dishwashing [washing-up] liquid	жидкость для мытья посуды *zhidkast' dlya mitya pasoodi*
garbage [refuse] bags	полиэтиленовые мешки *palee-eteelyenaviye meeshkee*
detergent [washing powder]	стиральный порошок *steeral'niy parashok*

Crockery/Cutlery Посуда

cups	чашки *chashkee*
knives/forks	ножи/вилки *nazhi/veelkee*
spoons	ложки *loshkee*
glasses	стаканы *stakani*
mugs	кружки *krooshkee*
plates	тарелки *taryelkee*

Jeweler Ювелирные изделия

Russia is well-known for its amber (янтарь **eentar'**), and you will find amber jewelry and that jewelry made from other semi-precious stones in foreign-currency stores.

Could I see …?	Можно посмотреть …? _mozhna pasmatryet'_ …
this/that	это/то _eta/to_
It's in the window/ display cabinet.	что в витрине/в горке _shto v veetreenye/f gorkye_
I'd like a(n)/some …	Я хочу купить … _ya khachoo koopeet'_ …
bracelet	браслет _braslyet_
brooch	брошь _brosh_
clock	часы _chyasi_
earrings	серьги _syer'gee_
necklace/chain	ожерелье/цепочку _azheryelye/tsepochkoo_
ring	кольцо _kal'tso_
watch	наручные часы _naroochniye chasi_

Materials Материалы

Is this real silver/gold?	Это настоящее серебро/золото? _eta nastoyashchyeye seereebro/zolata_
Is there a certificate for it?	На это есть сертификат? _na eta yest' seerteefeekat_
Do you have anything in …?	У Вас есть изделия из …? _oo vas yest' eezdyeleeya eez_ …
copper	меди _myedee_
crystal (quartz)	хрусталя _khroostalya_
cut glass	резного стекла _reeznova steekla_
diamond	брильянтов _breelyantaf_
enamel	эмали _emalee_
gold/gold-plate	золота/позолоты _zolata/pazaloti_
pearl	жемчуга _zhemchyooga_
platinum	платины _plateeni_
silver/silver-plate	серебра/посеребренные _seereebra/paseereebryonniye_
stainless steel	нержавеющей стали _neerzhavyeyooshchyeey stalee_

Newsstand [Newsagent]/
Tobacconist Газетный киоск/Табак

Russian newspapers and magazines can be bought near subway [metro] stations (marked with a large M for Метро **meetro**) and at kiosks with the sign Печать. The latter may also sell envelopes and postcards.

Locally published English-language newspapers are offered free in many hotels, supermarkets, and stores. For foreign language newspapers and magazines, your best bet is the newsstand in your hotel.

Lots of imported and Russian brands of cigarettes are sold in stores and kiosks – and are much cheaper than in Western countries.

Do you sell English-language books/newspapers?	Есть в продаже английские книги/газеты? *yest' f pradazhe angleeyskeeye kneegee/gazyeti*
I'd like a(n)/some ...	Дайте, пожалуйста ... *daytye pazhalsta ...*
book	книгу *kneegoo*
candy [sweets]	конфеты *kanfyeti*
chewing gum	жевательную резинку *zheevateel'nooyoo reezeenkoo*
chocolate bar	шоколадку *shakalatkoo*
cigarettes (pack of)	пачку сигарет *pachkoo seegaryet*
cigars	сигары *seegari*
dictionary	словарь *slavar'*
English-Russian	англо-русский *anglo/roosskee*
guidebook of ...	путеводитель по ... *pooteevadeeteel' ...*
lighter	зажигалку *zazheegalkoo*
magazine	журнал *zhoornal*
map of the town	карту города *kartoo gorada*
matches	спички *speechkee*
newspaper	газету *gazyetoo*
American	американскую *ameereekanskooyoo*
English	английскую *angleeskooyoo*
pen/paper	ручку/бумагу *roochkoo/boomagoo*
road map of ...	карту автомобильных дорог ... *kartoo aftamabeel'nikh darok...*
stamps	марки *markee*
tobacco	табак *tabak*

Photography Фотография

Film is probably more expensive in Russia than where you live, so it may be worthwhile taking some with you.
Warning: Don't photograph objects of a military nature, airports, or harbors.

I'm looking for a(n) … camera.	Я ищу … фотоаппарат. *ya eeshchyoo … fataapparat*
automatic	автоматический *aftamateechyeeskeey*
compact	компактный *kampaktniy*
disposable	одноразовый *adnarazaviy*
SLR	зеркальный *zeerkal'niy*
battery	батарейка *bataryeyka*
camera case	футляр *footlyar*
electronic flash	вспышка *fspishka*
filter	фильтр *feel'tar*
lens	объектив *ab'ekteef*
lens cap	крышка объектива *krishka ab'ekteeva*

Film/Processing Фотография /Обработка

I'd like a … film.	Дайте, пожалуйста … плёнку. *daytye pazhalsta … plyonkoo*
black and white	чёрно-белую *chyorna byelooyoo*
color	цветную *tsvyetnooyoo*
I'd like this film developed, please.	Я хотел(а) бы проявить плёнку. *ya khatyel(a) bi praeeveet' plyonkoo*
Would you enlarge this, please?	Можно это увеличить? *mozhna eta ooveeleechyeet'*
How much do … exposures cost?	Сколько стоит сделать … фото? *skol'ka stoeet zdyelat' … fota*
When will the photos be ready?	Когда фотографии будут готовы? *kagda fatagrafeeyee boodoot gatovi*
I'd like to collect my photos.	Я хочу забрать фотографии. *ya khachyoo zabrat' fatagrafeeyee*
Here's the receipt.	Вот квитанция. *vot kveetantsiya*

Police Милиция

Crime is a big problem all over Russia, and particularly in Moscow and St. Petersburg. Sensible precautions include making photocopies of your passport and visa, leaving tickets and valuables in your hotel safe, and taking out only the money you need. Crime that affects tourists is mostly of a "petty" nature: theft from cars and hotel rooms, and pickpocketing. The police are recognized by their blue-gray uniforms with red lapels and cap bands. To contact the police in an emergency ☎ 02.

Where's the nearest police station?	Где ближайшее отделение милиции? *gdye bleezhaysheye addeelyeneeye meeleetsiee*
Does anyone here speak English?	Здесь кто-нибудь говорит по-английски? *zdyes' ktoneebood' gavareet pa angleeyskee*
I want to report a(n) …	Я хочу заявить о … *ya khachyoo zaeeveet' a …*
accident/attack	несчастном случае/нападении *neeshchyastnam sloochyaye/napadyeneeyee*
mugging/rape	краже/изнасиловании *krazhe/eeznaseelavaneeyee*
My child is missing.	У меня пропал ребёнок. *oo meenya prapal reebyonak*
Here's a photo of him/her.	Вот его/её фотография. *vot eevo/eeyo fatagrafeeya*
I need an English-speaking lawyer.	Мне нужен адвокат, говорящий по-английски. *mnye noozhen advakat gavaryashchyeey pa angleeyskee*
I need to make a phone call.	Мне нужно позвонить *mnye noozhna pazvaneet'*
I need to contact the … Consulate.	Мне нужно связаться с … консульством. *mnye noozhna sveezat'sa s … konsool'stvam*
American/British	американским/британским *ameereekanskeem/breetanskeem*

Вы можете описать его/её?	Can you describe him/her?
мужчина/женщина	male/female
блондин(ка)/брюнет(ка)	blond(e)/brunette
рыжий(-ая)/седые волосы	red-headed/gray haired
длинные/короткие волосы/лысый	long/short hair/balding
роста …/возраста …	height …/aged …
Был(а) одет(а) в …	He/She was wearing …

152

CLOTHES ➤ 144; COLORS ➤ 143

Lost property/Theft Пропажа/Кража

I want to report a theft/ break-in.
Я хочу заявить о краже/ взломе. *ya khachyoo zaeeveet' a krazhe/vzlomye*

My car's been broken into.
У меня взломали машину. *oo meenya vzlamalee mashinoo*

I've been robbed/mugged.
Меня обокрали. *meenya abakralee*

I've lost my ...
Я потерял(а) ... *ya pateeryal(a) ...*

My ... has been stolen.
У меня украли ... *oo meenya ookralee ...*

bicycle
велосипед *veelaseepyet*

camera
фотоаппарат *fataapparat*

(rental) car
машину *mashinoo*

credit card
кредитную карточку *kreedeetnooyoo kartachkoo*

handbag
сумочку *soomachkoo*

money
деньги *dyen'gee*

passport
паспорт *paspart*

purse
кошелёк *kasheelyok*

wallet
бумажник *boomazhneek*

watch
часы *chyasi*

What shall I do?
Что мне делать? *shto mnye dyelat'*

I need a police report for my insurance claim.
Мне нужно свидетельство из милиции для получения страховки. *mnye noozhna sveedyeteel'stva eez meeleetsiee dlya paloochyeneeya strakhofkee*

Что пропало?	What's missing?
Когда украли?	When was it stolen?
Когда это случилось?	When did it happen?
Где вы остановились?	Where are you staying?
Откуда украли?	Where was it taken from?
Где вы были в это время?	Where were you at the time?
Мы пригласим вам переводчика	We're getting an interpreter for you.
Мы всё проверим.	We'll look into the matter.
Пожалуйста, заполните эту форму.	Please fill out this form.

Post office Почта

The main post offices in Moscow and St. Petersburg offer round-the-clock service. Other post offices are generally open Monday through Saturday from 8 a.m. to 7 p.m. and Sunday from 9 a.m. to 7 p.m. Major hotels have their own branches for postal, telegraph, and telephone services. Note: International money orders can only be cashed at banks. Also, both incoming and outgoing postal services are slow, so allow plenty of time.

General queries Общие вопросы

Where is the nearest/main post office?	Где здесь ближайшая почта/главпочтамт? *gdye zdyes' bleezhayshaya pochta/glavpachtamt*
What time does the post office open/close?	Во сколько почта открывается/закрывается? *va skol'ka pochta atkrivaeetsa/zakrivaeetsa*
Does it close for lunch?	Закрывается на обед? *zakrivaeetsa na abyet*
Where's the mailbox [postbox]?	Где здесь почтовый ящик? *gdye zdyes' pachtoviy yashchyeek*
Is there any mail for me? My name is …	Есть почта для меня? Моя фамилия … *yest' pochta dlya meenya. maya fameeleeya …*

Buying stamps Марки

A stamp for this postcard/letter, please.	Дайте марку на эту открытку/это письмо, пожалуйста. *daytye markoo na etoo atkritoo/eto pees'mo pazhalsta*
A … ruble stamp, please.	Марку за … рублей, пожалуйста. *markoo za … rooblyey pazhalsta*
What's the postage for a postcard/letter to …?	Сколько стоит послать открытку/письмо в …? *skol'ka stoeet paslat'*

> – *zdrastvooytye. ya khachyoo paslat' etee atkritkee v ameereekoo.*
>
> – *skol'ka atkritok?*
>
> – *dyeveet' pazhalsta.*
>
> – *tak pa tree rooblya dyeveet' ras. s vas dvatsats syem' rooblyey.*

154

Sending packages Посылки

I want to send this package [parcel] by …	Я хочу послать эту посылку … *ya khachyoo paslat' etoo pasilkoo…*
air mail	авиа *aveeya*
special delivery [express]	экспресс *ekspryess*
registered mail	заказной почтой *zakaznoy pochtay*
It contains …	Там … *tam …*

Пожалуйста, заполните таможенную декларацию.	Please fill in the customs declaration.
Какая стоимость?	What's the value?
Что там?	What's inside?

Other services Другие услуги

I'd like a phone card, please.	Я хочу телефонную карточку, пожалуйста. *Ya khachoo teeleefonooyoo kartochkoo pazhalsta*
10/20/50 units	на десять/двадцать/пятьдесят единиц *na dyesyat'/dvattsat'/peedeesyat' yedeeneets*
Do you have a photocopier/ fax machine here?	Здесь есть ксерокс/факс? *zdyes' yest' ksyeraks/ faks*
I'd like to send a telex/fax.	Мне нужно послать телекс/факс. *mnye noozhna paslat' tyeleeks/faks*
I'd like to send a message by e-mail.	Мне нужно послать сообщение по электронной почте. *mnye noozhna paslat' sapshchyeneeye pa eeleektronay pochtee*
What's your e-mail address?	Какой у вас адрес электронной почты? *kakoy oo vas adrees eeleektronay pochtee*
Can I access the Internet here?	Можно ли здесь войти в Интернет? *mozhna lee zdyes' vayetee v eenteernyet?*
What are the charges per hour?	Сколько стоит в час? *skol'ka stoyeet f chyas*

МАРКИ	stamps
ТЕЛЕГРАММЫ	telegrams
ДО ВОСТРЕБОВАНИЯ	general delivery [poste restante]
ВЫЕМКА ПОЧТЫ В …	next collection …
ПОСЫЛКИ	packages

Souvenirs Сувениры

When buying antiques remember that anything dating from before 1917 is likely to be considered a national treasure not to be taken out of the country. Thus, you can only export antique paintings, sculptures, antique samovars, and icons after securing permission from the Ministry of Culture and upon payment of customs duties. Rules and regulations are subject to change. Obtain up-to-date information from your travel agent or the Russian embassy before setting off.

amber	янтарь *eentar'*
balalaika	балалайка *balalayka*
caviar	икра *eekra*
chess set	шахматы *shakhmati*
fur hat	меховая шапка *meekhavaya shapka*
icon	икона *eekona*
nesting dolls	матрёшка *matryoshka*
Palekh boxes	палехские шкатулки *paleekhskeeye shkatoolkee*
poster	плакат *plakat*
rugs from *Tekin*	текинские ковры *teekeenskeeye kavri*
samovar	самовар *samavar*
shawl	шаль *shal'*
wood carving	резьба по дереву *reez'ba pa dyereevoo*
wooden spoons	деревянные ложки *deereevyaniye loshkee*

Gifts Подарки

bottle of wine	бутылка вина *bootilka veena*
box of chocolates	коробка шоколада *karopka shakalada*
calendar	календарь *kaleendar'*
key ring	брелок *breelok*
postcard	открытка *atkritka*
souvenir guide	путеводитель *pooteevadeeteel'*
tea towel	кухонное полотенце *kookhonnaye palatyentse*
T-shirt	майка *mayka*

Music Музыка

Locally produced audio- and videocassettes and compact
discs are inexpensive, especially for classical music.

I'd like a …	Я хочу купить … *ya kha<u>chyoo</u> koo<u>peet'</u> …*
cassette	кассету *ka<u>sye</u>too*
compact disc	компакт-диск *kam<u>pakt</u> deesk*
record	пластинку *pla<u>steen</u>koo*
videocassette	видеокассету *veedeeoka<u>sye</u>too*
Who are the popular native singers/bands?	Кто сейчас популярные певцы/группы? *kto see<u>chyas</u> papoo<u>lyar</u>niye peev<u>tsi</u>/<u>groop</u>pi*

Toys and games Игрушки и игры

I'd like a toy/game …	Я хочу купить игрушку/игру … *ya kha<u>chyoo</u> koo<u>peet'</u> ee<u>groosh</u>koo/ ee<u>groo</u> …*
for a boy	для мальчика *dlya <u>mal'</u>cheeka*
for a 5-year-old girl	для пятилетней девочки *dlya peetee<u>lyet</u>nee <u>dye</u>vachkee*
chess set	шахматы *<u>shakh</u>mati*
doll	куклу *<u>koo</u>kloo*
electronic game	электронную игру *eleek<u>tron</u>nooyoo ee<u>groo</u>*
pail and shovel [bucket and spade]	ведёрко и совок *vee<u>dyor</u>ka ee sa<u>vok</u>*
teddy bear	мишку *<u>meesh</u>koo*

Antiques Старинные вещи

How old is this?	Какой это век? *ka<u>koy</u> eta vyek*
Do you have anything of the … era?	У Вас есть что-нибудь … века? *oo vas yest' <u>shto</u>neebood' … <u>vye</u>ka*
Can you send it to me?	Вы можете переслать это мне по почте? *vi <u>mozhe</u>tye peeree<u>slat'</u> eta mnye pa <u>pach</u>tye*
Will I have problems with customs?	Могут быть проблемы на таможне? *<u>mogoot</u> bit' prab<u>lye</u>mi na ta<u>mozh</u>nye*
Is there a certificate of authenticity?	Есть сертификат подлинности? *yest' seertee<u>fee</u>kat pad<u>lyeen</u>nastyee*

WHO/WHAT/WHEN? ➤ 104

Supermarket/Minimart
Универсам/Павильон

There are big supermarkets with a wide choice of food and Western imports in large cities which only accept cash. Credit cards can only be used in Western-owned shops. However, many of the large supermarkets have ATMs which accept Visa and MasterCard. For beer, spirits, and tobacco, it is better to go to kiosks or minimarts, where prices are lower.

At the supermarket В Универсаме

Excuse me. Where can I find (a) …?	Извините. Где можно купить ...? *eezvee*nee*tye gdye mozhna koopeet'* …
Do I pay for this here or at the checkout?	Где платить здесь или в кассу? *gdye plateet' zdyes' eelee f kassoo*
Where are the shopping carts [trolleys]/baskets?	Где здесь тележки/корзинки? *gdye zdyes' teelyeshkee/karzeenkee*
Is there a … here?	Здесь есть ...? *zdyes' yest'* …
bakery	булочная *boolachnaya*
delicatessen	магазин деликатесов *magazeen deeleekatyessaf*
pharmacy	аптека *aptyeka*

ХЛЕБ И КОНДИТЕРСКИЕ ИЗДЕЛИЯ	bread and cakes
МОЛОЧНЫЕ ПРОДУКТЫ	dairy products
РЫБА	fresh fish
МЯСО/ПТИЦА	fresh meat/poultry
СВЕЖИЕ ПРОДУКТЫ	fresh produce
МОРОЖЕНЫЕ ПРОДУКТЫ	frozen foods
ХОЗЯЙСТВЕННЫЕ ТОВАРЫ	household goods
КОНСЕРВИРОВАННЫЕ ФРУКТЫ/ОВОЩИ	canned fruit/vegetables
ВИНА И КРЕПКИЕ НАПИТКИ	wines and spirits

Weights and measures

- 1 kilogram or kilo (kg.) = **1000 grams (g.)**; **100 g.** = 3.5 oz.;
  1 kg. = 2.2 lb.; 1 oz. = **28.35 g.**; 1 lb. = **453.60 g.**
- 1 liter (l.) = 0.88 imp. quart or 1.06 U.S. quart; 1 imp. quart = **1.14 l.**
  1 U.S. quart = **0.951 l.**; 1 imp. gallon = **4.55 l.**; 1 U.S. gallon = **3.8 l.**

Food hygiene Гигиена питания

РЕАЛИЗАЦИЯ В ТЕЧЕНИЕ … ДНЕЙ	eat within … days of opening
ХРАНИТЬ В ХОЛОДИЛЬНИКЕ	keep refrigerated
ДЛЯ МИКРОВОЛНОЙ ПЕЧИ	microwaveable
ПОДОГРЕТЬ ПЕРЕД УПОТРЕБЛЕНИЕМ	reheat before eating
ДИЕТИЧЕСКОЕ ПИТАНИЕ	suitable for vegetarians
ГОДЕН ДО …	use by …

At the minimart В павильоне

I'd like some of that/those.	Дайте, пожалуйста, вон то/вот это *daytye pazhalsta von to/vot eta*
I'd like …	Дайте, пожалуйста, … *daytye pazhalsta …*
this one/these	вон эту/вон эти *von etoo/von etee*
that one/those	вон ту/вон те *von too/von tye*
on the left/right	направо/налево *naprava/nalyeva*
over there/here	вон там/вон здесь *von tam/von zdyes'*
Where is/are the …?	Где у вас …? *gdye oo vas …*
a kilo of apples	килограмм яблок *keelagram yablak*
a half-kilo of tomatoes	полкило помидоров *palkeelo pameedoraf*
100 grams of cheese	100 грамм сыра *sto gramm sira*
a liter of milk	литр молока *leetr malaka*
10 eggs	десяток яиц *deesyatak eeeets*
… slices of ham	… ломтиков ветчины *… lomteekaf veetchyeeni*
a piece of cake	кусочек торта *koosochyeek torta*
a bottle of wine	бутылку вина *bootilkoo veena*
a carton of milk	пакет молока *pakyet malaka*
a jar of jam	банку варенья *bankoo varyenya*
a bag of potato chips [crisps]	пакет чипсов *pakyet chyeepsaf*

– <u>day</u>tye pa<u>zhal</u>sta palkee<u>lo</u> <u>si</u>ra?
– *vot e<u>ta</u>va?*
– da pa<u>zhal</u>sta ra<u>see</u>skava.
– khara<u>sho</u> ... shto ee<u>shchyo</u>?
– ee shest' <u>lom</u>teekof veet<u>chyee</u>ni pa<u>zhal</u>sta.
– *vot pa<u>zhal</u>sta.*

Provisions/Picnic Продукты/Пикник

beer	пиво *<u>pee</u>va*
butter	масло *<u>mas</u>la*
cheese	сыр *sir*
cold meats	мясные изделия *mees<u>ni</u>ye eez<u>dye</u>leeya*
cookies [biscuits]	печенье *pee<u>chye</u>nye*
eggs	яйца *<u>yay</u>tsa*
grapes	виноград *veena<u>grat</u>*
ice cream	мороженое *ma<u>ro</u>zhenaye*
instant coffee	растворимый кофе *rastva<u>ree</u>niy <u>ko</u>fye*
loaf of bread	булка хлеба *<u>bool</u>ka <u>khlye</u>ba*
margarine	маргарин *marga<u>reen</u>*
milk	молоко *mala<u>ko</u>*
oranges	апельсины *apeel'<u>see</u>ni*
potato chips [crisps]	чипсы *<u>cheep</u>si*
rolls	булочки *<u>boo</u>lachkee*
sausages	сосиски *sa<u>see</u>skee*
soft drinks	безалкогольные напитки *beezalka<u>gol</u>'niye na<u>peet</u>kee*
wine	вино *vee<u>no</u>*

Russian bakeries and supermarkets sell a rich variety of black and white bread. In addition, each region has its own special varieties and forms of bread. Well-known types of bread include Московский (**mas<u>kof</u>skeeye**), Рижский (**<u>reezh</u>skeeye**), and Бородинский (**bora<u>deen</u>skeeye**). Sliced bread is available in many supermarkets.

MEAT ➤ 46; VEGETABLES ➤ 47

Health

Medical treatment is supposed to be free in Russia, but it is customary to offer the doctor a present: a box of chocolates or a bottle of something. State hospitals are generally run-down and uncomfortable. Food may not be provided. And you will have to pay for medicine.

More and more private hospitals and clinics are opening in big towns and cities with imported drugs and equipment. These charge American rates, so it is advisable to take out medical insurance before traveling.

Visitors to Russia are advised to get booster shots for diphtheria, tetanus, and polio. If you are on prescription medication, you should bring sufficient supplies with you.

Doctor (General) Врач/Общие вопросы

Where can I find a hospital/dentist?	Мне нужен врач/зубной врач. *mnye noozhen vrach/zoobnoy vrach*
Where's there a doctor who speaks English?	Где есть врач говорящий по-английски? *gdye yest' vrach gavaryashchyeey pa angleeyskee*
What are the office [surgery] hours?	Когда открыта поликлиника? *kagda atkrita paleekleeneeka*
Could the doctor come to see me here?	Можно вызвать врача на дом? *mozhna vizvat' vrachya na dam*
Can I make an appointment for …?	Можно записаться к врачу на …? *mozhna zapeesat'sa k vrachyoo na …*
today/tomorrow	сегодня/завтра *seevodnya/zaftra*
as soon as possible	как можно скорее *kak mozhna skaryeye*
It's urgent.	Это срочно. *eta srochna*
I've got an appointment with Doctor …	Я по записи к доктору … *ya pa zapeesee k doktaroo …*

– <u>mozh</u>na zapee<u>sat</u>'sa k vra<u>chyoo</u>?

– <u>zapees</u>' na pree<u>yom</u> za<u>kon</u>cheena <u>seevodnya</u>. <u>eta</u> <u>sroch</u>na?

– da.

– <u>kharasho</u>. mo<u>zheem</u> vam preedla<u>zheet</u>' na <u>dyeseet</u>' peet<u>natsat</u>' k <u>dok</u>taroo Sheev<u>chyen</u>koo.

– na <u>dyeseet</u>' peet<u>natsat</u>'. spa<u>seeba</u> vam bal<u>shoye</u>.

Accident and injury
Несчастный случай и травма

My ... is hurt/injured.	Мой(-я) ... ушибся(-лась).
	moy (maya) ... oo<u>shipsa</u> (oo<u>shiblas</u>')
husband/wife	муж/жена moosh/<u>zhena</u>
son/daughter	сын/дочь sin/doch'
friend	друг drook
child	ребёнок ree<u>byo</u>nak
He/She is unconscious.	Он/она без сознания.
	on/<u>ana</u> byes saz<u>na</u>neeya
He/She is bleeding (heavily).	У него/неё кровотечение (сильное).
	oo <u>nee</u>vo/nee<u>yo</u> kravatee<u>chye</u>neeye (<u>seel</u>'naye)
He/She is (seriously) injured.	Он/она (тяжело) ранен(а).
	on/<u>ana</u> (teezhe<u>lo</u>) <u>ra</u>nyen(a)
I have a(n) ...	У меня ... oo mee<u>nya</u> ...
blister	волдырь val<u>dir</u>'
boil	нарыв na<u>riv</u>
bruise	синяк see<u>nyak</u>
burn	ожог a<u>zhok</u>
cut/graze	порез/ссадина pa<u>ryes</u>/<u>ssa</u>deena
insect bite	укус oo<u>koos</u>
lump	шишка <u>shish</u>ka
rash	сыпь sip'
strained muscle	растянута мышца ras<u>tya</u>nootaya <u>mish</u>tsa
My ... is swollen.	У меня распухло ...
	oo mee<u>nya</u> ras<u>pookh</u>la ...
My ... hurts.	У меня болит ... oo mee<u>nya</u> ba<u>leet</u> ...

Symptoms Симптомы

I've been feeling ill for … days.	Я заболел(а) … дня/дней назад. *ya zabalyel(a) … dnya/dnyey nazat*
I feel …	У меня … *oo meenya …*
faint	слабость *slabast*
feverish	жар *zhar*
sick	тошнота *tashnata*
I've been vomiting.	Меня тошнило. *meenya tashneela*
I have diarrhea.	У меня понос. *oo meenya panos*
It hurts here.	Мне больно вот здесь. *mnye bol'na vot zdyes'*
I have (a/an) …	У меня … *oo meenya …*
backache	болит спина *baleet speena*
cold	простуда *prastooda*
cramps	судороги *soodaragee*
earache	болит ухо *baleet ookha*
headache	болит голова *baleet galava*
stomachache	болит живот *baleet zhivot*
sore throat	болит горло *baleet gorla*
sunstroke	солнечный удар *solneechniy oodar*

Health conditions Состояние здоровья

I have arthritis.	У меня артрит. *oo meenya artreet*
I have asthma.	У меня астма. *oo meenya astma*
I am …	Я … *ya …*
deaf	глухой(-ая) *glookhoy (-aya)*
diabetic	диабетик *deeabyeteek*
epileptic	эпилептик *epeelyepteek*
handicapped	инвалид *eenvaleet*
(… months) pregnant	(… месяца) беременна (*… myeseetsa) beeryemeenna*
I have a heart condition/ high blood pressure.	У меня больное сердце/высокое кровяное давление. *oo meenya bolynoye syerttse/visokaye kravyanoye davlyeneeye*
I had a heart attack … years ago	У меня был сердечный приступ … года/лет назад. *oo meenya bil seerdyechniy preestoop … goda/lyet nazat*

Doctor's inquiries Вопросы врача

Давно Вы себя так чувствуете?	How long have you been feeling like this?
Это у Вас первый раз?	Is this the first time you've had this?
Вы принимаете другое лекарство?	Are you taking any other medication?
Аллергия на что-нибудь?	Are you allergic to anything?
Вам делали прививку против столбняка?	Have you been vaccinated against tetanus?
У Вас есть аппетит?	Is your appetite okay?

Examination Осмотр

Я измерю Вам температуру/давление.	I'll take your temperature/ blood pressure.
Засучите рукава.	Roll up your sleeve, please.
Разденьтесь до пояса.	Please undress to the waist.
Ложитесь, пожалуйста.	Please lie down.
Откройте рот.	Open your mouth.
Дышите глубоко.	Breathe deeply.
Покашляйте.	Cough, please.
Где болит?	Where does it hurt?
Здесь болит?	Does it hurt here?

Diagnosis Диагноз

Вам нужно сделать рентген.	I want you to have an X-ray.
Вам нужно сдать кровь/кал/ мочу на анализ.	I want a specimen of your blood/stools/urine.
Я Вас направлю к специалисту.	I want you to see a specialist.
Я Вас направлю в стационар.	I want you to go to hospital.
Это сломано/растянуто.	It's broken/sprained.
Это вывихнуто/порвано.	It's dislocated/torn.

У Вас ...	You have (a/an) ...
аппендицит	appendicitis
цистит	cystitis
грипп	flu
отравление	food poisoning
перелом	fracture
гастрит	gastritis
грыжа	hernia
воспаление ...	inflammation of ...
корь	measles
пневмония	pneumonia
ишиас	sciatica
ангина	tonsilitis
опухоль	tumor
венерическое заболевание	venereal disease
У Вас заражение.	It's infected.
Это инфекционное заболевание.	It's contagious.

Treatment Лечение

Я Вам дам ...	I'll give you ...
антисептическое средство	an antiseptic
болеутоляющее средство	a painkiller
Я Вам пропишу ...	I'm going to prescribe ...
курс антибиотиков	a course of antibiotics
свечи	some suppositories
У Вас есть аллергия на лекарства?	Are you allergic to any medication?
Принимайте одну таблетку ...	Take one pill ...
каждые ... часа	every ... hours
раз в день	... times a day
перед едой	before meals
Сходите к врачу, когда приедете домой.	Consult a doctor when you get home.

Parts of the body   Части тела

English	Russian
arm	рука *rooka*
back	спина *speena*
bladder	мочевой пузырь *machyeevoy poozir'*
bone	кость *kost'*
breast	грудь *grood'*
chest	грудная клетка *groodnaya klyetka*
ear/eye	ухо/глаз *ookha/glas*
face	лицо *leetso*
finger/thumb	палец/большой палец *paleets/bal'shoy paleets*
foot	нога *naga*
glands (tonsils)	гланды *glandi*
hand	рука *rooka*
head	голова *galava*
heart	сердце *syertse*
jaw	челюсть *chyelyoost'*
joint	сустав *soostaf*
kidney	почка *pochka*
knee	колено *kalyena*
leg	нога *naga*
lip	губа *gooba*
liver	печень *pyechyeen'*
mouth	рот *rot*
muscle	мышца *mishtsa*
neck	шея *sheya*
nose	нос *nos*
rib	ребро *reebro*
shoulder	плечо *pleechyo*
skin	кожа *kozha*
stomach	живот/желудок *zhivot/zheloodak*
thigh	бедро *beedro*
throat	горло *gorla*
toe	палец ноги *paleets nagee*
tongue	язык *eezik*
vein	вена *vyena*

Gynecologist Гинеколог

I have …	У меня … *oo meenya* …
abdominal pains	боли в животе *bolee v zhivatye*
period pains	боли при менструации *bolee pree meenstrooatsiee*
a vaginal infection	воспаление влагалища *vaspalyeneeye vlagaleeshchya*
I haven't had my period for … months.	У меня нет менструации уже … месяца. *oo menya nyet meenstrooatsiee oozhe …* *myeseetsa*
I'm on the Pill.	Я принимаю противозачаточные таблетки. *ya preeneemayoo* *prateevazachyatachniye tablyetkee*

Hospital Больница

Please notify my family.	Пожалуйста, сообщите моей семье. *pazhalsta saabshchyeetee mayey seemye*
What are the visiting hours?	Когда часы посещений? *kagda chyasi paseeshchyeneey*
I'm in pain.	У меня боли. *oo meenya bolee*
I can't eat/sleep.	Я не ем/сплю. *ya nee yem/splyoo*
When will the doctor come?	Когда придёт врач? *kagda preedyot vrach*
Which ward is … in?	В какой палате …? *f kakoy palatye* …
I'm visiting …	Я посещаю … *ya paseeshchyayoo* …

Optician Оптика

I'm near- [short-] sighted/ far- [long-] sighted.	У меня близорукость/дальнозоркость. *oo meenya bleezarookast'/dal'nazorkast'*
I've lost …	Я потерял(а) … *ya pateeryal(a)*
one of my contact lenses	контактную линзу *kantaktnooyoo leenzoo*
my glasses	мои очки *maee achkee*
a lens	линзу *leenzoo*
Could you give me a replacement?	Можно заменить? *mozhna zameeneet'*

Dentist Зубной врач

I have toothache.	У меня болит зуб. *oo meenya baleet zoop*
This tooth hurts.	Вот этот зуб болит. *vot etat zoop baleet*
I've lost a tooth/cap.	Я потерял(а) зуб/коронку. *ya pateeryal(a)/ slamal(a) zoop/karonkoo*
I've lost a filling.	Пломба выпала. *plomba vipala*
Can you repair this denture?	Вы можете починить этот протез? *vi mozhetye pachyeeneet' etat pratyes*
I don't want it extracted.	Можно не удалять? *mozhna nee oodalyat'*

Я Вам сделаю укол/ обезболивание.	I'm going to give you an injection/ a local anesthetic.
Вам нужно поставить пломбу/ коронку.	You need a filling/cap [crown].
Придётся удалить.	I'll have to take it out.
Это можно поправить только временно.	I can only fix it temporarily.
Приходите через ... дня (дней).	Come back in ... days.
Нельзя есть ... часа.	Don't eat anything for ... hours.

Payment and insurance Оплата и страховка

Do I pay you now?	Платить сейчас? *plateet' seechyas*
How much do I owe you?	Сколько с меня? *skol'ka s meenya*
I have insurance.	У меня есть страховка.
Can I have a receipt for my health insurance?	Дайте мне квитанцию для медицинского страхования. *daytee mnye kveetantseeyoo dlya meedeetseenkava strakhavaneeya*
Would you fill out this health insurance form, please?	Не могли бы Вы заполнить бланк для страхования, пожалуйста? *nee maglee bi vi zapolneet' blank dlya strakhavaneeya*
Can I have a medical certificate?	Можно получить медицинское свидетельство? *mozhna meedeetsinskaye sveedyeteel'stva*

Dictionary
English–Russian

Most terms in this dictionary are either followed by an example or cross-referenced to pages where the word appears in a phrase. Only the masculine ending (-ый, -ой, -ий) of adjectives is given in the dictionary. The feminine and neuter endings are -ая, -ое respectively.

The notes below provide some basic grammar guidelines.

Nouns

There are three genders in Russian: masculine (m), feminine (f), and neuter (n) ▶15. The endings of nouns vary according to their "role" in the sentence. There are six different cases in both the singular and plural. Adjectives agree in number and gender with the noun they modify.

The following notes give an overview of how the cases are used.

Nominative (N): refers to the subject of the sentence – the person or thing performing the action.
Genetive (G): is used to designate a person/object to whom/which somebody or something belongs (it can often be translated by "of" in English).
Dative (D): designates the person/object to whom/which something is given or done.
Accusative (A): usually denotes the direct object of an action.
Instrumental (I): answers the questions "by whom?", "by what means?", "how?".
Prepositional (P): is always used with a preposition. The most common are в, на, (on, in) and о (about).

Verbs (For information about the verb "to be" ▶17.)

The infinitive of most verbs ends in **т́** (-ть). Russian verbs conjugate (change their endings) according to the subject of the verb (I, you, he/she/it, we, you (pl.), they.)

The negative is formed by adding **nee** (не) before the verb.

Past tense

The past tense is formed by removing the -ть of the infinitive and adding:

-л (**-l**)	masculine ending	-ла (**-la**)	feminine ending
-ло (**-lo**)	neuter ending	-лы (**-li**)	plural ending

It is the gender and number of the subject that control the choice of ending, for example: I spoke (said by a man) = говорил, I spoke (said by a woman) = говорила.

"to have"

When "to have" means "possess" it is expressed by the preposition у followed by the genitive case of the word denoting the possessor + есть (in the present tense) + the thing possessed (in the nominative case). In the present tense есть may be omitted. For example, У меня (есть) машина.
(**oo meenya (yest') masheena**) = "in the possession of me is a car" = I have a car.

A

a few немного/несколько neemnoga/nyeskal'ka 15

a little немного neemnoga 15

a lot много mnoga 15

a.m. до полудня da paloodnya

abbey аббатство m abatstva 99

abdominal pains боли в животе fpl bolee v zheevatye 167

about (approximately) около okala 15

abroad заграницей zagraneetsey

accept: do you accept ...? Вы принимаете ...? Vi preeneemayetee...? 42, 136

access (n) допуск m dopoosk 100

accessories принадлежности fpl preenadlyezhnastee 144

accident несчастный случай m neshchasniy sloochay 152; (road) авария f avareeya 92

accidentally случайно sloochayna 28

accompaniments гарнир m garneer 38

accompany, to провожать pravazhat' 65

accountant бухгалтер m boogaltyer 121

acne прыщи mpl prishchee

across через chyereez 12

acrylic акрил m akreel

actor актёр m aktyor 110

actress актриса f aktreesa 110

adapter адаптер m adapteer 26, 148

address адрес m adrees 84, 126

adhesive bandages пластырь m plastir 141

adjoining room совмещённые комнаты/номера fpl/mpl savmeshchyenyeye komnaty/nomeera 22

admission charge входная плата f fkhadnaya plata 114

adult взрослый vzrosliy 81

adult (n) взрослый m vzrosliy

aerobic class класс аэробики m klas ayerobeekee 115

after (time/place) после poslee 13, 95

after-shave лосьон после бритья m lasyon poslee breetya 142

afternoon, in the днём m dnyom 221

age: what age? какой возраст? m kakoy vozrast? 113

agree: I don't agree я не согласен ya nee saglaseen

air: ~ conditioning кондиционер m kandeetseeonyer 22, 25; **~ pump** воздух m vozdookh 87; **~ sickness bag** гигиенический пакет m geegeeyeneecheskiy pakyet 70; **~mail** авиапочта f aveeapochta 155

airport аэропорт m aeraport 96

aisle seat боковое место n bakavoye myesta 74

alarm clock будильник m boodeel'neek 149

alcoholic (drink) алкогольный alkagol'niy

all все vsyo

all-night ночный nachnoy 140

allergic, to be аллергия f aleergeeya 164

allergy аллергия f aleergeeya 165

allowance разрешение n razryeshyeneeye 67

almost почти pachtee

alone только tol'ka

already уже oozhe 28

also также tagzhe 19

alter, to переделывать peereedyelivat' 137

alumin(i)um foil фольга f fal'ga 148

always всегда fseegda 13

amazing поразительный parazeetyelniy 101

ambassador посол m pasol

ambulance скорая помощь f skoraya pomashch 92

American *(adj)* американский
ameereekanskeey 150, 152
amount сумма f sooma 42
amusement arcade аттракционы
mpl atrakseeoni 113
anaesthetic обезболивающее n
abeezboleevayooshcheye
and и, а ee/a 19; **and so on** и так
далее ee tag daleeye 19
animal животное n
zheevotnaya 106
anorak куртка f koortka
another другой(ая) m/f
droogoy(aya) 21; *(time)* в другой
раз v droogoy ras 125
antacid средство от изжоги n
sryetstva at eezzhogee
antibiotics антибиотики mpl
anteebeeoteekee 165
antifreeze антифриз m anteefreez
antique антиквар m anteekvar 157;
~ store антикварный магазин m
anteekvarniy magazeen 130
antiseptic антисептическое средство
n anteeseepteecheskoye sretstva
165; **~ cream** антисептическая
мазь f anteeseepteecheskaya
maz' 141
any какой-либо kakoy-leeba
anyone: does anyone speak English?
здесь кто-нибудь говорит по-
английски? zdyes' kto-neebood'
gavareet pa angleeyskee
anything else? что-нибудь еще?
chto-neebood' eeshchyo
apartment квартира f
kvarteera 28, 123
apologize: I apologize прошу
прощения prashoo
prashchyeneeya
appendicitis аппендицит m
apeendeetseet 165
appendix аппендикс m
apyendeeks 166
apple яблоко n yablaka 160
appointment приём m preeyom
161; **to make an ~** записываться
zapeesivat'sya 147

approximately приблизительно
preebleezeeteel'na 152
April апрель m apryel' 218
architect архитектор m
arkheetektar 104
area code код m kod 127
arm рука f rooka 166
around *(place)* по pa 12; *(time)*
около okala 13
arrive, to прилетать preelyetat'
68, 70, 71
art gallery картинная галерея f
karteenaya galyeryeya 99
arthritic, to be иметь артрит
eemyet' artreet 163
artificial sweetener сахарин m
sakhareen 38
artist художник m khoodozhneek 104
ashtray пепельница f
pyepyel'neetsa 39
ask: I asked for ... я просил(а) ... ya
praseel(a) ... 41
asking просьба f pros'ba 37
aspirin аспирин m aspeereen 141
asthmatic *(n)* астматик m
astmateek 163
at last! наконец nakanyets 19
at *(place)* в, на v/f, na 12;
(time) в v 13
at least по крайней мере ра
krayney myerye 23
athletics атлетика f atlyeteeka 114
ATM *(automated teller)* банкомат
bankamat 139
attack нападение n
napadyeneeye 152
attractive привлекательный
preevleekateel'niy
August август m afgoost 218
aunt тётя f tyotya 120
Australia Австралия f
Afstraleeya 119
authentic: is it authentic? это
настоящее? eta nastayashcheey
authenticity подлинность f
podleenast' 157

A-Z

automatic (car) с автоматической трансмиссией s aftamateecheskay transmeeseeyey 86;
~ **camera** автоматический фотоаппарат m aftamateecheskiy fotaaparat 151
automobile машина f masheena 86
autumn осень f oseen' 219
available (unoccupied) свободный svabodniy 77
avalanche лавина f laveena

B baby ребёнок m reebyonak 39, 113, 162; ~ **food** детское питание n dyetskaye peetaneeye 142; ~ **wipe** подгузник m padgoozneek 142; ~-**sitter** няня f nyanya 113; ~-**sitting** присмотр за детьми m preesmotar za deet'mee 113
back спина f speena 166; ~**ache** боль в спине f bol' v speenye 163
backpacking туризм m tooreezm
bad плохой plakhoy 14
baggage багаж m bagazh 32, 67, 71; ~ **check** багажное отделение n bagazhnoye adelyeneeye 71, 73
bakery булочная f boolachnaya 130, 158
balcony балкон m balkon 29
ball мяч m myach 157
ballet балет m balyet 108, 111
bananas банан m banan 160
band (musical group) группа f groopa 111, 157
bandages бинт m beent 141
bank банк m bank 130, 138
bar (hotel, etc.) бар m bar 26, 112
barber парикмахер m pareekhmakheer
basement подвал m padval 132
basket корзинка f karzeenka 158
basketball баскетбол m baskeetbol 114

bath towel банное полотенце n banoye palatyentse 27
bathroom туалет m tooalyet 26, 98
battery (car) аккумулятор m akamoolyatar 88; (camera, etc.) батарейка f batareyka 137, 151
battle site место сражения n myesta srazhyeneeya 99
be, to быть byt' 17
beach пляж m plyazh 116
beard борода f barada
beautiful красивый kraseeviy 14; прекрасный preekrasniy 101
because потому что patamoochto 16; ~ **of** из-за eez-za 16
bed кровать/постель f kravat'/pastel' 21; ~ **and breakfast** с завтраком m s zavtrakam 24
bedding постельное бельё n pastel"noye byelyo 29
bedroom спальня f spal'nya 29
beer пиво n peeva 40, 160
before (time) до da 13, 221;
~ **meals** перед едой pyereet eedoy
begin, to начинать nacheenat'
beginner новичок m naveechyok 117
beige бежевый byezheeviy 143
Belarus Белоруссия f Beelaroosseeya 119
belong: this belongs to me это принадлежит мне eta preenadleezheet mnye
belt ремень/пояс m reemyen'/poyas 144
berth полка f polka 74, 77
best лучший loochshiy
better лучше loochshe 14
bib салфетка f salfyetka
bicycle велосипед m vyelaseepyet 75, 83
bidet биде n beede
big большой bal'shoy 14, 134; великий veeleekeey 117;
bigger больше bol'shye 24
bikini бикини pl beekeenee 144
bill счёт m schyot 32, 35, 42

bin liner мешок для мусора m meeshok dlya moosara

binoculars бинокль m beenokal'

bird птица f pteetsa 106

birthday день рождения m dyen' razhdyeneeya 219

biscuits печенье n peechyenye 160

bite (insect) укус m ookoos

bitten: I've been bitten by a dog меня укусила собака meenya ookooseela sabaka

bitter горький gor'kiy 41

bizarre причудливый preechoodleeviy 101

black чёрный chyorniy 143; **~ and white film** (camera) чёрно-белая chyorna-byelaya 151; **~ coffee** чёрный кофе m chyorniy kofye 40

bladder мочевой пузырь m macheevoy poozir' 166

blanket одеяло n adyeyala 27

bleach отбеливатель m atbyeleevateel' 148

bleeding кровотечение n kravateechyeneeye 92, 162

blinds (n) шторы fpl shtora 25

blister волдырь m valdir' 162

blocked, to be засорен(а) zasaryon/zasoryena 25

blood кровь f krov' 164; **~ group** группа крови f groopa krovee; **~ pressure** кровяное давление n kraveenoye davlyeneeye 164

blouse блузка f bloozka 144

blow-dry фен m fyen 147

blue синий seeniy 143

blush [rosé] wine розовое вино n rozovoye veeno 40

boarding card посадочный талон m pasadachniy talon 70

boat лодка f lotka 81; **~ trip** водная экскурсия f vodnaya ekskoorseeya 81

boil (medical) нарыв m nariv 162

boiled вареный varyoniy

boiler бойлер m boyleer 29

bone кость f kost' 166

book книга f kneega 150

book, to (reserve) заказывать zakazivat'

booking заказ m zakaz

booklet of tickets талоны mpl taloni 79

bookstore книжный магазин m kneezhniy magazeen 130, 150

booted, to be надеть штрафной башмак nadyet' shtrafnoy bashmak 87

boots сапоги mpl sapagee 145; (for sport) спортивная обувь f sparteevnaya oboov' 115

boring скучный skoochniy 101

born: I was born in я родился в ... ya radeelsya v

borrow: may I borrow your ...? можно мне взять взаймы ваш ...? mozhna mnye vzyat' vzaymi vash ...

botanical garden ботанический сад m bataneecheskiy sat 99

bottle бутылка f bootilka 37, 159; **~ of wine** бутылка вина f bootilka veena 156; **~-opener** открывалка f atkrivalka 148

bowel кишечник m keeshyechneek

box of chocolates коробка шоколада f karopka shakalada 156

boy мальчик m mal'cheek 120, 157

boyfriend друг m drook 120

bra бюстгальтер m byoostgal'tyer 144

bracelet браслет m braslyet 149

bread хлеб m khlyeb 38

break, to сломать slamat' 28; **~ down** (car) сломаться slamat'sya 88

break-in взлом m vzlom 153

breakdown truck буксир m bookseer 88

breakfast завтрак m zaftrak 27

breast грудь f grood' 166

breathe, to дышать dishat' 92, 164

breathtaking захватывающий zakvativayooshchiy 101

bridge мост m most 107

briefs трусики pl trooseekee 144

bring somebody, to привести preeveestee 125

A-Z

Britain Великобритания f Vyeleekabreetaneeya 119
British (adj) британский breetanskeey 152
brochure брошюра f brashoora
broken сломан sloman 137; **to be ~** сломаться slamat'sya 25; (bone) сломать slamat' 164
bronchitis бронхит m brankheet
brooch брошь f brosh 149
brother брат m brat 120
brown коричневый kareechneeviy 143
browse, to смотреть smatryet' 133
bruise синяк m seenyak 162
bucket ведёрко n veedyorka 157
build, to строить stroyeet' 104
building здание n zdaneeye 104
built построенный pastroyeniy 104
bureau de change обмен валюты m abmyen valyooti 138
burger гамбургер m gamboorgyer 40; **~ stand** кафе-гамбургер n kafye gamboorgyer 35
burn ожог m azhok 162
bus автобус m aftoboos 70, 78, 98; **~ route** автобусный маршрут m aftoboosniy marshroot 96; **~ station** автобусная станция f aftoboosnaya stantseeya 78; **~ stop** автобусная остановка f aftoboosnaya astanofka 65, 96; стоянка f stayanka 78
business бизнес m beeznees 121; **~ class** бизнес класс m beeznees klas 68; **~ trip** командировка f kamandeerofka 123; **on ~** по делу n pa dyeloo 66
busy, to be (occupied) занят(а) zanyat 125
but но no 19
butane gas газовый баллон m gazaviy balon 30, 31
butcher мясной магазин m myasnoy magazeen 130
butter масло n masla 38, 160
button кнопка f knopka

buy, to покупать pakoopat' 67, 80, 133
by (time) к k 13; **~ car** на машине na masheene 17, 94; **~ credit card** кредитной карточкой kredeetnoy kartochkoy 17
bye! пока! paka

C cab такси n taksee 84
cabaret кабаре n kabare 112
cabin каюта f kayoota 81
café кафе n kafye 35, 40
cagoule плащ m plashch 145
cake пирожное n peerozhnoye 40
calendar календарь m kaleendar' 156
call, to вызвать vizvat' 92; (phone) звонить zvaneet' 127, 128; **~ collect** звонить по коллекту zvaneet' pa kalyektoo 127; **~ for somebody** заходить за zakhadeet' 125; **call the police!** вызовете милицию vizaveetee meeleetsiyoo 92
camera фотоаппарат m fotaaparat 151; **~ case** футляр m footlyar 151; **~ store** фототовары mpl fotatavari 130, 151
campbed раскладушка f raskladooshka 31
camping кемпинг m kyempeeng 30; **~ equipment** снаряжение n snaryazhyeneeye 31
campsite кемпинг m kyempeeng 123
can банка f banka 159; **~-opener** открывалка f atkrivalka 148
can: can I? можно мне ...? mozhno mnye ...? 18; **can I have?** можно мне ...? mozhno mnye ...? 18; **can you help me?** помогите мне pamageetye mnye 18; **can you recommend ...?** вы можете порекомендовать ...? vi mozheetee pareekamyendavat' ...? 112
Canada Канада f Kanada 119
cancel, to (reservation) отменять atmyenyat' 68

cancer (*disease*) рак m rak

candle свеча f sveecha 148

candy конфеты, сладости fpl kanfyeti, sladastee 150

cap (*dental*) коронка f karonka 168

car машина f macheena 81, 86, 87, 88, 89, 153; **~ ferry** грузовой паром m groozavoy parom 81; **~ hire** прокат автомобилей m prakat aftamabeeleyey 70, 86; **~ park** автостоянка f aftastayanka 26, 87, 96; **~ rental** прокат автомобилей m prakat aftamabeeleyey 70, 86

car (*compartment of train*) вагон m vagon 77

carafe графин m grafeen 37

caravan трейлер m treyler 30, 81

cards карты fpl karti 121

careful: be careful! будьте осторожны! bood'tee astarozhni

carpet (*rug*) ковер m kavyor

carrier bag авоська f avos'ka

carry-cot люлька f lool'ka

cart тележка f teelyeshka 158

carton пакет m pakyet 159

cash наличные pl naleechniye 136, 138; **~ desk** касса f kasa 132; **~ machine** банкомат bankamat 139

cashier касса f kasa 132

casino казино n kazeeno 112

cassette кассета f kasyeta 157

castle замок m zamak 99

catch, to (*bus*) успеть на автобус oospyet' na aftoobos

cathedral собор m sabor 99

Catholic католический kataleechyeskiy 105

cave пещера f peeshchyera 107

CD компакт-диск m kampakt deesk; **~-player** лазерный проигрыватель m lazeerniy praeegrivateel'

center (*of town*) центр (города) m tsentr (gorada) 21

central heating центральное отопление n tseentral'naya ataplyeneeye

ceramics керамика f keerameeka

certificate сертификат m seerteefeekat 149, 157; видетельство n sveedyeteel'stva 168

chain цепочка f tseepochka 149

change (*coins*) сдача f sdacha 136, **keep the change** оставьте сдачу f astav'tye zdachoo 84

change, to (*buses, trains*) делать пересадку dyelat' pyeryesatkoo 75, 79, 80; (*baby*) перепеленать pyeryepyelyonivat' 39; (*money*) обменять abmeenyat' 138; разменивать razmyeneevat' 87; (*alter*) поменять pamyenyat' 68

changing facilities (*baby*) место перепеленать ребёнка n myesta pyereepeeleenat' reebyonka 113

charcoal уголь m oogal' 31

charge плата f plata 30, 115

charter flight чартерный рейс m chartyerniy reys

cheap дешёвый deeshoviy 14, 134; **cheaper** дешевле deeshyevlee 21, 24, 109, 134

check: please check the … пожалуйста, проверьте... pazhalsta pravyertee; **~ in** регистрироваться reegeestreeravat'sya 68; **~ out** (*hotel*) выезжать vieezhat'

check-in desk регистрационная стойка f reegeestratseeonaya stoyka 69

checkout контроль m kantrol' 158

cheers! за ваше здоровье! za vashye zdarov'ye

cheese сыр m sir 157

chemist аптека f aptyeka 130, 140

check [cheque] book чековая книжка f chyekavaya kneeshka

chess шахматы pl shakhmati 121; **~ set** шахматы pl shakhmati 157

chest (*body*) грудная клетка f groodnaya klyetka 166

chewing gum жевательная резинка f zheevateel'naya reezeenka 150

A-Z

A-Z

child ребёнок m reeby<u>o</u>nak 98, 152; **children** дети npl dy<u>e</u>tee 22, 66, 74, 100, 113, 120; (adj.) детский dy<u>e</u>tskiy 39; **child seat** (in car) детское сиденье n dy<u>e</u>tskaye seedy<u>e</u>nye 86; **child's seat** (high chair) детский стульчик m dy<u>e</u>tskiy st<u>oo</u>lcheek 39; **child's cot** детская кроватка f d<u>e</u>tskaya krav<u>a</u>tka 22

childminder воспитатель m vaspeet<u>a</u>teel'

Chinese (cuisine) китайская (кухня) keet<u>a</u>yskaya (k<u>oo</u>khnya) 35

chips (crisps) чипсы pl ch<u>ee</u>psi 160

choc-ice шоколадное мороженое n shak<u>a</u>ladnaye mar<u>o</u>zhenoye 110

chocolate шоколад m shak<u>a</u>lat 160; (flavor) шоколадное shak<u>a</u>ladnaye 40; **hot ~** горячий шоколад m gary<u>a</u>chiy shak<u>a</u>lat 40; **~ bar** шоколадка f shak<u>a</u>latka 150

Christmas Рождество n Razdeestv<u>o</u> 219

church церковь f ts<u>e</u>rkav' 96, 99, 105

cigarettes, packet of сигареты fpl seegar<u>ye</u>ti 150

cigars сигары fpl seeg<u>a</u>ri 150

cinema кинотеатр m keenate<u>a</u>tr 96, 110

claim check багажная квитанция f bag<u>a</u>zhnaya kveet<u>a</u>ntseeya 71

clamped, to be надеть штрафной башмак nad<u>ye</u>t' shtrafn<u>o</u>y bashm<u>a</u>k 87

class (type of seat, etc.) класс m klas 68

clean чистый ch<u>ye</u>esti 14; чистый ch<u>ee</u>stiy 39, 41

clean, to чистить ch<u>ee</u>steet' 137

cliff обрыв m abr<u>i</u>v 107

cling film обёрточная бумага f ab<u>yo</u>rtachnaya boom<u>a</u>ga 148

clinic поликлиника f paleekl<u>ee</u>neeka 131

cloakroom гардероб m gardeer<u>o</u>p 109

clock часы pl chas<u>i</u> 149

close, to (store, etc.) закрываться zakriv<u>a</u>t'sya 100, 140

clothes одежда f ady<u>e</u>zhda 144; **~ peg** прищепка f preeshchy<u>e</u>pka 148; **~ store** одежда f ady<u>e</u>zhda 130

cloudy, to be облачно <u>o</u>blachna 122

clubs (golf) клюшки fpl kly<u>oo</u>shkee 115

coach (long-distance bus) междугородний автобус m myezhdoogar<u>o</u>dniy aft<u>o</u>boos 78; **~ bay** стоянка f stay<u>a</u>nka 78; **~ station** автобусная станция f aft<u>o</u>boosnaya st<u>a</u>ntseeya 78

coach (train compartment) вагон m vag<u>o</u>n 75

coast побережье n pabeer<u>ye</u>zhye

coat пальто n pal't<u>o</u> 144

coatcheck гардероб m gardeer<u>o</u>p 109

coathanger вешалка f vy<u>e</u>shalka

cockroach таракан m tarak<u>a</u>n

code (area, dialling) код m kod

coffee кофе m k<u>o</u>fye 40

coin монета f man<u>ye</u>ta

cola кока-кола f k<u>o</u>ka k<u>o</u>la 40

cold ('flu) простуда f prast<u>oo</u>da 141, 163

cold (adj.) холодный khal<u>o</u>dniy 14, 41, 122; **~ meats** мясные изделия npl myasn<u>i</u>ye eezdy<u>e</u>leeya 160

collapse: he's collapsed он потерял сознание on pateer<u>ya</u>l saznan<u>e</u>eye

collect, to забирать zabeer<u>a</u>t' 151

color цвет m tsvet 143; **~ film** цветная tsvyetn<u>a</u>ya 151

comb расчёска f rashch<u>yo</u>ska 142

come back приходить preekhad<u>ee</u>t' 36, 140

commission комиссионный сбор m kameeseeon<u>i</u>y sbor 138

compact camera компактный фотоаппарат m kam<u>pak</u>tniy <u>fo</u>taaparat 151

compact disc компакт-диск m kam<u>pak</u>t-deesk 157

company *(business)* предприятие n preetpree<u>ya</u>teeye

company *(companionship)* компания f kam<u>pa</u>neeya 126

compartment *(train)* купе n koo<u>pe</u>

complaint жалоба f <u>zha</u>loba 41

computer компьютер m kam<u>pyoo</u>teer

concert концерт m kan<u>tsyert</u> 108, 111; **~ hall** концертный зал m kan<u>tsyert</u>niy zal 111

concession скидка f <u>skeet</u>ka

concussion: he has concussion у него сотрясение мозга n oo nee<u>vo</u> satrya<u>sye</u>neeye <u>moz</u>ga

conditioner кондиционер m kandeetsee<u>a</u>nyer 142

condoms презервативы mpl preezeerva<u>tee</u>vi 141

conductor дирижёр m deeree<u>zhyor</u> 111

confirm, to *(reservation)* подтвердить pattveer<u>deet'</u> 68

congratulations! поздравляем! pazdrav<u>lya</u>eem

conscious: he's conscious он в сознании f saz<u>na</u>neeye

constipation запор m za<u>por</u>

Consulate консульство n kon<u>sool</u>'stva 152

consult, to консультироваться kansool'<u>tee</u>ravat'sya 165

contact, to связаться svya<u>zat'</u>sya 28

contact lenses контактные линзы CORR fpl kan<u>tak</u>niye <u>leen</u>zi 167

contagious инфекционный eenfeektsee<u>on</u>niy 165

contain, to содержать sadeer<u>zhat'</u> 39, 69, 155

contemporary dance современный танец m savree<u>mye</u>niy <u>ta</u>neets 111

contraceptive противозачаточное средство n proteevaza<u>cha</u>tachnaya <u>sry</u>etstva

cook повар m <u>po</u>var

cook, to готовить ga<u>to</u>veet'

cooker плита f <u>plee</u>ta 28, 29

cookies печенье n pee<u>chye</u>nye 160

cooking *(cuisine)* кухня f <u>kookh</u>nya

coolbox холодильник m khala<u>deel</u>'neek

copper медь f myed' 149

copy копия f <u>ko</u>peeya 155

corkscrew штопор m <u>shto</u>par 148

corner угол m <u>oo</u>gal 95

correct правильно pra<u>veel</u>'na 77

cosmetics косметика f kas<u>mye</u>teeka

cottage дача f <u>da</u>cha 28

cotton [cotton wool] вата f <u>va</u>ta 141

cough кашель m <u>ka</u>sheel' 141; **~ syrup** жидкость от кашля f <u>zheet</u>kast' at <u>kash</u>lya 141

cough, to кашлять <u>kash</u>lyat' 164

could I have ...? можно мне ...? <u>mozh</u>no mnye …?18

country *(nation)* страна f stra<u>na</u>

country music музыка кантри f <u>moo</u>zika <u>kan</u>tree 111

courier *(guide)* курьер m koo<u>ryer</u>

course *(part of meal)* блюдо n <u>blyoo</u>da

cousin кузен/кузина m/f koo<u>zyen</u>/koo<u>zee</u>na

craft shop магазин ремесленных изделий m maga<u>zeen</u> ree<u>mye</u>slyanikh eez<u>dye</u>leey

cramps судороги fpl <u>soo</u>daragee 163

creche ясли pl <u>ya</u>slee

credit card кредитная карточка f kree<u>deet</u>naya <u>kar</u>tachka 42, 136, 139; **~ number** номер кредитной карточки m <u>no</u>meer kree<u>deet</u>nay <u>kar</u>tachkee 109

crib детская кроватка f <u>dyet</u>skaya kra<u>vat</u>ka 22

crisps чипсы pl <u>cheep</u>si 160

A-Z

crockery посуда f pasooda 29, 148
cross (crucifix) распятие n raspyateeye
crossroad перекрёсток m peereekryostak 95
crowded тесно tyesna 30
crown (dental) коронка f karonka 168
cruise (n.) круиз m krooeez
crutches костыли mpl kastilee
crystal хрусталь m khroostal' 149
cup чашка f chashka 39, 148
cupboard шкаф m shkaf
currency валюта f valyoota 67, 138; ~ **exchange** (office) обмен валюты m abmyen valyooti 70, 73, 138
curtains занавеси fpl zanaveesee
customs таможня f tamozhnya 67, 157; ~ **declaration** таможенная декларация f tamozheenaya deeklaratseeya 155
cut порез m paryez 162
cut glass резное стекло n reeznoye steeklo 149
cut and blow-dry стрижка и сушка феном f streeshka ee sooshka fyenam 147
cut and style стрижка и укладка f streeshka ee ooklatka 147
cutlery прибор m preebor 29, 148
cycle route велосипедный маршрут m veelaseepyedniy marshroot 106
cycling велоспорт m vyelasport 114
cystitis цистит m tseesteet 165

D daily ежедневно eezheednyevna
damaged, to повредить pavryedeet' 71; **to be ~** повреждён(а) pavryezhdyon/ pavrezhdyena 28
damp (n.) сырость f sirast'; (adj.) сыро sira
dance (performance) танец m taneets 111

dancing, to go пойти потанцевать paytee patantseevat' 124
dangerous опасно apasna
dark тёмный tyomniy 14, 24, 134, 143
daughter дочь f doch 120, 162
dawn рассвет m rasvyet 221
day день m dyen' 97; (ticket) на день na dyen' 79
deaf (adj.) глухой glookhoy 163
December декабрь m deekabr' 218
deck chair шезлонг m shezlonk 116
declare, to предъявлять preedyavlyat' 67
deduct, to (money) вычитать vicheetat'
deep глубокий gloobokeey; ~ **freeze** замораживать zamarazheevat'
defrost, to размораживать razmarazheevat'
degrees (temperature) градусы mpl gradoosi
delay задержка f zadyerzhka 70
delicatessen магазин деликатесов m magazeen deeleekatyessaf 130, 158
delicious вкусный fkoosniy 14
deliver, to доставлять dastavlyat'
denim джинсовая ткань f dzheensovaya tkan' 146
dentist зубной врач m zoobnoy vrach 131, 161, 168
dentures протез m pratyez 168
deodorant дезодорант m deezadarant 142
depart, to (train, bus) отправляться atpravlyat'sya
department (in store) отдел m adyel 132; ~ **store** универмаг m ooneeveermag 130
departure lounge накопитель m nakapeetyel'
deposit аванс m avans 24, 83
describe, to описывать apeesivat' 152
destination место назначения n myesta naznachyeneeya
details подробности fpl padrobnastee

detergent моющее средство n moyooshcheeye sryetstva

develop, to (photos) проявлять praeevlyat' 151

diabetes диабет m deeabyet

diabetic (n.) диабетик m deeabyeteek 39, 163

diagnosis диагноз m deeagnas 164

dialling code код m kod 127

diamond брильянт m breelyant 149

diapers пелёнка f peelyonka 142

diarrhea понос m panos 141, 163; **I have ~** у меня понос oo meenya panos

dice кости fpl kostee

dictionary словарь m slavar' 150

diesel дизельное топливо n deezeel'naye topleeva 85, 87

diet: I'm on a ~ я на диете deeyeta

difficult трудный troodniy 14

dining: ~ car ресторан m ryestaran 75; **~ room** столовая f stalovaya 26, 29

dinner: to have ~ ужинать oozheenat' 124; **~ jacket** смокинг m smokeeng

dipped beam нижний свет m neezhniy svyet 86

direct (of train, etc.) прямой pryamoy 75

direct, to направлять napravlyat' 18

direction направление n napravlyeneeye 80; **in the ~ of** по направлению к ... pa napravlyeneeyoo k ... 95

directions указания npl ookazaneeya 94

director (of company) директор m deeryektar

directory (telephone) телефонный справочник m teeleefoniy spravechneek; **Directory Enquiries** справочная служба f spravachnaya sloozhba 127

dirty грязный gryazniy 14, 28

disabled (n) инвалид m eenvaleed 22

disabled (npl.) инвалиды mpl eenvaleedi 100

disco дискотека f deeskatyeka 112

discount скидка f skeedka 74

dish (meal) блюдо n blyooda 37

dish cloth тряпка f tryapka 148

dishwashing liquid средство для мытья посуды n sryetstva dlya mitya pasoodi 148

dislocated, to be вывихнуть viveekhnoot' 164

display cabinet/case витрина f veetreena 134, 149

disposable camera одноразовый фотоаппарат m adnarazaviy fotaaparat 151

distilled water дистиллированная вода f deesteeleerovanaya vada

disturb: don't disturb не беспокоить nee beespakoyeet'

dive, to нырять niryat' 116

diving equipment акваланг m akvalank 116

divorced, to be разведён razveedyon 120

dizzy: I feel ~ у меня кружится голова oo meenya kroozheetsya galava

do: what do you do? ваша профессия? vasha prafyeseeya? 121; **do you have ...?** у Вас есть ...? oo vas yest' 37

doctor врач m vrach 131, 161, 167

doll кукла f kookla 157

dollar доллар m dolar 67, 138

don't mention it не за что nye za shta 10

door дверь f dvyer' 25

double двухместный dvookhmyesniy 81; **~ bed** двуспальная кровать f dvoospal'naya kravat' 21; **~ room** двухместный номер m dvookhmyestnyi nomer 21

downtown area центр города m tsyentr gorada 99

A-Z

dozen дюжина f <u>dyoo</u>zheena 217

dress платье n <u>plat'</u>yee 144

drink, to пить peet' 70, 124, 126; выпить <u>vi</u>peet' 125

drinking water питьевая вода f peet'ye<u>va</u>ya va<u>da</u> 30

drip, to: the faucet [tap] drips кран протекает kran prate<u>ka</u>yeet

drive, to ехать <u>ye</u>khat' 93

driver водитель m va<u>dee</u>tyel'; **driver's licence [license]** водительские права npl va<u>dee</u>teel'<u>skee</u>ye pra<u>va</u> 93

drop off, to (children) приводить preeva<u>deet'</u> 113; высадить <u>vi</u>sadeet' 83

drowning: someone is drowning кто-то тонет <u>kto</u>-ta to<u>neet</u>

drugstore аптека f ap<u>tye</u>ka 130

drunk (adj.) пьяный <u>pya</u>niy

dry cleaner химчистка f kheem<u>chee</u>stka 131

dry cut сухая стрижка f soo<u>khaya</u> <u>stree</u>shka 147

dry clean, to отдавать в химчистку ada<u>vat'</u> f kheem<u>chee</u>skoo

dubbed, to be дублирован doo<u>blee</u>ravan 110

during во время vo <u>vrye</u>mya

dustbins мусорные баки mpl <u>moo</u>sornye <u>ba</u>kee 30

duty: to pay duty платить пошлину f pla<u>teet'</u> <u>posh</u>leenoo 67

duvet пододеяльник m pada<u>dyeal'</u>neek

E **e-mail** электронная почта f ele<u>ektro</u>naya <u>poch</u>ta 155

ear ухо n <u>oo</u>kha 166; **~ drops** капли для ушей fpl <u>kap</u>lee dlya <u>oo</u>shey; **~ache** боль в ухе f bol' v <u>oo</u>khee 163

earlier раньше <u>ran'</u>she 125, 147

early ранний <u>ran</u>neey 14, 221

earrings серьги fpl <u>syer'</u>gee 149

east восток m va<u>stok</u> 95

Easter Пасха f <u>Pa</u>skha 219

easy лёгкий <u>lyokh</u>keey 14

eat, to есть yest' 41, 167

eat: places to eat места где поесть mee<u>sta</u> gdye pa<u>yest'</u> 123

economy class пассажирский класс m pasa<u>zheer</u>skiy klas 68

egg яйцо n yay<u>tso</u> 160

either ... or или ... или <u>ee</u>lee ... <u>ee</u>lee 16

elastic (adj.) эластичный ela<u>steech</u>niy

electric: ~ outlet розетка f ra<u>zyet</u>ka 30; **~ shaver** электробритва f elyektra<u>bree</u>tva

electricity электричество n eleek<u>tree</u>chestva 28; **~ meter** счётчик m <u>schyot</u>cheek 28

electronic: ~ flash вспышка f <u>vspi</u>shka 151; **~ game** электронная игра f ele<u>ektro</u>naya ee<u>gra</u> 157

elevator лифт m leeft 26, 132

else: something else что-то еще <u>chto</u>-ta ee<u>shchyo</u>

embassy посольство n pa<u>sol'</u>stva

emerald изумруд m eezoom<u>root</u>

emergency крайний случай m <u>kray</u>niy <u>sloo</u>chay 152; **~ exit** аварийный выход m ava<u>ree</u>yniy <u>vi</u>khat; **it's an emergency** это срочно <u>eta</u> <u>sroch</u>na 127

empty пустой poo<u>stoy</u> 14

enamel эмаль f ee<u>mal'</u> 149

end, to кончаться kan<u>chat'</u>sya 108

engaged, to be обручиться abroo<u>cheet'</u>sya 120

engineer инженер m eenzhe<u>nyer</u> 121

England Англия f <u>Ang</u>leeya 119

English (adj.) английский ang<u>leey</u>skeey 11, 67, 110, 150, 152, 161; **~-speaking** говорящий по-английски gava<u>rya</u>shcheey pa ang<u>leey</u>skee 98, 152

enjoy, to нравиться <u>nra</u>veet'sya 110, 121, 124

enlarge, to *(photos)* увеличивать ooveeleecheevat' 151

enough достаточно dastatachna 15, 42, 136

ensuite bathroom ванна в номере f vana v nomeeree

entertainment guide путеводитель по местам отдыха m pooteevadeeteel' pa meestam otdikha

entrance fee входная плата f fkhadnaya plata 100

entry visa въездная виза f vyezdnaya veeza

envelope конверт m kanvyert 150

epileptic *(n.)* эпилептик m epeelyepteek 163

equipment *(sports)* снаряжение n snaryazhyeneeye 115

error ошибка f asheepka

escalator эскалатор m eeskalatar 132

essential основной asnavnoy 89

EU Европейский союз m yevrapeyskeey sayooz

Eurocheque еврочек mpl yevrachyek

evening: in the ~ вечером m vyecheeram 109, 221; **~ dress** вечернее платье veechyerneeye plat'ye 112

events представление n preetstavlyeneeye 108

every: ~ day каждый день m kazhdiy dyen'; **~ week** каждую неделю kazhdooyoo nedyelyoo 13; **every ... hours** каждые ... часа kazhdiye ... chasa

examination *(medical)* осмотр m asmotr

example, for например napreemyer

except кроме kromee

excess baggage перевес багажа m pyeryevyes bagazha 69

exchange, to обменивать abmyeneevat' 138

exchange rate курс обмена m koors abmyena 138

excluding meals без питания n bez peetaneeya 24

excursion экскурсия f ekskoorseeya 97

excuse me извините/ простите eezveeneetye/ prasteetye 10, 94, 224

exhausted, to be уставать oostavat' 106

expected, to be обязательно abeezateel'na 111

expensive дорогой daragoy 14, 134

experienced опытный opitniy 117

expiration date срок действия m srok deystveeya 109

expiry date срок действия m srok deystveeya 109

exposure *(photos)* фотография/фото f/n fotagrafeeya/fota 151

express экспресс m ekspryes 155

extension добавочный номер m dabavachniy nomeer 128

extra *(additional)* ещё yeshchyo 23

extracted, to be *(tooth)* удалять oodalyat' 168

extremely крайне krayne 17

eye глаз m glas 166

F **fabric** *(material)* ткань f tkan' 146

face лицо n leetso 166

facial чистка лица f cheestka leetsa 147

facilities удобства npl oodobstva 22

factor ... номер ... m nomyer 142

faint, to feel чувствовать слабость choofstvavat' slabast' 163

fairground луна-парк m loona-park 113

fairly bad довольно плохо davol'na plokha 19

fall *(season)* осень f oseen' 219

family семья f seemya 66, 74, 120, 167

famous знаменитый znameeneetiy

fan *(air)* вентилятор m veenteelyatar 25

far далеко daleeko 12; **is it ~?** это далеко? eta dalyeko 73; **far-sighted** дальнозоркость f dal'nazorkast' 167

fare плата f plata 79
farm ферма f fyerma 107
fast быстро bistra 93; (clock) спешат speeshat 221
father отец m atyets 120
faucet кран m kran 25
faulty: this is faulty это испорчено eta eesporcheena
favorite любимый lyoobeemiy
fax факс m faks 22, 155
February февраль m feevral' 218
feed, to кормить karmeet' 39
feeding bottle бутылка для кормления f bootilka dlya karmlyeneeya
feel sick, to тошнить tashneet' 98
female женщина f zhyenshcheena 152
ferry паром m parom 81
fever жар m zhar 163
few несколько nyeskal'ka 15
field поле n polye 107
fifth пятый pyatiy 217
fight (brawl) драка f draka
fill in , to заполнять zapalnyat' 155
filling (dental) пломба f plomba 168
film (movie) фильм m feel'm 108, 110; (camera) плёнка f plyonka 151
filter фильтр m feel'tar 151
fine (well) хорошо kharasho 118
finger палец m paleets 166
fire: ~ alarm пожарная тревога f pazharnaya treevoga; **~ department [brigade]** пожарная бригада f pazharnaya breegada 92; **~ escape** пожарная лестница f pazharnaya lyesneetsa; **~ extinguisher** огнетушитель m agneetoosheeteel'; **there's a fire!** пожар! m pazhar
firewood дрова pl drava
first первый pyerviy 68, 75, 81, 217
first class (train) мягкий вагон m myahkiy vagon 74; (plane) первый класс m pyerviy klas 68

fish: ~ counter рыбный отдел m ribniy adyel 158; **~ restaurant** рыбный ресторан ribniy ryestaran 35; **~ store [fishmonger]** рыба m riba 130
fit, to (clothes) под ходить patkhadeet' 146
fitting room примерочная preemyerachnaya 146
flashlight фонарь m fanar' 31
flat (puncture) прокол m prakol 83, 88
flea блоха f blakha
flight рейс m reys 70; **~ number** номер рейса m nomyer reysa 68
flip-flops шлёпанцы mpl shlyopantsee 145
floor (level) этаж m etazh 132; **~ show** варьете n var'yetye 112
florist цветы mpl tsvyeti 130
flower цветок m tsveetok 106
flu грипп m greep 165
flush: the toilet won't flush в туалете не спускается вода v tooalyetee nee spooskayeetsya vada
fly (insect) муха f mookha
foggy, to be туман m tooman 122
folk: ~ art народное искусство n narodnaye eeskoostva; **~ music** народная музыка f narodnaya moozika 111
follow, to (pursue) преследовать preeslyedavat' 152
food еда/пища f yeda/peeshcha; (cuisine) кухня f kookhnya 119; **~ poisoning** отравление n atravlyeneeye 165
foot нога f naga 166
football футбол m footbol 114
footpath тропинка f trapeenka 107
for: ~ a day на день na dyen' 86; **~ a week** на неделю na nyedyelyoo 86
foreign currency иностранная валюта f inastranaya valyoota 138
forest лес m lyes 107
forget, to забывать zabivat' 41, 42
fork вилка f veelka 39, 41, 148

form бланк/форма m/f
blank/fo_r_ma 71, 153, 168
formal dress вечернее платье n
veech_yer_neeye plat'ye 111
fortunately к счастью k
shch_yas_yoo 19
fountain фонтан m fan_tan_ 99
four-door car с четырьмя дверями s
chyeetir'_mya_ dveer_ya_mee 86
four-wheel drive с полным приводом
s po_l_nim pr_ee_vadam 86
fourth четвёртый cheet_vyor_tiy 217
foyer (hotel, theater) фойе n fa_ye_
fracture (of a bone) перелом m
peer_ee_lom 165
frame (glasses) оправа f ap_ra_va
free (not busy) свободный sva_bo_dniy
124; (available) свободный
sva_bo_dniy 77
freezer морозильная камера f
maraz_eel_naya _ka_meera 29
frequent: how frequent? как часто?
kak _chas_ta 19
frequently часто _chas_ta
fresh свежий sv_ye_zhey 41
Friday пятница f p_ya_tneetsa 218
fried жареный _zha_ryeniy
friend друг m drook 162; **friendly**
дружеский droo_zhee_skeey
fries жареный картофель m
_zha_ryeniy kar_to_fyel' 38
frightened, to be бояться ba_yat_'sya
fringe чёлка f ch_yol_ka 147
from от/из at/eez 12; **from ... to**
(time) с ... до z ... da 13
front door key ключ от входной
двери m klyooch at fkhad_noy_
_dvye_ree 28
frosty, to be мороз m ma_roz_ 122
fruit juice сок m sok 40
frying pan сковорода f skavara_da_ 29
fuel (gasoline/petrol) бензин m
been_zeen_ 86
full полный _pol_niy 14; **~ beam**
верхний свет m v_yerkh_niy svyet
86; **~ board** с полным питанием
s _pol_nem peeta_nee_eyem 24;
~ insurance полная страховка f
_pol_naya stra_khof_ka 86

fun: to have ~
веселье: веселиться
n vees_yel_'ye:
veese_leet_'sya
furniture мебель f
_mye_beel'
fuse пробка f _prob_ka 28; **~ box**
распределительный щит m
raspryedy_eleet_yel'ny shcheet 28

G **gallon** галлон m ga_lon_
game игра f ee_gra_ 157;
матч m mach 114
garage гараж m ga_razh_ 26;
станция обслуживания f
_stant_seeya ap_sloo_zheevanya 88
garbage bags полиэтиленовые
мешки m palee-eteel_yen_aviye
_mee_shkee 148
garden сад m sat
gas (fuel) бензин m been_zeen_ 88;
~ station заправочная станция f
za_pra_vachnaya _stant_siya 87
gas: I smell gas! я чувствую запах
газа! m ya _choof_stvooyoo _za_pakh
_ga_za 28; **~ bottle** газовый баллон m
_ga_zovy ba_lon_ 28
gastritis гастрит m ga_street_ 165
gate (airport) выход m _vi_khad 70
gauze бинт m beent 141
gay club клуб гомосексуалистов m
kloop gomaseeksooa_lees_taf 112
general delivery до востребования
do va_strye_bavaneeya 155
gentle лёгкий _lyokh_keey 106
genuine настоящий nastay_ash_chiy 134
Georgian (adj.) грузинский
groo_zeen_skeey 35
get off, to (bus, etc.) выходить
vikha_deet_' 79, 80
get, to (find) взять vzyat' 84; **~ to**
добираться/доехать dabeera_t'sya_/
da_ye_khat' 73, 94; **how do I get
to ...?** как мне добраться до ...?
kak mne dab_ra_t'sya do ... 73
gift подарок m pa_da_rak 67, 156;
~ store подарки mpl pa_dar_kee 130

girl девочка f dyevachka 120, 157
girlfriend подруга f padrooga 120
give, to давать davat'
glands гланды fpl glandi 166
glass стакан m stakan 37, 39, 41, 148
glasses (optical) очки pl achkee 167
glossy finish (photos) глянец m glyaneets
glove перчатка f peerchatka
go: ~ on дальше dal'she 19; **~ for a walk** пойти погулять paytee pagoolyat' 124; **~ shopping** пойти по магазинам paytee pa magazeenam 124; **let's go!** пошли! pashlee; **go away!** уходите! ookhadeetee; **where does this bus go?** идти: куда идет этот автобус? eetee: kooda eedyot etat aftoboos
goggles очки pl achkee
gold золото n zolata 149; **~-plate** позолоченный pazalocheniy 149
golf гольф m gol'f 114; **~ course** гольф корт m gol'f kort 115
good хороший kharosheey 14, 35, 42; **~ afternoon** добрый день dobriy dyen' 10; **~ evening** добрый вечер dobriy vyechyer 10; **~ morning** доброе утро dobraye ootra 10; **~ night** спокойной ночи spakoynigh nochyee 10
good-bye до свидания 10
gram грамм m gram 159
grandparents бабушка и дедушка f/m babooshka ee dyedooshka
grapes виноград m veenagrat 160
grass трава f trava
gray серый syeriy 143
graze ссадина f sadeena 162
great блестяще bleestyashchye 19
green зелёный zeelyoniy 143
greengrocer овощи и фрукты mpl ovashchee ee frookti 130
grey серый syeriy 143
grilled жареные на гриле zhareeniye na greelee

grocery store бакалея f bakalyeya
ground (camping) кемпинг m kyempeeng 30; **groundcloth [groundsheet]** полотнище n palotneeshchye 31
group группа f groopa 66, 100
guarantee гарантия f garanteeya 135
guide (tour) гид m geet 98; **~book** путеводитель m pooteevadeeteel' 100, 150
guided tour экскурсия f ekskoorsiya 100
guitar гитара f geetara
gum десна f deesna
guy rope оттяжка f attyashka 31
gynecologist гинеколог m geeneekolak 167

H **hair** волосы mpl volasi 147; **~ brush** щётка для волос f shchyotka dlya valos 142; **~ mousse** мусс для волос m moos dlya valos 142; **~ spray** лак для волос m lak dlya valos 142; **~cut** стрижка f streeshka 147; **~dresser** парикмахер m pareekhmakheer 147; **~stylist** мастер m masteer 147
half половина f palaveena 217; **~ board** с завтраком и ужином m s zavtrakam ee oozheenam 24; **~ past** пол m pol 220
hand рука f rooka 166; **~ luggage** ручная кладь f roochnaya klad' 69; **~ washable** ручная стирка f roochnaya steerka 144
handbag сумка f soomka 144
handicap (golf) гандикап m gandeekap
handicapped (n.) инвалид m eenvaleed 163
handicrafts ремесла npl reemyosla
handkerchief платок m platok
hanger вешалка f vyeshalka 27

hangover похмелье n pakh<u>myel</u>'ye 141

happy: I'm not happy with the service я не доволен обслуживанием ya nee dav<u>o</u>len aps<u>loo</u>zheevan<u>ee</u>yem

harbor гавань f <u>gav</u>an' 81

hat шапка f <u>shap</u>ka 144

have to, to (must) должен/должна d<u>o</u>lzhen/dolzhn<u>a</u>

hayfever сенная лихорадка f seen<u>a</u>ya leekhar<u>a</u>tka 141

head голова f galav<u>a</u> 166; **~ waiter** метрдотель m myetrdat<u>el</u>' 41; **~ache** болит голова bal<u>ee</u>t galav<u>a</u> 163

heading, to be (in a direction) ехать в <u>ye</u>khat' 83

health: ~ food store диетические продукты mpl deeyet<u>ee</u>cheeskeeye prad<u>oo</u>kti 131; **~ insurance** медицинское страхование n meed<u>ee</u>ts<u>ee</u>nskaya strakhav<u>a</u>neeye 168

hear, to слышать sl<u>i</u>shat'

hearing aid слуховой аппарат m slookhav<u>o</u>y apar<u>a</u>t

heart сердце n s<u>ye</u>rtsee 166; **~ attack** сердечный приступ m seerd<u>ye</u>chniy pr<u>ee</u>stoop 163; **~ condition** заболевание сердца n zabalev<u>a</u>neeye s<u>ye</u>rtsa

hearts (cards) червы fpl ch<u>ye</u>rvi

heater обогреватель m abagreev<u>a</u>teel'

heating отопление n atapl<u>ye</u>neeye 25

heavy тяжёлый teezh<u>o</u>liy 14, 134

height рост m rost 152

hello здравствуй(те) zdr<u>a</u>stvooy(tye) 10, 118

help, to помогать pamag<u>a</u>t' 18, 94; **can you help me?** помогите мне pamag<u>ee</u>tee mnye 92

hemorrhoids реморрой m geemar<u>o</u>y

her её ey<u>o</u> 16

here здесь/сюда zdyes'/syood<u>a</u> 12

hernia грыжа f gr<u>i</u>zha 165

hers её ey<u>o</u> 16; **it's hers** это ее <u>e</u>ta ey<u>o</u>

hi привет preev<u>y</u>et 10

high высокий vis<u>o</u>keey; **~ beam** верхний свет m v<u>ye</u>rkhniy svyet 86; **~ blood pressure** высокое кровяное давление n v chyetv<u>ee</u>rt'kaee kravee<u>no</u>ye davl<u>ye</u>neeye 163; **~ street** главная улица f <u>glav</u>naya <u>oo</u>leetsa 96

highlight, to (hair) осветлить asvetl<u>ee</u>t' 147

highway (авто)шоссе n (afta)shass<u>e</u> 92, 94

hike (walk) поход m pakh<u>o</u>t 106

hiking поход m pakh<u>o</u>t; **~ boots** ботинки mpl bat<u>ee</u>nki 145; **~ gear** туристское снаряжение n toor<u>ee</u>skaya snareezh<u>y</u>eneeye

hill холм n kholm 107

him ему eem<u>oo</u> 16

hire (out), to давать/взять напрокат dav<u>a</u>t'/vsyat' napr<u>o</u>kat 29, 86, 115, 116, 117

his его ev<u>o</u> 16; **it's his** это его <u>e</u>ta ev<u>o</u>

hitchhiking голосовать galasav<u>a</u>t' 83

HIV-positive положительная реакция на СПИД f palazh<u>ee</u>tel'naya ree<u>a</u>ktseeya na speed

hobby (pastime) хобби n kh<u>o</u>bee 121

hold on, to подождать padazhd<u>a</u>t' 128

hole (in clothes) дырка f d<u>i</u>rka

holiday: on ~ в отпуске v <u>o</u>tpooskee 66, 123; **~ resort** курорт m koor<u>o</u>rt

home: to go ~ ехать домой <u>ye</u>khat' dam<u>o</u>y 123; **we're going home** мы идем домой mi eed<u>yo</u>m dam<u>o</u>y

homosexual (adj.) гомосексуальный gomaseeksoo<u>a</u>l'niy

honeymoon: we're on honeymoon у нас медовый месяц oo nas meed<u>o</u>viy m<u>ye</u>syats

horse лошадь f l<u>o</u>shad'; **~-racing** конные скачки fpl k<u>o</u>niye sk<u>a</u>chkee 114

A-Z

hospital больница f bal'neetsa 131, 161, 164, 167
hot горячий garyachyeey 14, 122; (weather) жаркая zharkaya 122; **~ dog** хот-дог m khot-dok 110; **~ spring** горячий источник m garyacheey eestochneek; **~ water** горячая вода f garyachaya vada 25
hotel гостиница f gasteeneetsa 21, 123; **~ room** номер m nomyer 21
hour час m chas 97; **in an ~** через час cheryes chas 84; **hours** (opening) часы работы mpl chasi raboti 161
house дом m dom
housewife домохозяйка f domakhazyayka 121
hovercraft ракета rakyeta 81
how? как? kak 17; **how are you?** как дела? kak deela? 118; **how far ...?** как далеко...? kak daleeko 94, 106; **how long?** сколько/как долго skol'ka/kak dolga 75, 76, 78, 94, 98, 135; **how many?** сколько? skol'ka 15, 80; **how much?** сколько? skol'ka 15, 21, 69, 84, 109; **how much? ...?** skolka 69; **how often?** как часто kak chasta 140; **how old?** сколько лет? skol'ka lyet? 120
hundred сто sto 216
hungry голодный galodniy
hurry: I'm in a ~ я спешу ya speeshoo
hurt, to be ушибиться oosheebeet'sya 92, 162; **it hurts** у меня болит ... oo meenya baleet ... 162
husband муж m moozh 120, 162

I
I'd like (some) ... я хотел(а) бы ... ya khatyel(a) bi 18, 36, 40
I'll have ... я возьму ... ya vaz'moo 37
ice лёд m lyod 38

ice cream мороженое n marozheenaye 40, 160; **ice-cream parlor** кафе-мороженое n kafye marozheenaye 35
icy гололёд m galalyot 122
identification удостоверение n oodastaveeryeneeye 136, 155
ill, to be заболеть zabalyet' 152
illegal: is it illegal? это незаконно? eta neezakona
imitation искусственный eeskoostveeniy 134
immediately немедленно neemyedleenna
in (place) в, на v/na 12; (time) через chyereez 13
included, to be входить fkhodeet' 86, 98
incredible невероятный neeveeerayatniy
indicate, to указывать ookazivat'
indigestion изжога f eezzhoga
indoor pool закрытый бассейн m zakritiy basyeyn 116
inexpensive недорогой needaragoy 35
infected, to be заразиться zarazeet'sya 165
infection воспаление n vaspalyeneeye 167
inflammation воспаление n vaspalyeneeye 165
informal (dress) форма одежды свободная f forma adyezhdi svabodnaya
information: ~ desk справочное бюро n spravachnoye byooro 73; **~ office** справочное бюро n spravachnaya byooro 96; **Information** справочная служба f spravachnaya sloozhba 127
injection воспаление n vaspalyeneeye 168
injured, to be получить травму paloocheet' travmoo 92
innocent невинный neeveeniy
insect насекомое n naseekomoye 25

insect: ~ bite укус насекомого m
ookoos naseekomava 141, 162;
~ repellent средство от комаров
sryetstva at kamaraf 141

inside внутри vnootree 12

insist: I insist я настаиваю уа
nastayeevayoo

insomnia бессонница f beesoneetsa

instant coffee растворимый кофе m
rastvareemiy kofee 160

instead of вместо vmyesta

instructions инструкция f
eenstrooktsiya 135

instructor инструктор m
eenstrooktar

insulin инсулин m eensooleen

insurance страховка f strakhofka
86, 89, 93; **~ claim** страховой иск
m strakhavoy eesk; **~ company**
страховая компания f strakhavaya
kampaneeya 93

interest (hobby) интересы/хобби n
eenteeryesi/khobee 121

interesting интересный
eenteeryesniy 101

International Student Card
студенческий билет m
stoodyenchyesky beelyet 29

interpreter переводчик m
peereevotcheek 153

intersection пересечение n
peereeseechyeneeye 95

introduce oneself, to представляться
preetstavlyat'sya 118

invitation приглашение n
preeglashyeneeye 124

invite, to приглашать
preeglashat' 124

iodine йод m yot

Ireland Ирландия f Eerlandeeya 119

is there ...? (➤ 17) есть yest' 17

it is ... (➤ 17) это eta 17

Italian итальянский
eetalyanskeey 35

itemized bill счёт по пунктам m
shchyot pa poonktam 32, 42

J **jacket** пиджак
m peedzhak 144
jam варенье n
varyenye

jammed, to be застревать
zastrevat' 25

January январь m eenvar' 218

jar банка f banka 159

jaw челюсть f chyelyoost' 166

jazz джаз m dzhas 111

jeans джинсы pl dzheensi 144

jellyfish медуза f meedooza

jet-ski джет-ски pl dzhyet-skee 116

jeweler ювелирный магазин m
yooveeleerniy magazeen 131, 149

job: what's your job? кем вы
работаете? f kyem vi rabotayeetee

join in, to вступать в fstoopat' v 115

joint сустав m soostaf 166;
~ passport совместный паспорт
m savmyestniy paspart

joke шутка f shootka

journalist журналист m
zhoornaleest

journey поездка f payezdka 76, 78

jug графин m grafeen

July июль m eeyool' 218

jump leads кабель с зажимами m
kabeel s zazheemamee

jumper джемпер m dzhyempeer 144

junction (intersection) перекресток m
peereekryostak

June июнь m eyooon' 218

K **keep: keep the change!**
оставьте себе сдачу astav'tee
seebye sdachoo

kerosene керосин m keeraseen;
~ stove примус m preemoos 31

ketchup кетчуп m kyetchoop

kettle чайник m chyayneek 29

key ключ m klyooch 27, 28, 88;
~ ring брелок m breelok 156

kiddie pool детский бассейн m
dyetskiy baseyn 113

kidney почка f pochka 166

kilo кило n keelo 159
kilogram килограмм m keelagram 69
kilometer километр m keelamyetar
kind (pleasant) любезный lyoobyezniy
kiss, to целовать tseelavat' 126
kitchen кухня f kookhnya 29
knapsack рюкзак m ryoogzak 31, 145
knee колено n kalyena 166
knickers трусики pl trooseekee
knife нож m nozh 39, 41, 148
kosher кошерный kashyerniy

L label ярлык m yarlik
lace кружево f kroozheeva
ladder стремянка f streemyanka
lake озеро n ozeera 107
lamp лампа f lampa 25, 29
land, to приземляться preezyemlyat'sya 70
language course языковые курсы mpl yazikaviye koorsi
large (adj.) большой balshoy 40, 110
last последний paslyedneey 14, 68, 75, 80, 81
last, to длиться dleet'sya
late (adj.) поздний pozneey 14; I **to be** (delayed) задерживаться zadyerzheevat'sya 70; (adv.) позже pozhe 221
later позже pozhe 125
laugh, to смеяться smeeyat'sya 126
laundromat прачечная f pracheechnaya 131
laundry: ~ **service** прачечная f prachechnaya 22; ~ **soap** стиральный порошок m steeral'niy parashok 148
lawyer адвокат m advakat 152
laxative слабительное n slabeeteelnaya
lead, to (road) вести veestee 94
leader (of group) руководитель m rookavadeeteel'

leaflet брошюра f brashoora 97
leak, to (roof, pipe) течь tyech
learn, to (language) изучать eezoochat'
leather кожа f kozha 146
leave, to уезжать ooyezhat' 32; (plane) вылетать vilyetat' 68; (train, etc.) отправляться atpravlyat'sya 76, 81, 98; ~ **from** (transport) отправляться atpravlyat'sya 78; **leave me alone!** оставьте меня в покое! astaftee meenya v pakoye 126
left, on the налево nalyeva 76, 95
left-luggage office багажное отделение n bagazhnoye adelyeneeye 71
leg нога f naga 166
legal: is it legal? это законно? eta zakona
leggings леггинги pl lyegeengee
lemon лимон m leemon 38
lemonade лимонад m leemanat 40
lend: could you lend me ...? не могли бы вы дать мне взаймы ...? nee maglee bi vi dat' mnye vzaymi
length (of) длина f dleena
lens (camera) объектив m 151; (optical) стекла npl styokla 167; ~ **cap** крышка объектива f krishka abyekteeva 151
lesbian club лесбийский клуб m leesbeeyskeey kloop
less меньше myen'she 15
lesson урок m oorok 115
let, to: let me know! дайте мне знать! daytee mnye znat'
letter письмо n pees'mo 154; ~**box** почтовый ящик m pachtoviy yashcheek
level (ground) площадка f plashchadka 30
library библиотека f beebleeatyeka 99, 131
license plate регистрационный номер m reegeestratsioniy nomeer 93

lifebelt спасательный пояс m spasateel'niy poyas

lifeboat спасательная лодка f spasateel'naya lotka

lifeguard спасатель m spasatyel' 116

lifejacket спасательный жилет m spasateel'niy zheelyet

lift лифт m leeft 26, 132; **~ pass** пропуск на лифт m proopoosk na leeft 117; (hitchhiking) подвозить padvazeet' 83

light (opp. heavy) лёгкий lyokhkeey 14, 134; (opp. dark) светлый svetliy 14, 134, 143

light (bicycle) фара f fara 83; (electric) свет m svyet 25; **~ bulb** лампочка f lampachka 148

lighter (cigarette) зажигалка f zazheegalka 150

like, to нравиться nraveet'sya 101, 124; **do you like?** вам нравится? vam nraveetsya 125; **I don't like it** мне это не нравится mnye eta nee nraveetsya; **I like it** мне это нравится mnye eta nraveetsya; **I'd like ...** я хотел(а) бы ... ya khatyel(a) bi ... 18, 36, 40

like this (similar to) как это kak eta

limousine лимузин m leemoozeen

line (metro) линия f leeneeya 80

line (profession) профессия f prafeseeya 121

linen лён m lyon 146

lip губа f gooba 166; **~stick** губная помада f goobnaya pamada

liqueur ликер m leekyor

liquor store винный магазин m veeniy magazeen 131

liter литр m leetr 87, 159

little (small) маленький maleen'keey

live together, to жить вместе zheet' vmyestee 120

liver печень f pyecheen' 166

living room гостиная f gasteenaya 29

loaf of bread буханка хлеба f bookhanka khlyeba 160

lobby (theater, hotel) фойе n faye

local местный myestniy 37; **~ anesthetic** обезболивание n abeezboleevaneeye 168

lock замок m zamok 25; **~ oneself out, to** захлопнуть дверь zaklopnoot' dvyer' 27

long длинный dleeniy 146; **long-distance bus** междугородний автобус m myezhdoogarodniy aftoboos 78

long-sighted дальнозоркость f dal'nazorkast' 167

look: ~ for искать eeskat' 18, 133; **to have a ~** (check) посмотреть pasmatryet' 89; **I'm just looking** я просто смотрю ya prosta smatryoo

loose (clothing) свободный svabodniy 146

lorry грузовик m groozaveek

lose, to потерять pateeryat' 28, 153; **I've ~ ...** я потерял(а) ... ya pateeryal(a) ... 100, 153

lost-and-found office [lost property] бюро находок n byooro nakhodak 73

louder громче gromchee 128

love, to любить lyoobeet'

lovely прекрасный preekrasniy 125

low beam нижний свет m neezhniy svyet 86

low-fat низкое содержание жира neezkaye sadeerzhaneeye zheera

lower нижний neezhneey 74

luggage багаж m bagash 32, 71; **~ carts** багажные тележки fpl bagazhniye tyelyezhkee 71; **~ locker** камера хранения f kameera khranyeneeya 71, 73; **~ trolleys** багажные тележки fpl bagazhniye tyelyezhkee 71

lump (medical) шишка f shishka 162

lunch обед m abyet 98

lung лёгкое n lyokhkaya 166

M

machine washable машинная стирка f masheenaya steerka 146
madam госпожа f gaspazha
magazine журнал m zhoornal 150
magnificent великолепный veeleekalyepniy 101
maid горничная/уборщица f gorneechnaya 27, 28
mail *(n.)* почта f pochta 27, 155; **by ~** письмом m pis'mom 22; **~box** почтовый ящик m pachtoviy yashcheek
mail, to отправлять atpravlyat'
main главный glavniy 130; **~ course** второе n ftaroye; **~ street** главная улица f glavnaya ooleetsa 95, 96
make: ~ a complaint жаловаться zhalavat'sya 137; **~ an appointment** записаться на приём zapeesat'sya na preeyom 161
make-up грим m greem
male мужчина m moozhcheena 152
mallet деревянный молоток m deereevyanniy malatok 31
man *(male)* мужской mooshskoy
manager директор m deeryektar 25, 41, 137
manicure маникюр m maneekyoor 147
manual *(car)* с ручным переключением передач s roochnim peereeklyochyeneeyem peereedach
many много mnoga 15
map карта f karta 94, 99, 106, 150
March март m mart 218
margarine маргарин m margareen 160
market рынок m rinak 99, 131
married, to be женат *(for men)*/замужем *(for women)* zheenat/zamoozheem 120
mascara тушь f toosh
mask *(diving)* маска f maska
mass месса f myesa 105
massage массаж m masazh 147
mat finish *(photos)* матовый matoviy
match *(sport)* матч m mach 114
matches спички fpl speechkee 31, 148, 150
matinée дневное представление n dnevnoye preetstavlyeneeye 109
matter: it doesn't matter это не имеет значения eta nee eemyeet znachyeneeya; **what's the matter?** в чем дело? f chyom dyela
mattress матрас m matras 31
May май m may 218
may I ...? Можно мне ... mozhna mnye ... 37
maybe может быть mozheet bit'
me *(to, for)* мне mnye 16
meal блюдо n blyooda 38
mean, to зничить znacheet' 11
measles корь f kor' 165
measure, to снять мерку snyat' myerkoo 146
measurement измерение n eezmeeryeneeye
meat мясо n myasa 41
medical certificate медицинское свидетельство n meedeetseenskaya
medication [medicine] лекарство n leekarstva 141, 164
medium *(adj.)* средний sryedneey 40, 106
meet, to встречаться fstreechat'sya 106, 125; **pleased to meet you** очень приятно ocheen' preeyatna 118
member *(of club)* член m chlyen 112, 115
men *(toilets)* мужской mooshskoy
menu меню n meenyoo
message передача f pyeredacha 27
metal металл m meetal
metro station станция метро f stantseeya myetro 80
microwave *(oven)* микроволновая печь f meekravalnovaya pyech
midday полдень m poldeen' 221
midnight полночь f polnach 221
migraine мигрень f meegryen'

mileage километраж m keelamye<u>trash</u> 86

milk молоко n ma<u>la</u>ko 160; **with ~** с молоком s mala<u>kom</u> 40

million миллион meellee<u>on</u> 216

mind: do you mind? (вы) не возражаете? (vi) nee vazra<u>zh</u>ayetee? 77, 126

mine мой moy 16; **it's mine!** это мой! eta moy

mineral water минеральная вода f meenee<u>ral</u>'naya va<u>da</u> 40

mini-bar мини-бар m <u>mee</u>nee bar 32

minimart гастроном m gastra<u>nom</u> 158

minute минута f mee<u>noo</u>ta 15

mirror зеркало n <u>zyer</u>kala

missing, to be не хватать nee khva<u>tat</u>' 137; пропасть pra<u>past</u>' 152

mistake ошибка f a<u>sheeb</u>ka 32, 41, 42

misunderstanding: there's been a ~ это недоразумение n <u>e</u>ta needarazoo<u>mye</u>neeye

mobile home караван m kara<u>van</u>

modern современный savree<u>myen</u>niy 14

moisturizer (cream) увлажняющий крем m oovlazh<u>nya</u>yooshcheey krem

monastery монастырь m mana<u>stir</u>' 99

Monday понедельник m panee<u>dyel</u>'neek 218

money деньги pl <u>dyen</u>'gee 42; **~ order** почтовый перевод m pach<u>to</u>viy peeree<u>vot</u>

month месяц m <u>mye</u>syats 218; **monthly** (ticket) на месяц na <u>mye</u>syats 79

moped мопед m ma<u>pyed</u> 83

more больше <u>bol</u>'she 15; **I'd like some more** можно ещё ... <u>mozh</u>na ye<u>shchyo</u> ... 39

morning, in the утром m <u>oo</u>tram 221

mosque мечеть f mee<u>chyet</u>' 105

mosquito bite комариный укус m kama<u>ree</u>niy oo<u>koos</u>

mother мать f mat' 120

motion sickness морская болезнь f mar<u>skaya</u> ba<u>lyezn</u>' 141

motorbike мотоцикл m matat<u>seekal</u> 83

motorboat моторка f ma<u>tor</u>ka 116

motorway (авто)шоссе n (<u>af</u>ta)shas<u>se</u> 92, 94

mountain гора f ga<u>ra</u> 106, 107; **~ bike** горный велосипед m <u>gor</u>niy veelasee<u>pyet</u>; **~ pass** перевал m peeree<u>val</u> 107; **~ range** хребет m khree<u>byet</u> 107

mouth рот m rot 166; **~ ulcer** язвы во рту fpl <u>yaz</u>vi va rtoo

move, to переезжать pyeryee<u>zzhat</u>' 25; **don't move him!** не двигайте его! nee <u>dvee</u>gaytee evo 92

movie фильм m feel'm 108, 110; **~ theater** кинотеатр m keenatee<u>atar</u> 96

Mr. г-н m gaspa<u>deen</u>

Mrs. г-жа f gaspa<u>zha</u>

much много <u>mno</u>ga 15

mug кружка f <u>kroosh</u>ka 148

mugged, to be обокрали aba<u>kra</u>lee 153

mugging кража f <u>kra</u>zha 152

multiplex cinema многозальный кинотеатр m mnaga<u>zal</u>niy keenatee<u>atr</u> 110

mumps корь f kor'

muscle мышца f <u>mish</u>tsa 166

museum музей m moo<u>zey</u> 99

music музыка f <u>moo</u>zika 111, 121

musician музыкант m moozi<u>kant</u>

must: I must я должен ya <u>dol</u>zheen

mustache усы mpl oo<u>si</u>

mustard горчица f gar<u>cheet</u>sa 38

my мой moy 16

myself: I'll do it myself я сделаю это сам ya <u>sdye</u>layoo eta sam

N name (first name) имя n **ee**mya 118, 120; (family name) фамилия f fa**mee**leeya 22, 36; **my name is** меня зовут **mee**nya za**voot** 118; **what's your name?** как Вас зовут? n kak vas za**voot** 118

napkin салфетка f sal**fyet**ka 39

nappies пелёнка f pee**lyon**ka 142

narrow узкий **oos**keey 14

national национальный natseea**nal'**niy

nationality национальность f natseea**nal'**nast'

nature reserve заповедник m zapa**vyed**neek 107

nausea тошнота f tash**na**ta

near около **o**kala 12

nearby рядом **rya**dam 21, 87

nearest ближайший blee**zhay**sheey 80, 88, 92, 130, 140

neck шея f **shye**ya 166; (clothes) ворот m **vo**rat 144

necklace ожерелье n azhee**ryel'**ye 149

need: I need to ... мне нужно ... mnye **noozh**na 18

nephew племянник m plee**mya**neek

nerve нерв m nyerf 166

nervous system нервная система f **nyerv**naya sees**tye**ma 166

never никогда nee**kag**da 13; **~ mind** ничего neechye**vo** 10

new новый **no**viy 14; **New Year** Новый Год m **no**viy got 219

New Zealand Новая Зеландия f **no**vaya zee**lan**deeya 119

newsagent's (newsdealer) газетный киоск m ga**zyet**niy kee**osk** 150

newspaper газета f ga**zye**ta 150

next следующий **slye**dooyoosh**chyee**y 68, 75, 78, 80, 81, 87; **next stop!** на следующей! na **slye**dooyoosh**chyey** 79; **next to** рядом с **rya**dam s 12, 95

nice хороший kha**ro**sheey 14

niece племянница f plee**mya**neetsa

night: at ~ ночью f **no**chyoo 221

nightclub ночной клуб m nach**noy** kloop 112

no нет nyet 10

no one никому neeka**moo** 16

noisy шумный **shoom**niy 14, 24

non-alcoholic безалкогольный beezalka**gol'**niy

non-smoking (adj.) некурящий neekoo**ryash**chyeey 36

nonsense ерунда eeroon**da** 19

noon полдень m **pol**deen' 220

normal нормальный nar**mal**niy 67

north север m **sye**veer 95

nose нос m nos 166

not: not bad неплохо neep**lo**kha 19; **not good** не очень хорошо nee **o**cheen' kha**ra**sho 19; **not that one** не тот(та) nye tot (ta) 16; **not yet** нет ещё nyet ees**chyo** 13

notebook записная книжка f zapees**na**ya **knee**shka 150

nothing ничего neechye**vo** 16; **~ else** ничего больше neechye**vo** bol'she 15

notice board доска объявлений f das**ka** abyav**lye**niy 26

notify, to сообщать saap**sh**chat' 167

November ноябрь m na**yabr'** 218

now сейчас/теперь see**chyas**/ tee**pyer'** 13, 84

number (telephone) номер m **no**myer 84; **~ plate** номерной знак m nameer**noy** znak; **sorry, wrong number** извините, неправильный номер n eezvee**nee**tee neep**ra**veel'niy **no**meer

nurse сестра f sees**tra**

nylon нейлон m ney**lon**

O occasionally иногда eenag**da**

occupied занятый za**nee**tiy 14

October октябрь m ak**tyabr'** 218

odds (betting) шансы mpl **shan**si 114

of course конечно ka**nyesh**na 19

off-licence винный магазин m veeniy maga<u>zeen</u> 131

office контора f kan<u>to</u>ra

often часто <u>chya</u>sta 13

oil нефть f nyeft'

okay хорошо/о кей kharas<u>ho</u>/o ke 10, 19

old старый <u>stari</u>y 14; ~ **town** старый город m <u>stari</u>y <u>go</u>rat 96, 99; ~-**fashioned** старомодный staram<u>o</u>dniy 14

olive oil оливковое масло n al<u>eef</u>kavaya <u>mas</u>la

omelet омлет m aml<u>yet</u> 40

on (day, date) в v 13; (place) на na 12; ~ **foot** пешком pesh<u>kom</u> 17; ~ **my own** один a<u>deen</u> 120; ~ **the left** налево nal<u>ye</u>va 12; ~ **the other side** на другой стороне na droo<u>goy</u> staran<u>ye</u> 95; ~ **the right** направо nap<u>ra</u>va 12; **on/off switch** включено/выключено vklyoch<u>ee</u>no/<u>vi</u>klyoch<u>ee</u>na

once однажды/один раз ad<u>na</u>zhdi 217

one like that как тот(та) kak tot (ta) 16; ~-**piece** костюм m kast<u>yoom</u> 144; ~-**way ticket** в один конец v a<u>deen</u> kan<u>yets</u> 68, 74, 79

open (adj.) открытый at<u>kri</u>tiy 14, 100; ~-**air pool** открытый бассейн m at<u>kri</u>tiy bas<u>eyn</u> 116

open, to открываться atkri<u>vat</u>'sya 132, 140

opening hours часы работы mpl cha<u>si</u> ra<u>bo</u>ti 100

opera опера f <u>o</u>peera 108, 111; ~ **house** оперный театр m <u>o</u>peerniy tee<u>atr</u> 99, 111

operation операция f apee<u>rat</u>seeya

opposite напротив nap<u>ro</u>teef 12

optician оптик m <u>op</u>teek 131, 167

or или <u>ee</u>lee 19

orange (fruit) апельсин m apeel'<u>seen</u> 160; (color) оранжевый a<u>ran</u>zheeviy 143

orchestra оркестр m ar<u>kyes</u>tar 111

order, to заказывать za<u>ka</u>zivat' 32, 37, 41, 135

ordering заказ m za<u>kaz</u> 37

organized hike/walk турпоход m toorpa<u>khot</u>

Orthodox православный pravas<u>lav</u>niy 105

others другие droo<u>gee</u>ye 134

our наш nash 16; **ours** наш nash 16

outdoor на открытом воздухе na at<u>kri</u>tam <u>voz</u>dookhee

outside на улице na <u>oo</u>leetsye 36; снаружи snar<u>oo</u>zhee 12

oval овальный av<u>al</u>'niy 134

oven духовка f doo<u>khof</u>ka

over there вон там von tam 76

overcharge: I've been overcharged меня обсчитали mee<u>nya</u> apschee<u>ta</u>lee

overdone (adj.) пережареный pyerye<u>zha</u>ryeniy 41

overheat перегреться peeree<u>gryet</u>'sya

overnight одна ночь f ad<u>na</u> noch' 23; ~ **service** срочная <u>sroch</u>naya 151

owe: how much do I owe? сколько я должен? <u>skol</u>'ka ya vam <u>dol</u>zheen

own: on my own я один/одна уа a<u>deen</u>/ad<u>na</u> 65

owner владелец m vlad<u>ye</u>leets

P **p.m.** после полудня <u>pos</u>lee pal<u>oo</u>dnya

pacifier соска f <u>sos</u>ka

pack, to упаковывать oopa<u>ko</u>vivat' 69

package посылка f pa<u>sil</u>ka 155

packed lunch готовый завтрак m ga<u>to</u>viy <u>zaf</u>trak

packet пакет m pa<u>kyet</u>; ~ **of cigarettes** пачка сигарет f <u>pach</u>ka seega<u>ryet</u> 150

paddling pool детский бассейн m <u>dyet</u>skiy ba<u>seyn</u> 113

padlock замок m za<u>mok</u>

pail ведёрко n ve<u>dyor</u>ka 157

pain, to be in иметь боли ee<u>myet</u>' <u>bo</u>lee 167

painkillers болеутоляющее (средство) n boleeoot<u>alya</u>yooshchyeye (sretstva) 141, 165

paint, to написать napee<u>sat</u>' 104

painted написанный napee<u>san</u>iy 104

painter художник m khoo<u>dozh</u>neek 104

painting картина f kar<u>teen</u>a 104

pair of пара f <u>pa</u>ra 217

palace дворец m dva<u>ryets</u> 99

palpitations сердцебиение n <u>syerts</u>eebee<u>ye</u>neeye

panorama панорама f pano<u>ra</u>ma 107

pants (U.S.) брюки pl <u>bryoo</u>kee 144

panty hose колготки pl kal<u>got</u>kee 144

paper бумага f boo<u>ma</u>ga 150; **~ napkin** бумажная салфетка f boo<u>mazh</u>naya sal<u>fyet</u>ka 148

paracetamol парацетамол m parats<u>eeta</u>mol

paraffin керосин m kyera<u>seen</u> 31

paralysis паралич m para<u>leech</u>

pardon? извините? eezvee<u>nee</u>tye 11

parents родители mpl ra<u>dee</u>teelee 120

park парк m park 96, 99, 107

parking: ~ lot автостоянка f aftasta<u>yan</u>ka 26, 87, 96; **~ meter** автомат m afta<u>mat</u> 87

parliament building правительственное здание n pra<u>vee</u>tyel'stvyenaye <u>zda</u>neeye 99

parting (hair) пробор m pra<u>bor</u>

partner (boyfriend/girlfriend) друг/подруга m/f drook/ pad<u>roo</u>ga

party (social) вечер m <u>vye</u>cheer 124

pass (mountain) проход m pra<u>khot</u>

pass, to проезжать praye<u>zhat</u>' 77

passport паспорт m <u>pas</u>part 66, 69

pastry store кондитерская f kan<u>dee</u>tyerskaya 131

patch, to заштопать za<u>shto</u>pat' 137

path тропинка f tra<u>peen</u>ka 107

patient (n.) пациент m patsee<u>yent</u>

pavement тротуар m trat<u>too</u>ar; **on the ~** на тротуаре n na trat<u>oo</u>aree

pay phone телефон-автомат m tee<u>lee</u>fon afto<u>mat</u>

pay, to платить pla<u>teet</u>' 42, 136

payment оплата f a<u>pla</u>ta

peak пик m peek 107

pearl жемчуг m <u>zhyem</u>chook 149

pebbly (beach) галька f <u>gal</u>'ka 116

pedestrian: ~ crossing переход m peeree<u>khot</u> 96; **~ zone** [precinct] пешеходная зона f peeshee<u>khod</u>naya <u>zo</u>na 96

pedicure педикюр m peedee<u>kyoor</u>

pen ручка f <u>rooch</u>ka 150

pencil карандаш m karan<u>dash</u> 150

pensioner пенсионер m peensee<u>an</u>yer 100

people люди pl <u>lyoo</u>dee 92, 119

pepper перец m <u>pye</u>ryets 38

per: ~ day в/на день f/na dyen' 30, 83, 86, 87, 115; **~ hour** в/на час f/na chas 87, 115; **~ night** в сутки f <u>soot</u>kee 21; **~ week** в/на неделю f/na nye<u>dye</u>lyoo 83, 86

perhaps может быть <u>mo</u>zhet bit' 19

period (historical) период m pee<u>ree</u>at 105; (menstrual) менструация f meenstroo<u>at</u>siya 167; **~ pains** боли при менструации fpl <u>bo</u>lee pree meenstroo<u>at</u>see 167

perm, to делать химическую завивку <u>dye</u>lat' kheemee<u>chees</u>kooyoo za<u>veef</u>koo 147

petrol бензин m been<u>zeen</u> 86, 87, 88; **~ station** заправочная станция f za<u>pra</u>vachnaya <u>stan</u>tsiya 87

pewter олово n <u>ola</u>va 149

pharmacy аптека f ap<u>tye</u>ka 130, 140, 158

phone: ~ card телефонная карточка f tee<u>lee</u>fonaya <u>kart</u>achka 127; **~ call** звонок m zva<u>nok</u> 152

phone, to звонить zvan<u>ee</u>t'

photo: to take a ~ фотографировать fatagraf<u>ee</u>ravat'

photocopier ксерокс m ks<u>ye</u>raks 155

photographer фотограф m fat<u>og</u>raf

photography фотография f fatagraf<u>ee</u>ya

phrase фраза fr<u>a</u>za 11; **~ book** разговорник razgav<u>o</u>rneek 11

pick up, to (get) взять fzyat' 28, 109; (collect) забирать zabee<u>ra</u>t' 113

picnic пикник m peek<u>nee</u>k; **~ area** площадка для привала f plashch<u>a</u>tka dlya preev<u>a</u>la 107

piece кусочек m koos<u>o</u>chyeek 40, 159; (of baggage) место багажа n m<u>ye</u>sta bagazh<u>a</u> 69

Pill (contraceptive): **to be on the Pill** противозачаточные таблетки: принимать fpl proteevazach<u>a</u>tachniye tabl<u>ye</u>tkee: preenee<u>ma</u>t' 167

pill (tablet) таблетка f tabl<u>ye</u>tka 165

pillow подушка f pad<u>oo</u>shka 27; **~ case** наволочка f n<u>a</u>valachka

pilot light запальник m zap<u>a</u>l'neek

pink розовый r<u>o</u>zaviy 143

pipe (smoking) трубка f tr<u>oo</u>pka

pitch (for camping) разбивать лагерь razb<u>ee</u>vat' l<u>ag</u>eer

pizzeria пиццерия f peetser<u>ee</u>ya 35

place (space) место n m<u>ye</u>sta 29

place a bet, to поставить ставку past<u>a</u>veet' st<u>a</u>fkoo 114

plane самолёт m samal<u>yo</u>t 68

plans планы mpl pl<u>a</u>ni 124

plant (n.) растение n rast<u>ye</u>neeye

plasters пластырь m pl<u>a</u>stir 141

plastic bags пластиковый мешок m pl<u>a</u>steekaviy meesh<u>o</u>k

plate тарелка f tar<u>e</u>lka 39, 41, 148

platform платформа f platf<u>o</u>rma 73, 76, 77

platinum платина f pl<u>a</u>teena 149

play, to (games, etc.) играть eegr<u>a</u>t' 121; (perform) исполнять eespaln<u>ya</u>t' 111

play group детская группа f d<u>ye</u>tskaya gr<u>oo</u>pa 113

playground детская площадка f d<u>ye</u>tskaya plashch<u>a</u>tka 113

playing: ~ cards игральные карты fpl eegr<u>a</u>l'niye k<u>a</u>rti 150; **~ field** спортплощадка f sportplashch<u>a</u>tka 117

playwright драматург m dramat<u>oo</u>rk 110

pleasant приятный m preey<u>a</u>tniy 14

please пожалуйста pazh<u>a</u>lsta 10

plug штепсель m sht<u>ye</u>pseel 148

pneumonia пневмония f pneevman<u>ee</u>ya 165

point to, to показывать pak<u>a</u>zivat' 11

poison яд m yat 141

poles палки fpl p<u>a</u>lkee 117

police милиция f meel<u>ee</u>tseeya 92, 152, 153; **~ station** отделение милиции n atdeel<u>ye</u>neeye meel<u>ee</u>tseeye 96, 131, 152

polyester полистерол m paleesteer<u>o</u>l

pond пруд m proot 107

pop поп(-музыка) m pop(-m<u>oo</u>zika) 111

popcorn воздушная кукуруза f vazd<u>oo</u>shnaya kookoor<u>oo</u>za 110

popular популярный papool<u>ya</u>rniy 111, 157

port (harbor) порт m port

porter носильщик m nas<u>ee</u>l'shcheek 71

portion порция f p<u>o</u>rtseeya 39

possible: as soon as possible как можно скорей kak m<u>o</u>zhna skar<u>ye</u>y

post (n.) почта f p<u>o</u>chta; **~ office** почта f p<u>o</u>chta 96, 131, 154; **~box** почтовый ящик m pacht<u>o</u>viy y<u>a</u>shcheek 154

post, to отправлять atpravl<u>ya</u>t'

postcard открытка f atkr<u>i</u>tka 150, 154, 156

poste restante до востребования do vastr<u>ye</u>bavaneeya 155

potatoes картофель/
картошка m/f
kart<u>o</u>fyel'/kart<u>o</u>shka 38
pottery керамика f
k<u>ee</u>rameeka
pound (sterling) фунт m
foont 67, 138
power: ~ cut перебой в
электроснабжении m peer<u>ee</u>b<u>oy</u> v
el<u>ye</u>ktrasnabzh<u>ye</u>nee; **~ point**
розетка f raz<u>ye</u>tka 30
pregnant: I'm pregnant я беременна
ya beer<u>ye</u>meenna 163
premium (gas/petrol) бензин 98 m
been<u>zeen</u> dyevyan<u>o</u>sta vas'<u>moy</u>
prescribe, to выписывать
v<u>i</u>peesivat' 165
prescription рецепт m reets<u>y</u>ept 141
present (gift) подарок m p<u>a</u>darak 137
press, to гладить gl<u>a</u>deet' 137
pretty красивый kras<u>ee</u>viy
priest священник m svyashch<u>y</u>eneek
prison тюрьма f tyoor'ma
program программа f pragr<u>a</u>ma
108, 109
pronounce, to произносить
praeeznas<u>ee</u>t'
Protestant протестантский
prateest<u>a</u>ntskeey 105
pub пивная f peevn<u>a</u>ya
public: ~ building горсовет m
garsav<u>y</u>et 96; **~ holiday** праздники
mpl pr<u>a</u>zneekee 219
pump насос m nas<u>o</u>s 83
puncture прокол m prak<u>o</u>l 83, 88
puppet show кукольный театр m
k<u>oo</u>kal'niy tee<u>a</u>tat
pure (material) чистый ch<u>ee</u>stiy 146;
~ cotton чистый хлопок m
ch<u>ee</u>stiy khl<u>o</u>pak 146
purple алый <u>a</u>liy 143
purpose цель f tsyel' 89
push-chair инвалидное кресло n
eenval<u>ee</u>dnaya kr<u>y</u>esla
put, to поставить past<u>a</u>veet'
put: where can I put ...? куда можно
поставить ...? kooda m<u>o</u>zhna
past<u>a</u>veet'

Q **quality** качество n
k<u>a</u>cheestva 134
quarter четверть f ch<u>y</u>etveert' 217;
~ past (after/past of time) четверть f
ch<u>y</u>etveert' 220;
~ to (before/to of time) без четверти
byez ch<u>y</u>etveertee 220
queue, to стоять в очереди stay<u>a</u>t' v
<u>o</u>cheereedee 112
quick быстрый b<u>i</u>striy 14; **quickly**
быстро b<u>y</u>stra 17
quickest самый быстрый s<u>a</u>miy
b<u>i</u>striy; **what's the quickest way?**
как быстрее пройти к ...? kak
bistr<u>ye</u>ye pr<u>a</u>ytee k …
quiet тихий t<u>ee</u>kheey 14; **quieter**
потише pat<u>ee</u>shee 24, 126

R **ready** готовый gat<u>o</u>viy 89
rabbi раввин m rav<u>ee</u>n
racetrack [racecourse] ипподром m
eepadr<u>o</u>m 114
racket (tennis) ракетка f
rak<u>y</u>etka 115
railway железная дорога f
zheel<u>ye</u>znaya dar<u>o</u>ga
rain to идёт дождь eed<u>y</u>ot
dozhd' 122
raincoat плащ m plashch 144
rape изнасилование n
eeznas<u>ee</u>lavaneeye 152
rapids пороги mpl par<u>o</u>gee 107
rare (steak) с кровью s kr<u>o</u>vyoo;
(unusual) редкий r<u>y</u>etkeey
rash сыпь f sip' 162
ravine овраг m avr<u>a</u>k 107
razor бритва f br<u>ee</u>tva; **~ blade**
лезвие n l<u>ye</u>zveeye 142
read, to читать chyeet<u>a</u>t' 121
ready готовый gat<u>o</u>viy 137, 151
real (genuine) настоящий
nastay<u>a</u>shcheey 149
receipt квитанция f kveet<u>a</u>ntseeya
89, 151; чек m chyek 32, 136, 137
reception (desk) регистрация f
reegeestr<u>a</u>tseeya

receptionist регистратор m reegeestratar

reclaim tag багажная квитанция f ba*gazh*naya kvee*tan*seeya 71

recommend, to рекомендовать reekameenda*vat'* 21, 35, 141; **can you ~ ...?** Вы можете порекомендовать ...? vi *mozh*eetye pareekameenda*vat'* ... 97; **what do you ~?** что Вы рекомендуете? shto vi reekameendoo*ee*tye

record (L.P.) пластинка f plas*teen*ka 157; **~ store** пластинки fpl plas*teen*kee 157

red красный *kras*niy 143; **~ wine** красное вино n *kras*noye *vee*no 40

reduction (in price) скидка f *skeed*ka 24, 68, 74, 100

refrigerator холодильник m khala*deel'*neek 29

refund вернуть деньги veer*noot'* *dyen'*gee 137

refuse bag полиэтиленовые мешки m palee-eteel*yen*aviye *meesh*kee 148

region район m ra*yon* 106

registered mail заказное отправление n zaka*znoye* atprav*lyen*eeye

registration: ~ form регистрационная форма f ryegeestra*tsee*onaya *for*ma 23; **~ number** номер m *no*meer 88

regular (gas/petrol) бензин 93 m been*zeen* dyev*ya*nosta *tryet*iy been*zeen* 87; (size) средний *sryed*neey 110

religion религия f re*lee*geeya

remember, to помнить *pom*neet'; **I don't remember** я не помню ya nee *pom*nyoo

rent (out), to давать/взять напрокат da*vat'/*vsyat' napra*kat* 29, 86, 115, 116, 117; **I'd like to ~ ...** я хотел(а) бы взять напрокат ... ya kha*tyel*(a) bi vzyat' napra*kat* ... 83

repair, to (от)ремонтировать/ (по)чинить (at)reeman*teer*avat'/ (pa)chy*eeneet'* 89, 137, 168

repairs ремонт m ree*mont* 89

repeat, to повторять paftar*yat'* 94, 128; **please ~ that** повторите, пожалуйста paftar*ee*tye pa*zhal*sta 11

replacement (n.) замена f za*mye*na 167; **~ part** запасная часть f zapas*naya* chast' 137

report, to заявить zaya*veet'* 152

required (necessary) обязательно abee*zatel'*na 112

reservation заказ m za*kas* 22, 36, 68, 74, 77, 112; **reservations desk** касса f *ka*sa 109

reserve, to заказать zaka*zat'* 22, 36

rest, to отдыхать at*dikhat'*

restaurant ресторан m reesta*ran* 35, 112

retail торговля f tar*gov*lya 121

retired, to be на пенсии na *pyen*see 121

return, to (surrender) возвратить vazvra*teet'* 86

return ticket билет туда и обратно m bee*lyet* *too*da ee a*brat*na 68, 74, 79

reverse the charges, to оплата вызываемым f a*plata* vizi*vayem*im 86

revolting невкусный nee*fkoos*niy 14

rheumatism ревматизм m reevma*teezm*

rib ребро n ree*bro* 166

right (correct) правильный *praveel'*niy 14, 77, 79, 80, 94; **that's ~** правильно: это правильно *praveel'*na: eta *praveel'*na

right of way преимущество n preem*oosh*cheestva 93

right: on the ~ направо na*prava* 76, 95

ring кольцо n kal'*tso* 149

rip-off (n.) дорого *dor*aga 101

river река f *reeka* 107; **~ cruise** речной круиз m ryech*noy* kroo*eez* 81

road дорога f da*roga* 94, 95; **~ map** карта дорог m *karta* da*rog* 150

robbed: I've been robbed меня обокрали mee*nya* aba*kral*ee 153

robbery грабеж m grab**yosh**
rock рок(-музыка) m rok(-**moo**zika) 111
roll *(bread)* булочка f **boo**lachka 160
romantic романтичный raman**teech**niy 101
roof *(house, car)* крыша f **kri**sha; **~rack** багажник на крыше m ba**gazh**neek na **kri**she
room комната f **kom**nata 29
rope веревка f vee**ryof**ka
ruble [rouble] рубль m roobl 138, 139
round круглый **kroog**liy 134; **round-trip ticket** билет туда и обратно m bee**lyet too**da ee a**brat**na 68, 74, 79
round *(of golf)* раунд m **ra**oond 115
rowing boat лодка f **lot**ka 116
rubbish мусор m **moo**sar 28
rucksack рюкзак m ryook**zak**
ruins развалины fpl raz**va**leeni 99
run: ~ into *(crash)* врезаться **vrye**zat'sya 93; **~ out** *(fuel)* кончиться **kon**cheet'sya 88
running shoes кроссовки fpl kra**sof**kee 145
rush hour час пик m chas peek
Russia Россия f ra**see**ya 119
Russian *(adj.)* русский **roos**keey 35, 126; **~ language** русский язык m **roos**kee ya**zeek**

S **safe** *(lock up)* сейф m seyf 27
safe *(adj.)* безопасный beeza**pas**niy 116
safety безопасность f beeza**pas**nast'; **~ pin** булавка f boo**laf**ka 142
sailing boat яхта f **yakh**ta 116
salad салат m sa**lat**
sales торговля f tar**gov**lya 121; **~ tax** НДС m en de es 24
salt соль f sol 38, 39
salty соленый sa**lyo**niy
same тот же самый tot zhe **sa**miy 75
sand песок m pee**sok**
sandals сандалии mpl san**da**lee 145

sandwich бутерброд m booter**brot** 40
sand песок m pee**sok** 116
sandy beach песчаный пляж m pee**scha**niy plyazh
sanitary napkins [towels] гигиеническая салфетка f geegee**neech**eskaya sal**fyet**ka 142
satellite TV спутниковое телевидение n **spoot**neekavaya tyelye**vee**dyeneeye 22
satin сатин m sa**teen**
satisfied: I'm not satisfied with this я не доволен этим ya nee da**vo**leen **e**teem
Saturday суббота f soo**bo**ta 218
sauce соус m **so**-oos 38
saucepan кастрюля f ka**stryoo**lya 29
sauna сауна f **sa**oona 22
sausage сосиска/колбаса f sa**sees**ka/kal**ba**sa 160
say, to говорить gava**reet'**; **how do you ~ ...?** как вы говорите ...? kak vi gava**ree**tee …
scarf шарф m sharf 144
scenic route живописный маршрут m zheeva**pees**niy marsh**root** 106
scheduled flight регулярный рейс m reegoo**lyar**niy ryeys
sciatica ишиас m ee**shee**as 165
scissors ножницы pl **nozh**neetsi 148
scooter мотороллер m mata**ro**leer
Scotland Шотландия f shat**lan**deeya 119
screwdriver отвертка f at**vyor**tka 148
sea море n **mo**rye 107; **~front** берег моря m **bye**reek **mo**rya; **~sickness** морская болезнь f mar**ska**ya ba**lyesn'**; **I feel ~sick** у меня морская болезнь oo mee**nya** mar**ska**ya ba**lyesn'**
season ticket проездной билет m praees**noy** bee**lyet**
seasoning приправы fpl pree**pra**vi 38
seat место n **mye**sta 68, 74, 77, 109
second второй fta**roy** 217

second: ~ **class** *(train)* купейный вагон m koopeyniy vagon 74; **~-hand** подержанный padyerzhaniy

secretary секретарь m seekreetar'

sedative успокаивающее n oospakayeevayooshcheeye

see, to видеть/(по)смотреть veedyet'/(pa)smatryet' 24, 93

self-employed работать на себя m rabotat' na seebya 121

self-service самообслуживание n samaaploozheevaneeye 87

sell, to продавать pradavat' 133

send, to послать/посылать paslat'/pasilat' 88, 155

senior citizen пенсионер m pyenseeonyer 74

separated, to be не жить вместе nye zheet' vmyestee 120

separately отдельно adel'na 42

September сентябрь m seentyabr' 218

serious серьёзный seeryozniy

service *(religious)* служба f sloozhba 105

service *(in restaurant)* обслуживание n apsloozheevaneeye; **is ~ included?** счёт включает обслуживание? schyot fkloochayeet apsloozheevaneeye? 42

serviette салфетка f salfyetka 39

set menu меню n myenyoo 37

sexual сексуальный seeksooal'niy

shade тон m ton 143

shady в тени f tyenee 30

shallow мелкий melkeey

shampoo шампунь f shampoon' 142; **~ and set** вымыть и уложить vimat' ee oolazheet' 147

shape форма, покрой f forma, pakroy 134

share, to *(room)* делить deeleet'

shaver электробритва f elyektrabreetva 142

shaving: ~ **brush** кисточка для бритья f keestachka dlya breetya; **~ cream** крем для бритья f krem dlya breetya

she она ana

sheath *(contraceptive)* презерватив m preeseervateef

sheet *(bedding)* простыня f prastynya 28

ship пароход m parakhod 81

shirt рубашка f roobashka 144

shock *(electric)* электрошок m elektrashok

shoe(s) обувь/туфли f/fpl oboof'/tooflee 145; **~ repair** ремонт обуви m reemont oboovee; **~ store** обувь f aboof'; **~mender's** ремонт обуви m reemont oboovee 131

shop магазин m magazeen 130; **~ assistant** продавец m pradavyets

shopping: ~ **basket** корзинка f karzeenka; **~ mall [centre]** торговый центр m targoviy tsentar 99, 131; **~ trolley** тележка f teelyeshka; **~ to go** идти за покупками eetee za pakoopkamee

short *(vs. tall)* низкий neeskeey 14

short-sighted близорукость f bleezarookast' 167

shorts шорты pl shorti 144

shoulder плечо n pleecho 166

shovel совок m savok 157

show, to показывать pakazivat' 18, 94, 133; **can you ~ me …?** покажите мне … pakazheetee mnye … 133

shower душ m doosh 26, 30

shut *(adj.)* закрытый zakritiy 14

shut, to закрываться zakrivat'sya 132; **when do you shut?** когда вы закрываетесь? kagda vi zakrivayeetees'

shutters ставни mpl stavni 25

sick: I'm going to be sick меня тошнит meenya tashneet

side *(of road)* сторона f starana 95; **~ order** гарнир m garneer 37, 38; **~ street** боковая улица f bakavaya ooleetsa 95

A-Z

A-Z

sightseeing: ~ tour
обзорная экскурсия f
abzornaya ekskoorseeya
97; to go ~ осматривать
достопримечательности
asmatreevat'
dastapreemeechateel'nastee

sign (road) знак m znak 93

signpost дорожный знак m
darozhniy znak

silk шёлк m shyolk

silver серебро n seereebro 149;
~-plate посеребренный
paseeryebryaniy 149

singer певец m peevyets 157

single одноместный adnamyesniy
81; ~ room одноместный номер m
adnamyestnyi nomyer 21; ~ ticket
билет в один конец beelyet v
adeen kanyets 68, 74, 79

single (unmarried) холост(а)
kholast/khalasta 120

sink раковина f rakoveena 25

sister сестра f seestra 120

sit, to сесть syest' 77

size размер m razmyer 146

skates коньки mpl kon'kee 117

ski: ~ boots лыжные ботинки mpl
lizhniye bateenkee 117; ~-school
лыжная школа f lizhnaya shkola

skin кожа f kozha 166

skirt юбка f yoopka 144

skis лыжи mpl lizhee 117

sleep, to спать spat' 167

sleeping: ~ bag спальный мешок m
spal'niy meeshok 31; ~ pill
снотворное n snatvornaya

sleeve рукава mpl rookava 144

slice ломтик m lomteek 159

slippers тапочки fpl tapachkee 145

slow медленный myedleenniy 14;
(clock) отстать atstat' 221;
slow down! помедленнее
pamyedleeneeye 94

slowly медленно myedleena 11, 17

small маленький maleen'keey 14,
40, 110; (cramped) тесно tyesno 24;
smaller поменьше pamyen'she 134

smell запах m zapakh

smoke, to курить kooreet' 126

smoking (adj.) курящий
kooryashchiy 36

snack bar буфет m boofyet 73

snacks закуски fpl zakookskee

sneakers кроссовки fpl krasofkee

snorkel трубка f troopka

snow снег snyek 122

soap мыло n mila 142; ~ powder
мыльный порошок m mil'niy
parashok

soccer футбол m footbol 114

socket розетка f razyetka

socks носки mpl naskee 144

soft drink напиток m napeetak 110

sole (shoes) подошва f padoshva

soloist солист m saleest 111

soluble aspirin растворимый
аспирин m rastvareemiy
aspeereen

some какой-то kakoy ta

someone кто-то/кто-нибудь kto-
to/kto-nibood'

something что-то/что-нибудь chto-
to/chto-nibood'

sometimes иногда eenagda 13

son сын m sin 120, 162

soon скоро skora 13; as ~ as
possible как можно скорее kak
mozhna skaryeye 161

sore throat воспаление горла n
vaspalyeneeye gorla 141, 163

sorry! извините/простите
eezveeneetye/prasteetye 10

sour кислый keesliy 41

South Africa Южная Африка f
yoozhnaya afreeka

South African (n.) южно-африканец
m yoozhnaafreekaneets

south юг m yook 95

souvenir сувенир m sooveeneer 98,
156; ~ guide путеводитель m
pooteevadeeteel' 156; ~ store
сувениры m sooveeneeri 131

spa минеральные воды fpl
meeneeral'niye vodi 107

space место n myesta 30

spade совок m sa<u>vok</u> 157

spare *(extra)* лишний <u>leesh</u>neey

speak, to говорить (с) gava<u>reet'</u> (s) 11, 41, 67, 128; **do you ~ English/ Russian?** вы говорите по-английски/по-русски? vi gava<u>ree</u>tye pa-ang<u>lee</u>yskee/pa-<u>roo</u>skee 11, 110

special: ~ delivery экспресс m eks<u>pryes</u> 155; **~ rate** особый тариф m a<u>so</u>biy ta<u>reef</u> 86

specialist специалист m speetseea<u>leest</u> 164

specimen анализ m a<u>na</u>leez 164

spectacles очки pl ach<u>kee</u>

spell, to называть по буквам nazi<u>vat'</u> pa <u>book</u>vam 11

spend, to тратить <u>tra</u>teet'

spicy острый <u>o</u>striy

spine позвоночник m pazva<u>noch</u>neek 166

spoon ложка f <u>losh</u>ka 39, 41, 148

sport спорт m sport 114, 121; **sports club** спортклуб m sport<u>kloop</u> 115; **sports ground** спортплощадка f sportplash<u>chat</u>ka 96

sporting goods store спорттовары m sporta<u>va</u>ri 131

sprained, to be расстянуть rastya<u>noot'</u> 164

spring *(season)* весна f vees<u>na</u> 219

square квадратный kvad<u>rat</u>niy 134

stadium стадион m sta<u>dee</u>on 96

staff персонал m peer<u>sa</u>nal

stainless steel нержавеющая сталь f neerzha<u>vye</u>yooshchaya stal' 149

stamp марка f <u>mar</u>ka 150, 154

stand in line, to стоять в очереди sta<u>yat'</u> v <u>o</u>cheereedee 112

start, to начинаться nachee<u>nat'</u>sya 108, 112; *(car)* заводить zava<u>deet'</u> 88

starter закуска f za<u>koos</u>ka 37

station вокзал m vak<u>zal</u> 96

stationer канцелярские товары mpl kantsee<u>lyar</u>skeeye ta<u>va</u>ri

statue статуя f <u>sta</u>tooya 99

stay, to остаться as<u>tat'</u>sa 23, 123

steet kiosk уличный киоск m oo<u>leech</u>niy kee<u>osk</u> 150

sterilizing solution стерилизующий раствор m steereelee<u>zoo</u>yooshchey ras<u>tvor</u> 142

still: I'm still waiting я все еще жду ya vsyo <u>eesh</u>cho zhdoo

sting укус m oo<u>koos</u> 162

stockings чулки mpl chool<u>kee</u> 144

stolen, to украсть oo<u>krast'</u> 71

stomach живот/желудок m zhee<u>vot</u>/zhee<u>loo</u>dak 166; **~ache** болит живот ba<u>leet</u> zhee<u>vot</u> 163

stools *(faeces)* кал m kal 164

stop *(bus, etc.)* остановка f asta<u>nof</u>ka 79, 80

stop, to останавливаться asta<u>nav</u>leevat'sya 76, 77, 78, 98

stopcock запорный кран za<u>por</u>ny kran 28

store магазин m maga<u>zeen</u> 130; **~ guide** перечень отделов m <u>pye</u>reecheen' ad<u>ye</u>laf 132

stormy гроза f gra<u>za</u> 122

stove плита f plee<u>ta</u> 28, 29

straight ahead прямо <u>prya</u>ma 95

strained muscle растянута мышца rastya<u>noo</u>ta <u>mish</u>tsa 162

strange странный <u>stra</u>niy 101

straw *(drinking)* соломинка f sa<u>lo</u>meenka

stream ручей m roo<u>chey</u> 107

strong *(potent)* сильный <u>seel'</u>niy

student студент m stoo<u>dyent</u> 74, 100

study, to учиться oo<u>cheet'</u>sya 121

stunning ошеломляющий asheelam<u>lya</u>yooshchey 101

style стиль m steel' 104

subtitled с субтитрами s soob<u>tee</u>tramee 110

subway метро n mee<u>tro</u> 80; **~ station** станция метро f <u>stant</u>siya mee<u>tro</u> 96

sugar сахар m <u>sa</u>khar 38, 39

suggest, to предлагать preed<u>la</u>gat' 123

suit костюм m kastyoom 144
suitable for годный для godniy dlya
summer лето n lyeta 219
sun-tan cream/lotion крем для загара m krem dlya zagara 142
sunbathe, to загорать zagarat'
sunburn солнечный ожёг m solneechniy azhok 141
Sunday воскресенье n vaskreesyen'ye 218
sunglasses солнечные очки pl solneechniye achkee 144
sunny на солнце n na sontse 31
sunshade зонт m zont 116
sunstroke солнечный удар m solneechniy oodar 163
super (gas/petrol) бензин 98 m dyevyanosta vas'moy beenzeen 87
superb превосходный preevaskhodniy 101
supermarket универсам m ooneevyersam 131, 158
supervision присмотр m preesmotar
supplement доплата f daplata 68, 69, 74
suppositories свечи fpl svyechee 165
sure: are you sure? вы уверены? vi oovyereeni
surfboard доска f daska 116
surname фамилия f fameeleeya
suspicious подозрительный padazreeteel'niy 152
sweater пуловер m poolovyer 144
sweatshirt рубашка/фуфайка f roobashka/foofayka 144
sweet (taste) сладкий slatkeey
sweets конфеты fpl kanfyeti 150
swelling опухоль f opookhal' 162
swim, to плавать plavat' 116
swimming плавание n plavaneeye 114; ~ **pool** бассейн m baseyen 22, 26, 116; ~ **trunks** плавки pl plafkee 144
swimsuit купальник m koopal'neek 144

swollen, to be распухать raspookhat'
symptoms симптомы mpl seemtomi 163
synagogue синагога f seenagoga 105
synthetic синтетика f seenteteeka 146

T **T-shirt** майка f mayka 144, 156
table столик m stoleek 35, 112
take, to (carry) нести nyestee 71; (medication) принимать preeneemat' 165; (time) длиться dleet'sya 78; **I'll take it** я возьму это ya vaz'moo eta 24, 135; ~ **out** [take away] брать с собой brat' s saboy 40; ~ **photographs** фотографировать fatagrafeeravat' 98, 100
taken (occupied): **is this seat taken?** это место занято? eta meysta zanyata 77
talcum powder тальк m tal'k 142
talk, to разговаривать razgavareevat'
tall высокий visokeey 14
tampon тампон m tampon 142
tan загар m zagar
tap кран m kran 25
taxi такси n taksee 70, 71, 84; ~ **stand** [rank] стоянка такси f stayanka taksee 84, 96
tea чай m chay 40; ~ **bag** пакетик чая m pakyeteek chaya 160; ~ **towel** кухонное полотенце n kookhanaye palatyentse
teacher учитель m oocheeteel'
team команда f kamanda 114
teaspoon чайная ложка f chaynaya loshka 148
teddy bear мишка m meeshka 157
telephone телефон m teeleefon 22, 70, 92, 127; ~ **bill** счёт за телефон m shchyot za teeleefon 32; ~ **booth** телефон-автомат m teeleefon-aftamat 127; ~ **calls** телефонные звонки mpl teeleefoniye zvankee 32; ~ **directory** телефонный справочник m teeleefoniy spravachneek 127; ~ **number** номер телефона m nomeer teeleefona 127

telex телекс m <u>ty</u>eleeks 155

tell, to рассказывать ras<u>ka</u>zyvat'
18; **tell me** скажите мне ska<u>zhee</u>tye
mnye 79

temperature (*body*) температура f
teempeera<u>too</u>ra 164

temporarily временно <u>vry</u>emeena 89

tennis теннис m <u>te</u>nees 114;
~ **court** теннисный корт m
<u>ty</u>eneesniy kort 115

tent палатка f pa<u>lat</u>ka 30, 31; ~
pegs колышки mpl <u>ko</u>lishkee 31;
~ **pole** шест m shest 31

terminus (*bus*) кольцо n kal'<u>tso</u> 78

terrible ужасный oo<u>zhas</u>niy 19, 101

tetanus столбняк m stalb<u>ny</u>ak 164

thank you спасибо spa<u>see</u>ba 10

that: ~ **one** вон тот(та) von tot/(ta)
16; **that's all** это всё eta vsyo 133

theater театр m tee<u>a</u>tr 96, 99, 110

theft кража f <u>kra</u>zha 153

their их ikh 16

theirs их eekh 16

them (*to, for*) им eem 16

then (*time*) затем/потом za<u>ty</u>em/
pa<u>tom</u> 13

there там tam 17; там/туда
tam/<u>too</u>da 12

thermometer термометр m
teer<u>mo</u>meetar

thermos flask термос m <u>ter</u>mas

these эти <u>e</u>tee 134

they они a<u>nee</u>

thick толстый <u>tol</u>stiy 14

thief вор m vor

thigh бедро n beed<u>ro</u> 166

thin тонкий <u>ton</u>keey 14

think, to думать <u>doo</u>mat' 42;
~ **about it** подумать об этом
pa<u>doo</u>mat' ab <u>e</u>tam 135; **I think**
я думаю ya <u>doo</u>mayoo 42, 77

third третий <u>try</u>eteey 217

third, a третья часть f <u>try</u>etya
chast 217

thirsty: I'm thirsty я хочу пить ya
kha<u>choo</u> peet'

this: ~ **one** вот этот (эта) von <u>e</u>tot
(<u>e</u>ta) 16

those те tye 134

thousand тысяча
<u>ti</u>seecha 216

throat горло n
<u>gor</u>la 166

thrombosis тромбоз m
tram<u>boz</u>

through через <u>chy</u>ereez

thumb большой палец m bal'<u>shoy</u>
<u>pa</u>leets 166

Thursday четверг m cheet<u>vy</u>erk
218

ticket билет m bee<u>ly</u>et 68, 75, 77, 79,
80, 100, 114; ~ **office** билетные
кассы fpl bee<u>ly</u>etniye <u>ka</u>ssi 73

tie галстук m <u>gal</u>stook 144

tight (*loose*) тесно <u>ty</u>esna 144

tights колготки pl kal<u>got</u>kee 144

till receipt чек m chyek

time время n <u>vry</u>emya 76; ~ **of day**
время суток n <u>vry</u>emya <u>soo</u>tak
220; **on** ~ во время va <u>vry</u>emya
76; **free** ~ свободное время n
sva<u>bod</u>naye <u>vry</u>emya 98; **... times a
day** ... раз в день ...raz v dyen'

timetable расписание n
raspee<u>sa</u>neeye 75

tin банка f <u>ban</u>ka 159; ~ **opener**
открывалка f atkri<u>val</u>ka 148

tint, to тонировать ta<u>nee</u>ravat' 147

tire (*n.*) шина f <u>shee</u>na 83, 88

tired усталый oo<u>sta</u>liy

tissue бумажная салфетка f
boo<u>mazh</u>naya sal<u>fy</u>etka 142

to (*place*) в, на v(f)/na 12

tobacco табак m ta<u>bak</u> 17

today сегодня see<u>vod</u>nee 124, 218

toe палец ноги m <u>pa</u>leets na<u>gee</u> 166

together вместе v<u>mye</u>stye 42

toilet туалет m tooa<u>ly</u>et 25, 26, 29,
96, 98, 132; ~ **paper** туалетная
бумага f tooa<u>ly</u>etnaya boo<u>ma</u>ga
25, 142

tomorrow завтра <u>za</u>ftra 84, 124, 218

tongs щипцы pl shchy<u>eep</u>tsi 31

tongue язык m ya<u>zik</u> 166

tonight сегодня вечером see<u>vod</u>nya
<u>vy</u>echeeram 108, 110, 124

tonsillitis тонзиллит m tanzee<u>leet</u>

A-Z

A-Z

tonsils миндалины fpl meendaleeni
too слишком sleeshkam 17, 93; **~ much** слишком много sleeshkam mnoga 15
tooth зуб m zoop 168; **~ache** зубная паста f zoobnaya pasta; **~brush** зубная щётка f zoobnaya shchyotka 142; **~paste** зубная паста f zoobnaya pasta 142
top крышка f krishka
torch фонарь m fanar' 31
torn, to be (muscle) разорвать razarvat' 164
totally полностью polnostyoo 17
tough (food) жёсткий zhyoskiy 41
tour экскурсия f ekskoorseeya 81; **~ guide** представитель тура m pryedstaveetyel' toora 27
tourist турист m tooreest; **~ office** бюро интуриста n byooro intooreesta 97
tow truck буксир m bookseer 88
tow, to отбуксировать atbookseeravat' 88
towel полотенце n palatyentse 142
tower башня f bashnya 99
town город m gorat 70, 94; **~ hall** горсовет m gorsavyet 99
toy игрушка f eegrooshka 157; **~ store** игрушки fpl eegrooshkee 131
traditional традиционный tradeetsioniy 35
traffic дорожное движение n darozhnaya dveezhyeneeye; **~ jam** пробка f propka; **~ violation** [offence] нарушение n narooshyeneeye
trail просёлочная дорога f prasyolachnaya daroga 106
trailer трейлер m tryeylyer 30
train поезд m poyest 75, 76, 77, 80; **~ station** вокзал m vakzal 73; **~ times** расписание поездов raspeesaneeye poyezdov 75

training shoes кроссовки fpl krasofkee 145
tram трамвай m tranvay 78, 79
transfer пересаживаться peereesazheevat'sya
transit, in в пути v pootee
translate, to переводить peereevodeet' 11
translation перевод m peereevot
translator переводчик m peereevotcheek
trash мусор m moosar 28; **~ cans** мусорные баки mpl moosornye bakee 30
travel: ~ agency бюро путешествий n byooro pooteeshyestveey 131; **~ sickness** морская болезнь f marskaya balyezn' 141
traveler's checks [cheques] аккредитивы mpl akreedeeteevi 136, 138
tray поднос m padnos
tree дерево n dyereeva 106
trim (hair) подстричь patstreech 147
trip (journey) поездка f payestka 76, 78, 123
trolley тележка f teelyeshka 158
trouser press гладильный пресс m gladeel'niy pres
trousers брюки pl bryookee 144
truck грузовик m groozaveek
true правда f pravda; **that's not ~** это не правда eta nee pravda
try on, to примерять preemeeryat' 146
Tuesday вторник m ftorneek 218
tumor опухоль f opookhal' 165
tunnel тунель m toonel'
turn: ~ down (volume, heat) уменьшать oomen'shat'; **~ off** выключать viklyoochat' 25; **~ on** включать fklyoochat' 25; **~ up** (volume, heat) увеличивать ooveeleecheevat'
turning поворот pavarot 95
TV телевизор m televeezar 22
tweezers пинцет m peentsyet
twice дважды/два раза dvazhdi 217

twin bed две кровати fpl dv**ye** krav**a**tee 21

twist: I've twisted my ankle вывихнуть: я вывихнул лодыжку v**i**veekhnoot': ya v**i**veekhnool lad**i**shkoo

two-door car двухдверная CORR dvookhdv**ye**rnaya 86

type тип m teep 109; **what ~?** какой тип? kak**oy** teep 112

typical типичный teep**ee**chiy 37

tyre (tire) шина f sh**ee**na 83, 88

U **ugly** некрасивый/ безобразный neekras**ee**viy/ beeza**bra**zniy 14, 101

Ukraine Украина f ookra**ee**na 119

ulcer язва f y**a**zva

umbrella (sunshade) зонт m zont 116

uncle дядя m dy**a**dya 120

unconscious без сознания byes sazn**a**neeya 92, 162

under под pot

underdone (adj.) недожареный needazh**a**ryeniy 41

underground метро n mye**tro**; **~ station** станция метро f st**a**ntseeya mye**tro**

underpants трусы pl troo**si** 144

underpass подземный переход m padz**ye**mniy peer**ee**ekhot 76, 96

understand, to понимать paneem**at'** 11; **do you ~?** вы понимаете? vi paneem**a**yetye 11; **I don't ~** я не понимаю ya nye paneem**a**yoo 67; **I don't understand** я не понимаю ya nye paneem**a**yoo 11

undress, to раздеваться razdeev**at'**sya 164

uneven (ground) неровный m nyer**o**vniy 30

unfortunately к сожалению k sazhal**ye**neeyoo 19

uniform форма f f**o**rma

unit (for phonecard, etc.) единица f eedeen**ee**tsa 155

United States Соединенные Штаты mpl saeedeen**yo**niye sht**a**ti

unleaded (gas/petrol) очищенный ach**ee**shcheniy 87

unlock, to отпирать atpeer**at'**

unpleasant неприятный neepree**ya**tniy 14

unscrew, to отворачивать atvar**a**cheevat'

until до do 221

upper (berth) верхний vy**e**rkhneey 74

upset stomach расстройство желудка n rastr**oy**stva zhee**lo**otka 141

urgent срочно sr**o**chna 161

urine моча f m**a**cha 164

U.S.A. США mpl es she a

use, to пользоваться p**o**l'zavat'sya 139

V **vacancy** вакансия/свободное место f/n vak**a**nsiya/ svab**o**dnoye mest**a**

vacant свободный svab**o**dniy 14

vacate, to освободить asvabad**eet'** 32

vacation: on ~ в отпуске v **o**tpooskee 66, 123

vaginal infection воспаление влагалища n vaspal**ye**neeye vlagal**ee**shcha 167

valid действителен dyeystv**ee**tyelyen 75

valley долина f dal**ee**na 107

valuable ценный ts**ye**niy

value стоимость f sto**ee**mast' 155

valve запорный кран m zap**o**rny kran 28

VAT НДС m en de es 24

vegetables овощи m **o**vashchee 38

vegetarian вегетарианец m vyegyetar**ee**anyets 35, 39

vein вена f vy**e**na 166

venereal disease венерическое заболевание n veeneer**ee**cheeskoye zabalee**va**neeye 165

ventilator вентилятор m veenteelyatar
very очень ochen' 17; ~ **good** отлично atleechna 19
video: ~ **game** видеоигра f veedeeaeegra; ~ **recorder** видео m veedeea
view вид m veet
viewing point смотровая площадка f smatravaya plashchatka 99, 107
village деревня f deeryevnya 107
vineyard виноградник m veenagradneek 107
visa виза f veeza
visit визит m veezeet 66, 119
visit, to посещать paseeshchat' 123
visiting hours часы посещений mpl chasi paseeshchyeneey 167
vitamin tablets витамины mpl veetameeni 141
volleyball волейбол m valeeybol 114
voltage напряжение n napryazhyeneeye
vomit, to тошнить tashneet' 163

W **wait** ждать zhdat' 36, 41, 76, 89, 126, 140; **wait!** подождите! padazhdeetye! 98
waiter! официант! m afeetseeant 37
waiting room зал ожидания m zal azheedaneeya 73
waitress! официантка! f afeetseeantka 37
wake someone, to разбудить razboodeet' 27
Wales Уэльс m ooel's 119
walk, to идти eetee 65, 106
walking route пешеходный маршрут m peesheekhodniy marshroot 106
wallet кошелёк m kashyelyok 42
want, to хотеть khatet' 18
war memorial мемориал m myemareeal 99
ward (hospital) палата f palata 167
warm тёплая tyoplaya 14, 122; **warmer** теплее tyeplyeye 24

washbasin раковина f rakaveena
washing: ~ **instructions** инструкция к стирке f eenstrooktseeya k steerkee 146; ~ **machine** стиральная машина f steeral'naya masheena 29; ~ **powder** стиральный порошок m steeral'niy parashok 147; ~**-up liquid** средство для мытья посуды n sryetstva dlya mitya pasoodi 148
wasp оса f asa
watch часы pl chasi 149
water вода f vada 87; ~ **bottle** бутылка с водой f bootilka s vadoy; ~ **heater** водогрей m vadagrey 28; ~ **skis** водные лыжи fpl vodniye lizhee 116; ~ **temperature** температура воды f teempeeratoora vadi 122; ~**fall** водопад m vadapat 107
waterproof водонепроницаемый vodaneepraneetsaeemiy; ~ **jacket** дождевик m dazhdeeveek 145
wave волна f valna
waxing восковая ванна f voskavaya vana 147
way: I've lost my way я заблудился (лась) ya zabloodeelsya (zabloodeelas') 94; **on the way** по пути pa pootee 83
we мы mi
wear, to одевать adeevat' 152
weather погода f pagoda 122; ~ **forecast** прогноз погоды pragnoz pagodi 122
wedding свадьба f svad'ba; ~ **ring** обручальное кольцо n abroochal'naya kal'tso
Wednesday среда f sreeda 218
week неделя f nedelya 23, 97, 218
weekend: at the ~ на викенд na veekent 218
weekly (ticket) на неделю на nyedyelyoo 79
weigh вес m vyes
welcome to ... добро пожаловать в ... dabro pazhalavat' v

well-done (steak) хорошо прожаренный kharasho prazhareeniy

west запад m zapat 95

what? что? shto; **what kind of ...?** какой ...? kakoy ... 37, 106; **what time ...?** во сколько...? va skol'ka ... 68, 76, 81; **what's the time?** который час? katoriy chas 220; **what's wrong?** что случилось? shto sloocheelas' 89

wheelchair инвалидное кресло n eenvaleednaya kryesla

when? когда?/во сколько? kagda/va skol'ka 13

where? (motion) куда? kooda 12; (position) где? gdye 12; **where are you from?** откуда Вы? atkooda vi 119

which? который katoriy; **which stop?** какая остановка? kakaya astanofka? 80

white белый byeliy 143; ~ **wine** белое вино n byeloye veeno 40

who? кто? kto 16

whose? чей? chey 16

why? почему? pacheemoo 16

wide широкий shirokeey 14

wife жена f zheena 120, 162

windbreaker плащ m plashch 145

window окно n akno 25, 77; (in store) витрина f veetreena 134, 149; ~ **seat** место у окна n myesta oo akna 74

windscreen ветровое стекло n veetravoye steeklo

windsurfer виндсерфер m veendsyerfyer 116

windy ветер m vyeteer 122

wine вино n veeno 40; ~ **list** карта вин m karta veen 37

winter зима f zeema 219

with с/со s/so 17

withdraw, to снимать sneemat' 139

without без bez 17

wood лес m lyes 107

wool шерсть f shyerst' 146

work, to работать rabotat' 28, 83, 121: **it doesn't ~** (function) это не работает eto nye rabotayet 25

worse хуже khoozhe 14

worst худший khoodsheey 14

wound рана f rana 162

write down, to записать zapeesat' 136

writing pad блокнот blaknot 150

wrong неправильный neepraveel'niy 14, 136

X-ray рентген m reengyen 164

yacht яхта f yakhta

year год m got 218

yellow жёлтый zhyoltiy 143

yes да da 10

yesterday вчера fcheera 218

yoghurt йогурт m yogoort

you (formal) Вы vi; (informal) ты ti

young молодой maladoy 14

your ваш vash 16

yours ваш vash 16

youth hostel общежитие n abshchyezheeteeye 29

zebra crossing переход m peereekhot

zero ноль m nol'

zip(per) молния f molneeya

zoo зоопарк m zaapark 113

Glossary
Russian–English

The Russian-English glossary covers all the areas where you may need to decode written Russian: hotels, public buildings, restaurants, stores, ticket offices, airports, and stations. The Russian is written in large type to help you identify the character(s) from the signs you see around you.

General Общие знаки

НАЛЕВО	nalyeva	LEFT
НАПРАВО	naprava	RIGHT
ВХОД	vkhot	ENTRANCE
ВЫХОД	vikhat	EXIT
ТУАЛЕТ	tooalyet	TOILETS
МУЖСКОЙ ТУАЛЕТ	mooshskoy tooalyet	MEN (TOILETS)
ЖЕНСКИЙ ТУАЛЕТ	zhyenskeey tooalyet	WOMEN (TOILETS)
НЕ КУРИТЬ	nee kooreet'	NO SMOKING
ОПАСНО	apasna	DANGER
ВХОД ЗАПРЕЩЕН	vkhot zapreeshchyon	NO ENTRY

General Общие знаки

НА СЕБЯ/ОТ СЕБЯ	*na seebya/ at seebya*	PULL/PUSH
ПОИСК БАГАЖА	*poeesk bagazha*	LOST PROPERTY
КУПАТЬСЯ ЗАПРЕЩЕНО	*koopat'sya zapreeshcheeno*	NO SWIMMING
ПИТЬЕВАЯ ВОДА	*peetyevaya vada*	DRINKING WATER
ЧАСТНАЯ СОБСТВЕННОСТЬ	*chasnaya sopstveenast'*	PRIVATE
НЕ СОРИТЬ	*nee sareet'*	NO LITTER
ПОДЗЕМНЫЙ ПЕРЕХОД	*padzyemniy peereekhot*	UNDERPASS
БУДЬТЕ ОСТОРОЖНЫ ПРИ ВЫХОДЕ	*bood'tee astarozhni pree vikhadee*	MIND THE STEP
СВЕЖАЯ КРАСКА	*svyezhaya kraska*	WET PAINT
МЯГКИЙ ВАГОН	*myakhkeey vagon*	FIRST CLASS
КУПЕЙНЫЙ ВАГОН	*koopyeyniy vagon*	SECOND CLASS

Road signs Дорожные знаки

СТОП	*stop*	STOP
ДЕРЖИТЕСЬ ПРАВОЙ СТОРОНЫ	*deerzheetees' pravay starani*	KEEP RIGHT
ДЕРЖИТЕСЬ ЛЕВОЙ СТОРОНЫ	*deerzheetees' levay starani*	KEEP LEFT
ОДНОСТО-РОННЕЕ ДВИЖЕНИЕ	*adnastaroneeye dveezhyeneeye*	ONE WAY
ОБГОН ЗАПРЕЩЕН	*abgon zapreeshchyon*	NO PASSING [OVERTAKING]
СТОЯНКА ЗАПРЕЩЕНА	*stayanka zapreeshcheena*	NO PARKING
АВТОМА-ГИСТРАЛЬ	*aftamageestral'*	HIGHWAY [MOTORWAY]
ПЛАТА ЗА ДОРОГУ	*plata za darogoo*	TOLL
СВЕТОФОР	*sveetafor*	TRAFFIC LIGHTS
РАЗВЯЗКА	*razvyaska*	INTERSECTION [JUNCTION]

Airport/Station
Аэропорт/Вокзал

СПРАВКИ	*sprafkee*	INFORMATION
ПЛАТФОРМА 1	*platforma adeen*	PLATFORM 1
НАКОПИТЕЛЬ 1	*nakopeeteel' adeen*	GATE 1
ТАМОЖНЯ	*tamozhnya*	CUSTOMS
ПАСПОРТНЫЙ КОНТРОЛЬ	*paspartniy kantrol'*	IMMIGRATION
ПРИБЫТИЕ	*preebiteeye*	ARRIVALS
ОТПРАВЛЕНИЕ	*atpravlyeneeye*	DEPARTURES
КАМЕРЫ ХРАНЕНИЯ	*kameeri khranyeneeya*	LUGGAGE LOCKERS
ВЫДАЧА БАГАЖА	*vidacha bagazha*	LUGGAGE RECLAIM
АВТОБУС/ ПОЕЗД	*aftoboos/poeezt*	BUS/TRAIN
ПРОКАТ АВТОМОБИЛЕЙ	*prakat aftamabeeleey*	CAR RENTAL
МЕТРО	*meetro*	SUBWAY [METRO]

Hotel/Restaurant
Гостиница/Ресторан

СПРАВКИ	*sprafkee*	INFORMATION
ФОЙЕ	*faye*	RECEPTION
ЗАРЕЗЕРВИ РОВАНО	*zareezeerveeravana*	RESERVED
АВАРИЙНЫЙ/ ПОЖАРНЫЙ ВЫХОД	*avareeyniy / pazharniy vikhat*	EMERGENCY/ FIRE EXIT
ГОРЯЧАЯ ВОДА	*garyachaya vada*	HOT (WATER)
ХОЛОДНАЯ ВОДА	*khalodnaya vada*	COLD (WATER)
ДЛЯ СЛУЖЕБНОГО ПОЛЬЗОВАНИЯ	*dlya sloozhebnava pol'zavaneeya*	STAFF ONLY
ГАРДЕРОБ	*gardeerop*	COATCHECK [CLOAKROOM]
ТЕРРАСА/САД	*teerasa/sat*	TERRACE/GARDEN
БАР	*bar*	BAR

Stores Магазины

ОТКРЫТО	*atkrita*	OPEN
ЗАКРЫТО	*zakrita*	CLOSED
ОБЕД	*abyet*	LUNCH
ОТДЕЛ	*adyel*	DEPARTMENT
ЭТАЖ	*etazh*	FLOOR
ПОДВАЛЬНЫЙ ЭТАЖ	*padval'niy etazh*	BASEMENT
ЛИФТ	*leeft*	ELEVATOR [LIFT]
ЭСКАЛАТОР	*eskalatar*	ESCALATOR
КАССА	*kasa*	CASHIER
РАСПРОДАЖА	*raspradazha*	SALE

Sightseeing
Достопримечательности

Russian	Transliteration	English
ВХОД БЕСПЛАТНЫЙ	vkhot beesplatniy	FREE ADMISSION
ВЗРОСЛЫЕ	vzrosliye	ADULTS
ДЕТИ	dyetee	CHILDREN
ЛЬГОТЫ	l'goti	CONCESSIONS (students/pensioners)
СУВЕНИРЫ	sooveeneeri	SOUVENIRS
БУФЕТ	boofyet	REFRESHMENTS
НЕ ТРОГАТЬ	nee trogat'	DO NOT TOUCH
НЕ ФОТОГРА-ФИРОВАТЬ	nee fatagrafeeravat'	NO PHOTOGRAPHY
ВХОДА НЕТ	vkhoda nyet	NO ACCESS

Public Buildings
Публичные здания

БОЛЬНИЦА	*bal'neetsa*	HOSPITAL
ВРАЧ	*vrach*	DOCTOR
ЗУБНОЙ ВРАЧ	*zoobnoy vrach*	DENTIST
МИЛИЦИЯ	*meeleetseeya*	POLICE
БАНК	*bank*	BANK
ПОЧТА	*pochta*	POST OFFICE
ПЛАВАТЕЛЬНЫЙ БАССЕЙН	*plavateel'niy basyeyn*	SWIMMING POOL
ГОРСОВЕТ	*gorsavyet*	TOWN HALL
СТОЯНКА ТАКСИ	*stayanka taksee*	TAXI STAND [RANK]
МУЗЕЙ	*moozyey*	MUSEUM

Reference

Numbers Числительные

GRAMMAR

Numbers in their basic nominative form
The number "one" and numbers ending in "one" are followed by the nominative singular and "one" agrees with the gender of the noun.

one book	**adna kneega** (f)
twenty-one books	**dvatsat' adna kneega** (f)

The numbers "two," "three," and "four," and numbers ending in them are followed by the genitive singular. The number "two" has two forms: masculine/neuter (два) and feminine (две).

two cars	**dva masheena** (m)
forty-two cars	**sorak dva masheena** (m)

Other numbers are followed by the genitive plural.

seven books	**syem' kneek** (f)
fifty cars	**peedeesyat masheenaf** (m)

For additional information ➤ 169.

0	ноль/нуль *nol'/nool'*		12	двенадцать *dveenatsat'*
1	один/одна/одно		13	тринадцать *treenatsat'*
	adeen/(adna)(adno)		14	четырнадцать
2	два/две *dva (dvye)*			*chyeetirnatsat'*
3	три *tree*		15	пятнадцать *peetnatsat'*
4	четыре *chyeetirye*		16	шестнадцать
5	пять *pyat'*			*shestnatsat'*
6	шесть *shest'*		17	семнадцать
7	семь *syem'*			*seemnatsat'*
8	восемь *voseem'*		18	восемнадцать
9	девять *dyeveet'*			*vaseemnatsat'*
10	десять *dyeseet'*		19	девятнадцать
11	одиннадцать			*deeveetnatsat'*
	adeenatsat'		20	двадцать
				dvatsat'

21	двадцать один *dvatsat' adeen*	35,750	тридцать пять тысяч семьсот пятьдесят *treetsat' pyat' tiseech syem'sot peedeesyat*
22	двадцать два *dvatsat' dva*		
23	двадцать три *dvatsat' tree*		
24	двадцать четыре *dvatsat' chyeetirye*	1,000,000	миллион *meelleeon*
25	двадцать пять *dvatsat' pyat'*	first	первый *pyerviy*
26	двадцать шесть *dvatsat' shest'*	second	второй *ftaroy*
27	двадцать семь *dvatsat' syem'*	third	третий *tryeteey*
28	двадцать восемь *dvatsat' voseem'*	fourth	четвёртый *chyeetvyortiy*
29	двадцать девять *dvatsat' dyeveet'*	fifth	пятый *pyatiy*
30	тридцать *treetsat'*	once	однажды/один раз *adnazhdi*
31	тридцать один *treetsat' adeen*	twice	два раза *dva raza*
32	тридцать два *treetsat' dva*	three times	три раза *tree raza*
40	сорок *sorak*	a half	половина *palaveena*
50	пятьдесят *peedeesyat*	half an hour	полчаса *polchyasa*
60	шестьдесят *sheezdeesyat*	half a tank	полбака *polbaka*
70	семьдесят *syemdeeseet*	a quarter	четверть *chyetveert'*
80	восемьдесят *voseemdeeseet*	a third	третья часть *tryetya chyast*
90	девяносто *deeveenosta*	a pair of ...	пара ... *para ...*
100	сто *sto*	a dozen ...	дюжина ... *dyoozheena ...*
101	сто один *sto adeen*	1998	тысяча девятьсот девяносто восьмой год *tiseechya deeveetsot deeveenosta vas'moy got*
102	сто два *sto dva*		
200	двести *dvyestee*		
500	пятьсот *peetsot*		
1,000	тысяча *tiseechya*	2001	две тысячи первый год *dvye tiseechyee pyerviy got*
10,000	десять тысяч *dyeseet' tiseech*		
		the 1990s	девяностые годы *deeveenostiye godi*

Days Дни

Monday	понедельник	*paneedyel'neek*
Tuesday	вторник	*ftorneek*
Wednesday	среда	*sreeda*
Thursday	четверг	*chyeetvyerk*
Friday	пятница	*pyatneetsa*
Saturday	суббота	*soobota*
Sunday	воскресенье	*vaskreesyenye*

Months Месяцы

January	январь	*eenvar'*
February	февраль	*feevral'*
March	март	*mart*
April	апрель	*apryel'*
May	май	*may*
June	июнь	*eeyoon'*
July	июль	*eeyool'*
August	август	*avgoost*
September	сентябрь	*seentyabr'*
October	октябрь	*aktyabr'*
November	ноябрь	*nayabr'*
December	декабрь	*deekabr'*

Dates Даты

It's … today.	Сегодня …	*seevodnya …*
July 10	десятое июля	*deesyataye eeyoolya*
Tuesday, March 1	вторник, первое марта	*ftorneek pyervaye marta*
yesterday	вчера	*fchyeera*
today/tomorrow	сегодня/завтра	*seevodnya/zaftra*
this/last week	на этой/прошлой неделе	*na etiy/proshliy needyelye*
this/last month/year	в этом/прошлом месяце/году	*v etam/proshlam myeseetse/gadoo*
next week	на следующей неделе	*na slyedooyooshcheey needyelye*
on [at] the weekend	в выходные дни	*v vikhadniye dnee*

Seasons Времена года

spring	весна *veesna*
summer	лето *lyeta*
fall [autumn]	осень *oseen'*
winter	зима *zeema*
in spring	весной *veesnoy*
during the summer	летом *lyetam*

Greetings Поздравления

Happy birthday!   С днём рождения! *z dnyom razhdyeneeya*

Merry Christmas!   С Рождеством! *s razhdeestvom*

Happy New Year!   С Новым годом! *s novim godam*

Happy Easter!   С Пасхой! *s paskhiy*

Best wishes!   Всего самого лучшего! *fseevo samava loochsheva*

Congratulations!   Поздравляю! *pazdravlyayoo*

Good luck!/All the best!   Удачи!/Всего самого хорошего! *oodachyee fseevo samava kharosheva*

Have a good trip!   Счастливого пути! *shchyastleevava pootee*

Give my regards to …   Передай(те) привет … *peereeday(tye) preevyet* …

Public holidays Праздничные дни

January 1	Новый Год	New Year's Day
March 8	Международный Женский День	International Women's Day
May 1–2	1-е мая	May Day/Labor Day
May 9	День Победы	Victory in Europe Day
October 7	День Конституции	Constitution Day
November 7–8	Праздник Октябрьской Революции	Revolution Day

Note: Christmas (Рождество) and Easter (Пасха) were not officially observed. However, from 1999 they are public holidays.

Time Часы

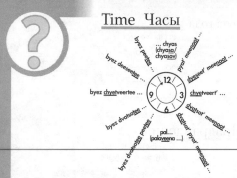

byez peetee …
byez deeseetee …
byez chyetveertee …
byez dvatsatee …
byez dvatsatee peetee …
pal… (palaveena …)
dvatsat' pyat' meenoot …
dvatsat' meenoot …
chyetveert' …
dveseet' meenoot …
pyat' meenoot …
… chyas (chyasa/ chyasov)

In Russian, times between the hour and the half hour are expressed as that number of minutes "of" the next hour. So, for example, "ten past two" would be "ten minutes of the third (hour)." Times between the half hour and the next hour are expressed by using the Russian word for "without" (без), the number of minutes remaining until the next hour, and the number of the next hour. So "twenty to eight" would be "without twenty eight."

Excuse me. Can you tell me the time?	Будьте добры! Который час? *bood'tye dabri katoriy chyas*
It's …	Сейчас … *seechyas* …
five past one	пять минут второго *pyat' meenoot ftarova*
ten past two	десять минут третьего *dyeseet' meenoot tryetyeeva*
a quarter past three	четверть четвёртого *chyetveert' chyeetvyortava*
twenty past four	двадцать минут пятого *dvatsat' meenoot pyatava*
twenty-five past five	двадцать пять минут шестого *dvatsat' pyat' meenoot shestova*
half past six	полседьмого *polseed'mova*
twenty-five to seven	без двадцати пяти семь *byez dvatsatee peetee syem'*
twenty to eight	без двадцати восемь *byez dvatsatee voseem'*
a quarter to nine	без четверти девять *byez chyetveertee dyeveet'*
ten to ten	без десяти десять *byez deeseetee dyeseet'*
five to eleven	без пяти одиннадцать *byes peetee adeenatsat'*
twelve o'clock	двенадцать часов *dveenatsat' chyasof*

noon/midnight	полдень/полночь *poldeen' polnach'*
at dawn	на рассвете *na rassvyetye*
in the morning	утром *ootram*
during the day	в течение дня *f teechyeneeye dnya*
before lunch	перед обедом *pyereed abyedam*
after lunch	после обеда *poslee abyeda*
in the afternoon/evening	днём/вечером *dnyom/vyechyeeram*
at night	ночью *noch'oo*
I'll be ready in five minutes.	Я буду готов(а) через пять минут. *ya boodoo gatof (gatova) chyerees pyat' meenoot*
He'll be back in a quarter of an hour.	Он вернётся через четверть часа. *on veernyotsa chyereez chyetveert' chyasa*
She arrived half an hour ago.	Она приехала полчаса назад. *ana preeyekhala palchyasa nazat*
The train leaves at …	Поезд отправляется в … *poeest atpravlyaeetsa v …*
13:04	тринадцать часов четыре минуты *treenatsat' chyasof chyeetiree meenooti*
0:40	ноль часов сорок минут *nol' chyasof sorak meenoot*
The train is 10 minutes late/early.	Поезд придёт на десять минут раньше/позже. *poeezt preedyot na dyeseet' meenoot ran'shee/pozhee*
It's five minutes fast/slow.	Часы на пять минут спешат/отстают. *chasi na pyat' meenoot speeshat/atstayoot*
from 9:00 to 5:00	с девяти до пяти *z deeveetee da peetee*
between 8:00 and 2:00	между восемью и двумя *myezhdoo voseemyoo ee dvoomya*
I'll be leaving by …	Я пойду часа … *ya paydoo chyasa …*
Will you be back before …?	Вы придёте до …? *vi preedyotye da …*
We'll be here until …	Мы здесь будем до … *mi zdyes' boodeem da …*

ARCTIC

NORWEGIAN SEA

BARANTS SEA

○ Murmansk

□ St. Petersburg

○ Archangel

○ Norilsk

Ural Mountains

□ Smolensk

□ **MOSCOW**

RUSSIAN

○ Yekaterinburg

Tomsk
○

○ Volgograd

○ Rostov-na-Donu

○ Omsk

○ Krasno-jarsk

CASPIAN SEA

OCEAN

Egvekinot

BERING
SEA

O Kazachye

Petropavlovsk-
Kamchatskiy O

PACIFIC OCEAN

SEA OF
OKHOTSK

O Yakutsk

FEDERATION

Korsakov

O Bratsk

Belogorsk

Ulan-Ude
O

O Vladivostok

SEA OF
JAPAN

Quick reference Выражения

Good morning.	Доброе утро.	*dobraye ootra*
Good afternoon.	Добрый день.	*dobriy dyen'*
Good evening.	Добрый вечер.	*dobriy vyecheer*
Hello.	Здравствуй(те).	*zdrastvooytye*
Good-bye.	До свидания.	*da sveedaneeya*
Excuse me. (getting attention.	Извините./Простите.	*eezveeneetye/prasteetye*
Excuse me? [Pardon?]	Извините?/Простите?	*eezveeneetye/prasteetye*
Sorry!	Извините!/Простите!	*eezveeneetye/prasteetye*
Please.	Пожалуйста.	*pazhalsta*
Thank you.	Спасибо.	*spaseeba*
Do you speak English?	Вы говорите по-английски?	*vi gavareetye pa angleeyskee*
I don't understand	Я не понимаю.	*ya nee paneemayoo*
Where is …?	Где ...?	*gdye …*
Where are the bathrooms [toilets]?	Где туалет?	*gdye tooalyet*

Emergency Срочно!

Help!	Помогите!	*pamageetye*
Go away!	Идите отсюда!	*eedeetye atsyooda*
Leave me alone!	Оставьте меня в покое!	*astaf'tye meenya f pakoye*
Call the police!	Вызовите милицию!	*vizaveetye meeleetsiyoo*
Stop thief!	Держите вора!	*deerzhitye vora*
Get a doctor!	Вызовите врача!	*vizaveetye vrachya*
Fire!	Пожар!	*pazhar*
I'm ill.	Я заболел(а).	*ya zabalyel(a)*
I'm lost.	Я заблудился(лась).	*ya zabloodeelsa (las')*
Can you help me?	Помогите мне, пожалуйста.	*pamageetye mnye pazhalsta*

Emergency ☎

Fire 01	Ambulance 03	Police 02

Embassies ☎

Australia: 095/956-6070
Canada: 095/956-6666
Eire: 095/288-4101

New Zealand: 095/956-3579
U.K.: 095/956-7200
U.S.: 095/252-2459

There are also consulates for Canada, the U.K., and the U.S. in St. Petersburg.